graphis posters 84

graphis posters 84

The International Annual of Poster Art

Das internationale Jahrbuch der Plakatkunst

Le répertoire international de l'art de l'affiche

Edited by: / Herausgegeben von: / Réalisé par:

Walter Herdeg

Graphis Press Corp., Zurich (Switzerland)

GRAPHIS PUBLICATIONS

GRAPHIS, International bi-monthly journal of graphic art and applied art
GRAPHIS ANNUAL, The international annual of advertising and editorial graphics
PHOTOGRAPHIS, The international annual of advertising and editorial photography
GRAPHIS PACKAGING VOL. 4, An international survey of package design
CHILDREN'S BOOK ILLUSTRATION VOL. 3, VOL. 4, An international survey of children's book illustration
GRAPHIS DIAGRAMS, The graphic visualization of abstract data
FILM + TV GRAPHICS 2, An international survey of the art of film animation
ARCHIGRAPHIA, Architectural and environmental graphics
GRAPHIS EPHEMERA, Artists' Self-Promotion

GRAPHIS-PUBLIKATIONEN

GRAPHIS, Die internationale Zweimonatsschrift für Graphik und angewandte Kunst
GRAPHIS ANNUAL, Das internationale Jahrbuch der Werbegraphik und der redaktionellen Graphik
PHOTOGRAPHIS, Das internationale Jahrbuch der Werbephotographie und der redaktionellen Photographie
GRAPHIS PACKUNGEN BAND 4, Internationales Handbuch der Packungsgestaltung
KINDERBUCH-ILLUSTRATION BAND 3, BAND 4, Eine internationale Übersicht über die Kinderbuch-Illustration
GRAPHIS DIAGRAMS, Die graphische Visualisierung abstrakter Gegebenheiten
FILM + TV GRAPHICS 2, Ein internationaler Überblick über die Kunst des Animationsfilms
ARCHIGRAPHIA, Architektur- und Umweltgraphik
GRAPHIS EPHEMERA, Künstler-Eigenwerbung

PUBLICATIONS GRAPHIS

GRAPHIS, La revue bimestrielle internationale d'arts graphiques et d'arts appliqués
GRAPHIS ANNUAL, Le répertoire international de l'art publicitaire et l'art illustratif
PHOTOGRAPHIS, Le répertoire international de la photographie publicitaire et rédactionnelle
GRAPHIS EMBALLAGES VOL. 4, Répertoire international des formes de l'emballage
ILLUSTRATIONS DE LIVRES D'ENFANTS VOL. 3, VOL. 4, Un aperçu international des illustrations de livres d'enfants
GRAPHIS DIAGRAMS, La visualisation graphique de données abstraites
FILM + TV GRAPHICS 2, Un panorama international de l'art du film d'animation
ARCHIGRAPHIA, La création graphique appliquée à l'architecture et à l'environnement
GRAPHIS EPHEMERA, Autopromotion des artistes

Distributors / Auslieferung / Distribution:

USA: WATSON-GUPTILL PUBLICATIONS, INC., 1515 Broadway, New York, N.Y. 10036 **(ISBN: 0-8230-2152-1)**
CANADA: HURTIG PUBLISHERS, 10560-105 Street, Edmonton, Alberta T5H 2W7, tel. (403) 426-2469
FRANCE: GRAPHIS DISTRIBUTION, Milon-la-Chapelle, F-78470 St-Rémy-lès-Chevreuse, tél. 052-13-26
ITALIA: INTER-ORBIS, Via Lorenteggio, 31/1, I-20146 Milano, tel. 422 57 46
SPAIN: COMERCIAL ATHENEUM, S.A., Consejo de Ciento, 130-136, Barcelona 15, tel. 223 14 51-3
AMERICA LATINA, AUSTRALIA, JAPAN AND OTHER ASIAN COUNTRIES, AFRICA:
FLEETBOOKS S.A., c/o Feffer & Simons, Inc., 100 Park Avenue, New York, N.Y. 10017, tel. (212) 686-0888

All other countries / Alle anderen Länder / Tout autres pays:

GRAPHIS PRESS CORP., 107 Dufourstrasse, CH-8008 Zurich (Switzerland)

PUBLICATION No.173 (ISBN 3-85709-384-6)

Contents

Inhalt

Sommaire

Advertising Posters

Werbeplakate

Affiches publicitaires

Cultural Posters

Kulturelle Plakate

Affiches culturelles

Social Posters

Soziale Plakate

Affiches sociales

Abbreviations   Abkürzungen   Abréviations

Australia	AUS	Australien	AUS	Allemagne (Est)	GDR
Austria	AUT	Belgien	BEL	Allemagne (Ouest)	GER
Belgium	BEL	Brasilien	BRA	Australie	AUS
Brazil	BRA	Bulgarien	BUL	Autriche	AUT
Bulgaria	BUL	Dänemark	DEN	Belgique	BEL
Canada	CAN	Deutschland (Ost)	GDR	Brésil	BRA
Czechoslovakia	CSR	Deutschland (West)	GER	Bulgarie	BUL
Denmark	DEN	Finnland	FIN	Canada	CAN
Finland	FIN	Frankreich	FRA	Danemark	DEN
France	FRA	Griechenland	GRE	Espagne	SPA
Germany (East)	GDR	Grossbritannien	GBR	Etats-Unis	USA
Germany (West)	GER	Hongkong	HKG	Finlande	FIN
Great Britain	GBR	Irland	IRL	France	FRA
Greece	GRE	Israel	ISR	Grande-Bretagne	GBR
Hong Kong	HKG	Italien	ITA	Grèce	GRE
Hungary	HUN	Japan	JPN	Hongkong	HKG
Ireland	IRL	Jugoslawien	YUG	Hongrie	HUN
Israel	ISR	Kanada	CAN	Irlande	IRL
Italy	ITA	Luxemburg	LUX	Israël	ISR
Japan	JPN	Mexiko	MEX	Italie	ITA
Luxemburg	LUX	Niederlande	NLD	Japon	JPN
Mexico	MEX	Norwegen	NOR	Luxembourg	LUX
Netherlands	NLD	Österreich	AUT	Mexique	MEX
Norway	NOR	Polen	POL	Norvège	NOR
Poland	POL	Rumänien	RUM	Pays-Bas	NLD
Rumania	RUM	Schweden	SWE	Pologne	POL
Soviet Union	USR	Schweiz	SWI	Roumanie	RUM
Spain	SPA	Sowjetunion	USR	Suède	SWE
Sweden	SWE	Spanien	SPA	Suisse	SWI
Switzerland	SWI	Tschechoslowakei	CSR	Tchécoslovaquie	CSR
USA	USA	Ungarn	HUN	Union Soviétique	USR
Venezuela	VEN	USA	USA	Venezuela	VEN
Yugoslavia	YUG	Venezuela	VEN	Yougoslavie	YUG

Cover / Umschlag / Couverture: Holger Matthies

In his introduction to this volume Jacques Richez takes a critical view of the artistic quality of the advertising poster. We are all the more pleased to be able to present—thanks to the thousands of entries from all parts of the world—posters satisfying high aesthetic standards in all fields, including product advertising. Our thanks go to all our numerous contributors.

In seiner Einführung zu diesem Band bedauert Jacques Richez die schlechte künstlerische Qualität vieler Plakate, vor allem auf dem Gebiet der Werbung. Um so erfreulicher ist für uns die Tatsache, dass wir für diese Ausgabe aus einer Vielzahl ausgezeichneter Plakate – auch auf dem Gebiet der Produktwerbung – auswählen konnten, dank des umfangreichen Materials, das wir aus aller Welt erhalten haben. Wir sagen allen Einsendern unseren herzlichen Dank.

Dans son introduction, Jacques Richez regrette le faible niveau de qualité de nombreuses affiches surtout publicitaires. Il n'en est que d'autant plus réjouissant que nous ayons pu opérer notre sélection parmi un choix d'affiches de toute première qualité, y compris les affiches de biens de consommation, et ce grâce à la multitude d'envois reçus du monde entier. Que tous ceux qui nous ont fait parvenir leurs travaux trouvent ici l'expression de notre reconnaissance.

HOLGER MATTHIES, who designed the cover of this issue, is one of the world's leading poster artists. His work has been reproduced on many occasions in GRAPHIS and in other professional publications, and has been exhibited all over the world. Among the many awards he has won are the following: "Edwin Scharff" prize, Hamburg, 1981; Gold Medal at the Poster Biennale in Warsaw, 1980; Gold Medal of the Poster Museum, Essen, 1976; "Prix de la Maison", Brno, 1970.

HOLGER MATTHIES, der Gestalter des Umschlags der diesjährigen Ausgabe, gehört weltweit zu den führenden Plakatgestaltern. Seine Arbeiten wurden in GRAPHIS- und anderen Fachpublikationen gezeigt und in aller Welt ausgestellt und ausgezeichnet: Edwin-Scharff-Preis, Hamburg (1981), Goldmedaille der Plakat-Biennale Warschau (1980), Goldmedaille des Deutschen Plakat-Museums, Essen (1976), «Prix de la Maison», Brünn (1970), um nur einige Beispiele zu nennen. Holger Matthies lebt in Hamburg.

HOLGER MATTHIES, l'auteur de notre couverture, est aujourd'hui l'une des têtes de liste de l'affichisme international. Ses travaux ont été publiés dans GRAPHIS et d'autres revues spécialisées, exposés dans le monde entier et dûment primés: «Edwin-Scharff-Preis» de Hambourg (1981), médaille d'or de la Biennale Internationale de l'Affiche à Varsovie (1980), médaille d'or du Musée de l'affiche d'Essen (1976), Prix de la Maison à Brno (1970), pour ne citer que quelques-unes de ses récompenses.

Jacques Richez

Just look at the fireworks!

JACQUES RICHEZ, born in France in 1918, today lives in Belgium. A poster artist himself, he has always taken a passionate interest in the poster. As far back as 1950 he wrote on the Belgian poster in GRAPHIS 29, and he has since authored numerous articles on the subject. His book *L'Art graphique appliqué à la communication* appeared in 1964, followed in 1980 by *Textes et Prétextes, 35 ans de réflexion(s) sur le graphisme*. Richez' own posters in recent times have mostly been cultural; best-known of them is perhaps that for the Expo in Brussels in 1958. Among his hobbies are photographic experiments and "colour traps", combinations of drawings, photographs, reliefs and colour reflections. He has always found time to take part in juries and in organizations, and has been a member of the Alliance Graphique Internationale since 1952.

The irony of things: if I have written rather often about posters, it has always been to denounce the incredible waste of money into which advertising men and posterists manage to inveigle their industrial clients. To understand my attitude, the reader should know that Belgium was rich after the war (uranium from the Congo, for uses we need not expatiate on), and we were even called the Americans of Europe. It was on our walls that the icons of the consumerist religion appeared in their most garish hues: *Coca-Cola* posters, huge and smiling, and illuminated at night by daylight lamps. This was the first wave of an unprecedented tide: within a few months the disembowelled city of Brussels was delivered over to the voracity of promoters and speculators, an immense building-yard surrounded by kilometre upon kilometre of hoardings to answer all the prayers of the sellers of wall space. The city was plastered over with huge billboards measuring 4.8 by 3.2 metres from which you were inevitably solicited by the idol of the new age, the pin-up. True, the ladies were not quite as seductive as their cousins from beyond the Atlantic: nobody in our parts was as yet skilled enough in the American techniques of realistic drawing. That made no difference, however: every advertiser, whatever the product or service he was selling, wanted his pin-up. I therefore started a crusade, taking every opportunity to state that the poster is a rudimentary means of communication, that its very function—transmitting a message in a minimum of time—is a pointer to its limitations, and that its cost is consequently out of all proportion to the results it is likely to achieve. Let me add at once that I got nowhere with my strictures, and commercial posters are still 20 square metres in size. While my opinion has not changed very much in the meantime, I am now less concerned, having distanced myself from advertising assignments. But the reader has been warned: the writer of this preface is biased, and his judgements are not likely to be impartial...

But is this really a judgement? To pass a fair one, it would be necessary to run around the world, or even to have the gift of ubiquity. But who, except perhaps for a few sociologists, would be interested in an exhaustive survey of the present status of the poster? What we have before us here, as in all publications devoted to communication graphics, is a *selection*. A selection based on what? On quality, of course. But what quality? On the qualities that interest graphic designers, illustrators, photographers, art directors, or those about to join their ranks. It is clear from the first that, over and above theory and statistics, an element of *pleasure* is involved. I am tempted to see GRAPHIS POSTERS as a superb picture-book, a "poeticization"—to coin a word—of the world we see daily in the raw, and often cruel, pictures of television. What we are looking at here is the same world, but seen through the sensibility and talent of image-makers.

In the preface to GRAPHIS POSTERS 75 Heinz Edelmann already drew attention to the embarrassment of exhibition juries when confronted with commercial posters, whereas in the heroic age of the poster the commercial production was considered the equal of its cultural counterpart. Which raises the question: is some discrimination going on, or have the pictures of the consumer society disqualified themselves? I have my own ideas on this matter, as you will have gathered. But I feel that the reader of GRAPHIS POSTERS will not have a very different impression: if we measure the space allotted in this work to strictly commercial posters (not counting a few remarkable efforts in the fields of clothing, cosmetics and food, which in a way border on the cultural), we must admit that the successful recipes of mass publicity seem not to interest us very much; and while we are no strangers to the idea of effectiveness, we use a different approach to try to achieve it. We are all fairly familiar with this long-standing debate, a dialogue between deaf interlocutors to which I for one regret having devoted so much of my time. I think today that the street offers us some qualitative choices—rather like the shows you can see "on Broadway", "off Broadway" and "off off Broadway"—and while we image-makers may deplore with Gilles de Bure (GRAPHIS POSTERS 80) and Pierre Restany (GRAPHIS POSTERS 82) the conformism, banality and poverty of the concepts, we know that we are hardly more than our own spectators, since our freedom, even when it is supposed to be complete, is almost always limited to the form and not to the essence. And it is perhaps to this fact—the paradox is only a seeming one—that we owe the present extraordinary florescence, the "Neo-Baroque and phantasmagoric patchwork discourse backed by muted irony and knowing smiles" (Restany), because that is the way we demonstrate and justify our existence. Some graphic designers, including some of the greatest of them, have not hesitated to state that form interests them more than function. This attitude, which might at first glance seem cynical, is founded, I am sure, on a deep personal conviction confirmed by experience. For while the notion may defy analysis (in the advertising sense), the conclusion it permits is an incontestable reality. How else should we explain the multiplication of poster museums, the proliferation of exhibitions, whether periodic or not, and the fascination shown by collectors?

Everything is considered suitable for use in the poster, from the laborious techniques of the past to the rough drafts of the counter-culture, whose sudden thrusts, related to social upheavals and economic disorders, are, upon closer scrutiny, only the oscillations of the barometer needle. (The counter-culture feeds culture proper, that is the essential meaning of its birth and its death. The marks it leaves are sometimes deep, but those who enthusiastically follow its lead soon turn them into mere ruts.) With the result that nothing is modern any more, but everything is sufficient unto the day. And since my opinion has been asked, I will admit that I let myself go in this maelstrom with pleasure and relish. A superb chaos, a salutary eruption, a sumptuous firework display. The sententious clowns are back, the goddesses astraddle bicycles or bottles of edible oil. The graphic pirouette is not prohibited even for the most serious of subjects. True, if there is anything left that gives me a rare sense of freedom, it is coming across a work like this one. I also see in the evident commitment of the best designers to the great human causes, as well as to culture and permanent education, an antidote to the poisons distilled by sectarians and fanatics of all denominations. Some will no doubt find this a rather idealistic attitude, but I am not so sure about that in view of the growing interest in the poster as object. This second life of the poster, after its death as a means of conveying information, is perhaps as important as its primary function, and it would surprise me if those who conceive posters did not give some thought to this question during their work. Thus the ephemeral survives itself and—miracle of miracles!—does so at the wish of those who are supposed to "have to live with" the poster. So why should anyone else put up a resistance?

Jacques Richez

Oh wie schön ist das alles!

JACQUES RICHEZ, 1918 in Frankreich geboren, lebt heute in Belgien. Er äussert sich hier über das Plakat aus seiner Sicht. In GRAPHIS 29 aus dem Jahre 1950 erschien bereits ein Beitrag des Autors über «Belgische Plakate». Neben verschiedenen Artikeln sind zwei Bücher von ihm erschienen: *L'Art graphique appliqué à la communication*, 1964, und *Textes et Prétextes, 35 ans de réflexion(s) sur le graphisme*, 1980. Der Graphiker Jacques Richez widmet sich seit einigen Jahren vorwiegend kulturellen Plakaten; international wird sein Plakat für die Weltausstellung in Brüssel 1958 am bekanntesten sein. Als «Hobbys» nennt er photo-graphische Experimente und «colour traps», Kombinationen aus Zeichnung, Photo, Relief und Farbspiegelungen. Daneben fand und findet er immer wieder Zeit, um in Jurys und Organisationen mitzuwirken; seit 1952 ist er Mitglied der Alliance Graphique Internationale.

Es mag ironisch klingen, doch habe ich noch jedesmal, wenn ich zur Feder griff, um mich über das Plakatwesen zu äussern, die Verschwendungssucht der Werbeleute und Plakat-Graphiker angeprangert, die der Industrie Unsummen aus den Taschen gezogen haben. Freilich war das Belgien der Nachkriegsjahre ein reiches Land, nicht zuletzt dank der Einkünfte aus dem Uran-Bergbau im Kongo, für Zwecke, die wir alle kennen. Man nannte uns die Amerikaner Europas, und auf unseren Plakatwänden fanden zum erstenmal die neuen leuchtenden Ikone der modernen Verbraucher-Religionen Eingang in unseren Alltag, in Form von riesengrossen *Coca-Cola*-Plakaten, nachts hell ausgeleuchtet und mit dem strahlenden Lächeln perfekter Pin-up-Girls aufgetakelt. Diesen Vorboten folgte nur wenige Monate später eine wahre Springflut von Riesenplakaten – 4,80 × 3,20 m –, die sich über die Umzäunungen der zahlreichen Bauplätze ergoss, die wie Pilze aus der Erde schossen, nachdem Brüssel zum Freiwild der Immobilienhändler und Spekulanten erklärt worden war. Hüben lachten die Pin-up-Girls nicht so verführerisch von den Bretterwänden herunter wie drüben, fehlte es uns doch noch an Könnern, die es mit den realistischen Zeichenkünsten der Amerikaner aufnehmen konnten. Und doch verlangte jeder Kunde eine makellose Schönheit zum Anpreisen seiner Ware oder Dienstleistung. Und da ging ich nun auf Kreuzzug gegen skrupellose Macher, erinnerte daran, dass das Plakat ein rudimentäres Informationsmittel darstellt, dem schon seiner Funktion nach (die Übermittlung einer Werbebotschaft in einem möglichst knapp bemessenen Zeitraum) enge Grenzen gezogen sind, so dass der Aufwand hier in gar keinem Verhältnis zu den erzielten Resultaten steht. Ich gestehe es reumütig ein: der Erfolg war gleich Null, und die Plakate messen noch immer 20 Quadratmeter. Zwar bin ich bei meiner Meinung geblieben, doch fühle ich mich weniger betroffen, von der Werbung im allgemeinen, vom Werbeplakat insbesondere. Damit ist der wohlgesonnene Leser gewarnt: der Verfasser dieses Vorwortes hat so seine Vorurteile, und die Bilanz, die er zu ziehen gedenkt, wird wohl kaum unparteiisch ausfallen ...

Doch geht es im Grunde um eine globale Bilanz? Eine solche zu erstellen würde bedeuten, dass man ständig um die Welt reisen müsste, am besten mit der Gabe der Allgegenwart ausgestattet. Und schliesslich mag eine Gesamtbilanz nur den Soziologen interessieren. Wie in jeder Veröffentlichung über Kommunikationsgraphik haben wir es hier mit einer *Auswahl* zu tun. Nach welchen Gesichtspunkten? Rein der Qualität nach, natürlich! Welche Qualität(en)? Diejenige(n), die für uns Graphiker, Illustratoren, Photographen, Art Directors sowie für die, die es werden wollen, von Interesse ist (oder sind). Womit bereits feststeht, dass weit mehr als Theorie und Statistik persönliches *Lustempfinden* im Spiele ist ... Ich bin versucht, in GRAPHIS POSTERS ein prachtvolles Bilderbuch zu sehen, in dem unsere tagtäglich in rohen und grausamen Bildern am Fernsehen vorgeführte Welt gleichsam poetisiert wird. Hier erblicken wir die gleiche Welt, doch in einer revidierten Fassung, die wir dem Empfindungsvermögen und dem Talent der Bildschöpfer verdanken.

In seinem Vorwort zu GRAPHIS POSTERS 75 unterstrich Heinz Edelmann bereits die Verlegenheit der Juroren, wenn es um die Beurteilung kommerzieller Plakate geht, die in heroischeren Zeiten noch den kulturellen gleichgestellt waren. Kann man hier von Diskriminierung sprechen, oder haben sich ganz einfach die Bilder der Konsumgesellschaft sukzessive entwertet? Wie Sie bereits wissen, habe ich mir da eine Meinung gebildet, die von derjenigen des GRAPHIS-POSTERS-Betrachters nicht sehr verschieden sein dürfte. Wenn man nämlich misst, wieviel Raum in diesem Werke das rein kommerzielle Plakat einnimmt (wobei von einigen ausserordentlich gelungenen Plakaten für Kleidung, Kosmetik und Nahrungsmittel abgesehen wird, die bereits an den Bereich Kultur heranrücken), so muss wohl zugegeben werden, dass die «guten Rezepte» der Massenwerbung uns kaum interessieren und dass wir der Werbewirksamkeit, die wir durchaus schätzen, mit ganz anderen Mitteln gerecht werden. Wer kann sich rühmen, von diesem alten und ewig neuen Streit unangetastet zu sein? Ich für meinen Teil bedauere es, soviel Zeit meines Lebens auf diese sinnlose Auseinandersetzung verschwendet zu haben. Ich glaube heute, dass ähnlich den Theaterstücken, die «on» oder «off» oder gar «off off Broadway» gespielt werden, die Strasse uns die Hand zur qualitativen Wahl bietet. Wenn wir Bilder-Macher mit Gilles de Bure (in GRAPHIS POSTERS 80) und Pierre Restany (in GRAPHIS POSTERS 82) den Konformismus, die Banalisierung und die Armut der Konzepte beklagen, so wissen wir doch zu genau, dass wir nur noch unsere eigenen Zuschauer sind, da unsere Freiheit, wie erhaben man sie uns auch vorstellen mag, fast immer auf die Form begrenzt wird und den Inhalt ausklammert. Vielleicht verdanken wir gerade diesem Umstand die nur scheinbar paradoxe gegenwärtige Blütezeit des Plakats, «ein neu-barockes, phantasmagorisches Gesprächs-Patchwork, mit leiser Ironie und allwissendem Lächeln umwoben» (Restany), denn nur so und nicht anders weisen wir unsere Existenz nach und rechtfertigen sie gleichzeitig. Manche Graphiker, darunter ganz bedeutende, haben nicht verschwiegen, dass die Form sie mehr interessiert als die Funktion. Das mag auf den ersten Blick zynisch wirken, doch bin ich sicher, dass eine solche Behauptung tiefbegründeter Überzeugung entspringt und von der Erfahrung bestätigt wird. Denn dieser Begriff mag wohl nicht im Sinne der Werbefachleute analysierbar sein, er führt uns dennoch zu einem unleugbaren Tatbestand. Wie sollte man denn anders die Gründung zahlreicher Plakatmuseen, die vielfachen regelmässigen oder Sonderausstellungen von Plakaten und die Begeisterung der Plakatsammler erklären?

Alles ist hochwillkommen, die ausgefeilte Technik von anno dazumal wie die ungestümen Ausbrüche der Gegenkultur, deren unerwartete Vorstösse im Zusammenhang mit sozialen Explosionen und wirtschaftlichen Umstürzen aus gebührendem Abstand betrachtet nur den Ausschlag der Barometernadel darstellen. (Die Gegenkultur speist die Kultur, das ist der Sinn ihrer Entstehung und ihres Untergangs. Die Spuren, die sie hinterlässt, sind manchmal tiefgründig, und doch verwandeln sie sich unter dem Ansturm begeisterter Nutzniesser rasch in ausgefahrene Geleise.) Somit gilt nichts mehr als modern, ist alles aktuell. Und da man mich um meine Meinung fragt, so will ich gern und ohne falsche Scham gestehen, dass ich mich mit Freude und Hingebung von diesem Strudel mitreissen lasse. Was für ein prachtvolles Chaos, was für ein wohltuender Ausbruch, was für ein unerhörtes Feuerwerk voller Köstlich- und Künstlichkeiten! Dies ist die Zeit der Rückkehr jener salbungsvollen Clowns, jener erhabenen Göttinnen hoch zu Ross – auf einem Fahrrad genausogut wie auf einer Flasche Speiseöl. Selbst für ernsthafteste Thematik ist eine graphische Pirouette nicht verpönt. Wahrhaft, wenn mir heutzutage noch irgend etwas den seltengewordenen Geschmack nach Freiheit vermittelt, so ist es, ein Werk wie das vorliegende anzutreffen. Ich sehe zudem im offensichtlichen Bemühen der besten Bildschöpfer zugunsten grosser menschlicher Werte, der Kultur, der Fortbildung aller ein wirksames Gegenmittel gegen die von Sektiererei und Fanatismus der übelsten und verschiedensten Sorten gestreuten Gifte. Sie mögen einwenden, das sei eine recht idealistische Sicht der Dinge. Ich bin dessen nicht so sicher, besonders, wenn man das wachsende Interesse für das Plakat als Sammelobjekt in Betracht zieht. Diesem Nachleben des Plakates über dessen Tod als Informationsmittel hinaus kommt vielleicht eine ebensogrosse Bedeutung zu wie seiner Werbefunktion. Ich würde mich sehr wundern, wenn die Plakatgestalter während ihrer Arbeit nicht ein klein wenig daran dächten. So überdauert das Vergängliche seine flüchtige Existenz, zudem noch – und das kommt einem Wunder gleich – dank des Wunsches derer, die angeblich das Plakat «ertragen» müssen. Warum also sollte man hier Widerstand leisten?

Jacques Richez

Oh, la belle bleue!

JACQUES RICHEZ, né en France en 1918, habite la Belgique.
Il nous confie ici ses réflexions sur l'affiche. Dès 1950,
il interrogeait «Les Affiches belges» dans GRAPHIS 29.
Essayiste prolifique, il a publié de nombreux articles et deux
ouvrages intitulés *L'Art graphique appliqué à la communication* (1964) et *Textes et Prétextes, 35 ans de réflexion (s) sur le
graphisme* (1980). Depuis plusieurs années, le graphiste
Jacques Richez se consacre surtout à l'affiche culturelle; son
affiche pour l'Exposition universelle de Bruxelles en 1958 a
fait le tour du monde. Au nombre de ses hobbies, il mentionne
ses recherches photo-graphiques et ses «colour traps», com-
binaisons de dessins, photos, reliefs et reflets colorés. Il a
toujours trouvé le temps nécessaire pour siéger dans des jurys
et organisations. Depuis 1952, Jacques Richez est membre de
l'Alliance Graphique Internationale.

Ironie des choses: s'il m'est arrivé souvent d'écrire à propos de l'affiche, cela a toujours été pour
dénoncer l'incroyable gaspillage d'argent auquel les publicitaires et les afficheurs poussent les
industriels. Pour comprendre, il faut savoir que la Belgique était riche, après la guerre (l'uranium
du Congo, destiné à l'usage que l'on sait...), on nous appelait les Américains de l'Europe. C'est
sur nos murs qu'on a pu voir d'abord les plus rutilantes icônes de la religion consumériste: les
affiches de *Coca-Cola*, tous sourires dehors, gigantesques, et, le soir, éclairées a giorno. Ce
n'était que la première vague annonciatrice d'un raz de marée sans précédent: en quelques mois,
Bruxelles, ville éventrée livrée à la voracité des promoteurs et des spéculateurs, immense chan-
tier entouré de kilomètres et de kilomètres de palissades providentielles pour les marchands
«d'espaces», Bruxelles se couvrit d'immenses placards de 4,80 × 3,20 m sur lesquels, imman-
quablement, vous aguichait l'idole des temps nouveaux: la «pin-up». Bien sûr, elles n'étaient pas
tout à fait aussi séduisantes que leurs cousines d'outre-Atlantique: personne n'était chez nous
préparé aux techniques du dessin réaliste à l'américaine. Qu'à cela ne tienne, chaque annonceur,
quel que fût le produit ou le service à promouvoir, exigeait sa pin-up. Je suis donc parti en croi-
sade, ne perdant pas une occasion d'affirmer que l'affiche est un moyen d'information rudimen-
taire, que sa fonction même (transmettre un message en un minimum de temps) donne la mesure
de ses limites et que, par conséquent, son coût est de loin hors de proportion avec les résultats
qu'on peut en attendre. Autant vous le dire tout de suite: cela n'a servi à rien, et les affiches com-
merciales ont toujours 20 m². Aujourd'hui, mon opinion n'a que peu changé, mais je me sens
moins «concerné»: il y a longtemps que j'ai volontairement pris mes distances vis-à-vis de la
publicité. Le lecteur est donc prévenu: le préfacier est de parti pris, et le bilan risque de n'être vrai-
ment pas impartial...

Mais après tout, ceci est-il un bilan? Pour en faire un, honnête, il faudrait constamment courir le
monde en tous sens, ou mieux, avoir le don d'ubiquité. Mais qui, en dehors peut-être des socio-
logues, serait intéressé par un constat exhaustif de la situation actuelle de l'affiche? Nous nous
trouvons bien ici, comme dans toutes les publications dédiées au graphisme appliqué à la communication, devant une *sélection*. Basée sur quoi? Mais sur la qualité, voyons! Quelle(s) qua-
lité(s)? Celle(s) qui nous intéresse(nt), nous graphistes, illustrateurs, photographes, art directors. Et ceux qui se préparent à le devenir. On voit d'emblée que, plus que la théorie et la statis-
tique, le *plaisir* y est pour quelque chose... Je serais donc tenté de voir GRAPHIS POSTERS comme
un superbe livre d'images, une «poétisation» – si j'ose dire – de notre monde tel qu'il apparaît
chaque jour dans les images crues – et cruelles – de la télévision. Nous revoyons ici ce même
monde, mais reconsidéré par la sensibilité et le talent des créateurs d'images.

Déjà, dans la préface à GRAPHIS POSTERS 75, Heinz Edelmann soulignait l'embarras des jurys
d'expositions devant les affiches «économiques», alors que, dans les temps héroïques, l'affiche
commerciale était considérée comme l'égale de celle à vocation culturelle. Dès lors la question,
s'agit-il d'une discrimination, ou bien les images de la société de consommation se sont-elles
disqualifiées? J'ai mon idée là-dessus, comme vous avez pu le voir. Mais surtout, il me semble
que le lecteur de GRAPHIS POSTERS ne doit pas avoir une impression tellement différente: si on
mesure la place qui est faite dans cet ouvrage à l'affiche strictement commerciale (à l'exception
de quelques remarquables réalisations dans le domaine de l'habillement, des cosmétiques et de
l'alimentation, qui touchent déjà à la culture, d'une certaine manière), on doit bien admettre que
les «bonnes recettes» de la publicité de masse ne nous intéressent guère, et que si la notion d'effi-
cacité ne nous est pas étrangère, c'est par des moyens tous autres que nous tentons d'y parvenir.
Qui d'entre nous n'a pas subi les effets de cette vieille et inépuisable querelle? Dialogue de
sourds auquel, pour ma part, je regrette d'avoir consacré tant de temps dans ma vie. Je crois
aujourd'hui que, comme les spectacles qui se jouent «on Broadway», «off Broadway» et «off off
Broadway», la rue nous offre des choix qualitatifs, et si nous, faiseurs d'images, pouvons déplo-
rer avec Gilles de Bure (cf. GRAPHIS POSTERS 80) et Pierre Restany (GRAPHIS POSTERS 82) le
conformisme, la banalisation et la pauvreté des concepts, nous savons bien que nous ne sommes
guère plus que nos propres spectateurs, puisque notre liberté, même lorsqu'on nous la présente
comme entière, se limite presque toujours à la forme et exclut le fond. Et c'est peut-être à cela – le
paradoxe n'est qu'apparent – que l'on doit l'extraordinaire efflorescence actuelle, «patchwork
néo-baroque et fantasmagorique, doublé d'ironie feutrée et de sous-entendus» (Restany),

parce que c'est ainsi, et pas autrement, que nous démontrons et justifions notre existence. Certains graphistes, et parmi les plus grands, n'ont pas hésité à affirmer que la forme les intéresse plus que la fonction. Ce propos, qui pourrait de prime abord paraître cynique, est, j'en suis certain, fondé sur une conviction intime profonde, confirmée par l'expérience. Car si cette notion échappe à l'analyse (au sens des publicitaires), le constat qu'on peut en tirer est bien, lui, une indiscutable réalité: comment expliquer autrement la multiplication des musées de l'affiche, la prolifération des expositions, périodiques ou non, et l'engouement des collectionneurs?

Tout est bon à prendre, des minutieuses techniques anciennes aux jetés bruts de la contre-culture, dont les poussées soudaines, liées aux explosions sociales et aux bouleversements économiques ne sont, distances prises, que les oscillations de l'aiguille du baromètre. (La contre-culture nourrit la culture, c'est le sens de sa naissance et le sens de sa mort. Les traces qu'elle laisse après elle sont quelquefois profondes, mais ceux qui s'y précipitent avec délectation les transforment aussitôt en ornières.) Ainsi, plus rien n'est moderne, et tout est actuel. Et puisqu'on me demande mon avis, je dirai sans honte que c'est avec gourmandise, avidité, jouissance que je me laisse porter par ce maelström. Superbe chaos, éclatement salutaire, somptueux feu d'artifice(s). Voici revenus les clowns sentencieux et les déesses à califourchon sur des bicyclettes ou des bouteilles d'huile de table. Même pour les sujets les plus graves, la pirouette graphique n'est pas interdite. Vrai, s'il est encore aujourd'hui une chose qui me donne le sentiment rare de la liberté, c'est bien de découvrir un ouvrage comme celui-ci. Je vois aussi, dans l'évident engagement des meilleurs créateurs pour les grandes causes humaines, comme pour la culture et l'éducation permanente, un antidote aux poisons distillés par les sectarismes et les fanatismes de toutes sortes. On me dira sans doute que voilà une vue bien idéaliste des choses: je n'en suis pas si sûr, à constater l'intérêt croissant pour l'affiche-objet. Cette deuxième vie de l'affiche, après qu'elle soit morte en tant que moyen d'information, est peut-être aussi importante que sa fonction première, et je serais fort étonné que ceux qui les conçoivent n'y pensent pas un peu pendant leur travail. Ainsi, l'éphémère se survit-il à lui-même et – miracle! – par la volonté de ceux dont on dit qu'ils «subissent» l'affiche. Pourquoi résister?

Index to Artists and Photographers
Verzeichnis der Künstler und Photographen
Index des Artistes et Photographes

Index to Designers
Verzeichnis der Gestalter
Index des Maquettistes

Index to Art Directors
Verzeichnis der künstlerischen Leiter
Index des Directeurs Artistiques

Index to Agencies and Studios
Verzeichnis der Agenturen und Studios
Index des Agences et Studios

Index to Advertisers
Verzeichnis der Auftraggeber
Index des Clients

■ Entry instructions may be requested by anyone interested in submitting samples of exceptional graphics or photography for possible inclusion in our annuals. No fees involved. Closing dates for entries:
GRAPHIS ANNUAL (advertising and editorial art and design): 31 January
PHOTOGRAPHIS (advertising and editorial photography): 30 June
GRAPHIS POSTERS (an annual of poster art): 30 June
Write to: Graphis Press Corp., Dufourstrasse 107, 8008 Zurich, Switzerland

■ Einsendebedingungen können von jedermann angefordert werden, der uns Beispiele hervorragender Photographie oder Graphik zur Auswahl für unsere Jahrbücher unterbreiten möchte. Es werden keine Gebühren erhoben.
Einsendetermine:
GRAPHIS ANNUAL (Werbe- und redaktionelle Graphik): 31. Januar
PHOTOGRAPHIS (Werbe- und redaktionelle Photographie): 30. Juni
GRAPHIS POSTERS (ein Jahrbuch der Plakatkunst): 30. Juni
Adresse: Graphis Verlag AG, Dufourstrasse 107, 8008 Zürich, Schweiz

■ Tout intéressé à la soumission de travaux photographiques et graphiques recevra les informations nécessaires sur demande. Sans charge de participation.
Dates limites:
GRAPHIS ANNUAL (art graphique publicitaire et rédactionnel): 31 janvier
PHOTOGRAPHIS (photographie publicitaire et rédactionnelle): 30 juin
GRAPHIS POSTERS (annuaire sur l'art de l'affiche): 30 juin
S'adresser à: Editions Graphis SA, Dufourstrasse 107, 8008 Zurich, Suisse

Editor and Art Director: Walter Herdeg
Assistant Editor: Stanley Mason
Project Managers: Romy Herzog, Heinke Jenssen
Designers: Marino Bianchera, Martin Byland, Ulrich Kemmner
Art Assistants: Peter Wittwer, Walter Zuber

1

Advertising Posters

Werbeplakate

Affiches publicitaires

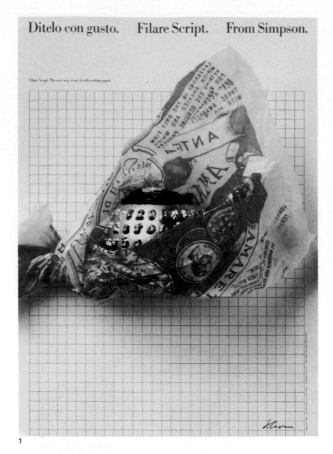

Ditelo con gusto.   Filare Script.   From Simpson.

METALLIC·DUAD

ARTIST / KÜNSTLER / ARTISTE:

1 James Cross
2 Viv Morris/Bruce Osborn
3, 4 Pasi Haaranen
5 Per Arnoldi

DESIGNER / GESTALTER:

1 James Cross
2 Toru Nakagawa
3, 4 Pentti Pilve
5 Per Arnoldi

ART DIRECTOR:

1 James Cross
2 Toru Nakagawa
3, 4 Pentti Pilve

AGENCY / AGENTUR / AGENCE:

1 Cross Associates
2 Dentsu Inc.
3, 4 Creator Oy

1 Advertising poster for *Filare Script*, a quality of paper manufactured by the *Simpson Paper Company*. (USA)
2 Poster in the New Wave style for *Sony* recording cassettes. Black-and-white shot combined with graphics in strong colours. (JPN)
3, 4 Trade posters for *Nokia* napkins. Fig. 3 in various blue shades, Fig. 4 in shades of brown and beige. (FIN)
5 Silkscreen poster for *Kevi* office furniture. (DEN)

1 «Die neue Art, es mit Schreibpapier zu sagen.» Plakatwerbung für die Qualität *Filare Script* des Papierherstellers *Simpson*. (USA)
2 Plakat im New-Wave-Stil für *Sony*-Tonbandkassetten. Schwarzweiss-Aufnahme kombiniert mit Graphik in leuchtenden Farben. (JPN)
3, 4 Für den Innenaushang bestimmte Plakate für *Nokia*-Servietten. Abb. 3 in Blautönen, Abb. 4 in Brauntönen. (FIN)
5 Siebdruck-Plakat für Büromöbel der Marke *Kevi*. (DEN)

1 «La nouvelle manière de le dire avec du papier à écrire.» Affiche publicitaire pour la qualité *Filare Script* du papetier *Simpson*. (USA)
2 Affiche style nouvelle vague pour les cassettes *Sony*. Photo noir et blanc combinée avec une composition graphique aux couleurs vives. (JPN)
3, 4 Affiches intérieures pour les serviettes *Nokia*. La fig. 3 est exécutée en divers bleus, la fig. 4 en divers bruns. (FIN)
5 Affiche sérigraphique pour les meubles de bureau *Kevi*. (DEN)

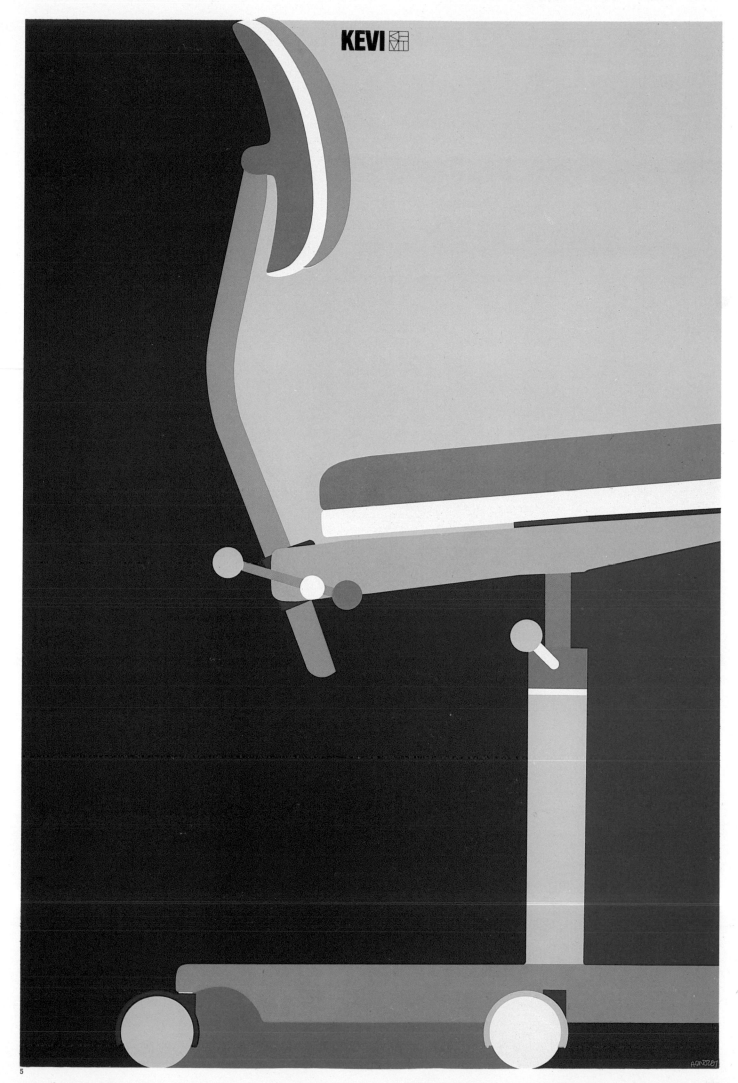

KEVI

Varia

ARTIST / KÜNSTLER / ARTISTE:

6 Clint Clemens
7, 8 Kazumasa Nagai
9 Günther Kieser
10 Shigeo Fukuda
11, 12 Yusaku Kamekura

DESIGNER / GESTALTER / MAQUETTISTE:

6 Keith Lane/Rod Smith
7, 8 Kazumasa Nagai
9 Günther Kieser
10 Shigeo Fukuda
11, 12 Yusaku Kamekura

ART DIRECTOR / DIRECTEUR ARTISTIQUE:

6 Keith Lane/Rod Smith
7, 8 Kazumasa Nagai
9 Günther Kieser
10 Shigeo Fukuda
11, 12 Yusaku Kamekura

AGENCY / AGENTUR / AGENCE – STUDIO:

6 Emerson, Lane, Fortuna
7, 8 Nippon Design Center
9 Günther Kieser

6 Advertisement for *Sperry Top-Sider* shoes. (USA)
7 Poster for image advertising of the *Shiseido* cosmetics company. (JPN)
8 Poster with a colour photograph and a geometrical composition, for a wall-paper manufacturer. (JPN)
9 Large-format poster for *Sofalet's*, made by the furniture designer Otto Zapf. (GER)
10 Poster for the image advertising of *Minolta*, a Japanese camera manufacturer. (JPN)
11 From a series of full-colour collectors' posters used as advertising for a music club. (JPN)
12 Poster in violet, blue, yellow, white and black for a lamp store. (JPN)

6 Werbung für Schuhe der Marke *Sperry Top-Sider* (top-side = die oben liegende Bootseite, also Luv). (USA)
7 Für die Image-Werbung des Kosmetik-Konzerns *Shiseido* bestimmtes Plakat. (JPN)
8 Mit Farbaufnahme und geometrischer Komposition gestaltetes Plakat für einen Tapeten-Hersteller. (JPN)
9 Grossformatiges Plakat für *Sofalet's* des Möbeldesigners Otto Zapf. (GER)
10 Zur Image-Werbung des japanischen Kameraherstellers *Minolta* gehörendes Plakat. (JPN)
11 Aus einer Reihe von mehrfarbigen Plakaten zum Sammeln, als Werbung für einen Musik-Club. (JPN)
12 «Die Sprache des Lichts.» Plakat (violett, blau, gelb, weiss auf Schwarz) für ein Lampengeschäft. (JPN)

6 Publicité pour les chaussures *Sperry Top-Sider* (de top-side = le côté du navire frappé par le vent). (USA)
7 Affiche destinée à la publicité globale de marque du groupe cosmétique *Shiseido*. (JPN)
8 Affiche pour un fabricant de papiers peints réalisée à l'aide d'une photo couleur et d'une composition géométrique. (JPN)
9 Affiche surdimensionnée pour le *Sofalet* du dessinateur d'ameublements Otto Zapf. (GER)
10 Affiche d'une campagne d'image de marque du fabricant japonais d'équipements photo *Minolta*. (JPN)
11 Elément d'une série d'affiches de collection polychromes. Publicité pour un club de musique. (JPN)
12 «Le langage de la lumière.» Affiche (violet, bleu, jaune, blanc sur noir) pour un magasin de lampes. (JPN)

8

9

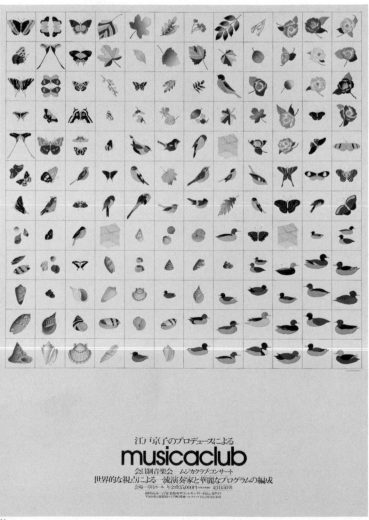

11

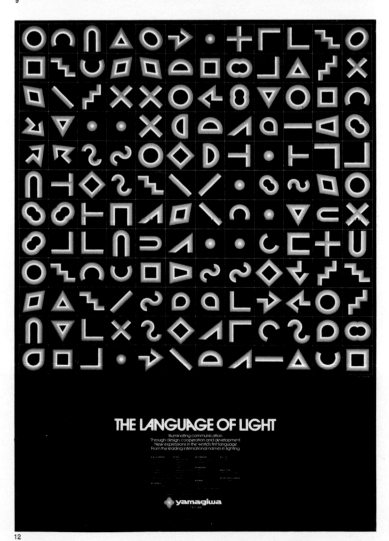

12

ARTIST / KÜNSTLER / ARTISTE:

13 Harry & Marion Zelenko
14, 16, 19 Masaki Ono
17, 18 Yasuo Kobayashi

DESIGNER / GESTALTER / MAQUETTISTE:

13 Harry & Marion Zelenko
14, 16, 19 Takanori Asaeda
15 Uwe Loesch
17, 18 Muneaki Andoh

ART DIRECTOR / DIRECTEUR ARTISTIQUE:

14, 16, 19 Takanori Asaeda
15 Claus Henseling
17, 18 Muneaki Andoh

AGENCY / AGENTUR / AGENCE – STUDIO:

14, 16, 19 Dentsu Inc./Kyushu Regional Office
15 Arbeitsgemeinschaft Uwe Loesch
17, 18 Dentsu Inc.

IFF GUIDE TO FRAGRANCES

13

16

17

13 Poster used as direct advertising for International Flavors and Fragrances Inc., addressed to its international clientele and showing various aromatic notes and their applications. (USA)
14, 16 Examples from a series of posters for the tenth anniversary of the department store *Matsuya*. The cloak in Fig. 14 is in brilliant red shades, and is worn over garments in dull yellow. (JPN)
15 Announcement of the international shoe fair in Düsseldorf. (GER)
17 Poster as part of the image advertising of the *Central Park* department store which is open every day of the week. Full-colour shot. (JPN)
18 Christmas poster for the *Central Park* department store. (JPN)
19 Further examples of advertising posters for women's fashions at the *Matsuya* department store (see also Figs. 14 and 16). (JPN)

14

15

18

19

13 Als Direktwerbung an die internationale Kundschaft gerichtetes Plakat eines Riechstoffherstellers, mit einer Übersicht der verschiedenen Duftnoten und ihrer Anwendung. (USA)
14, 16 Beispiele aus einer Serie von Plakaten zum zehnjährigen Bestehen des Kaufhauses *Matsuya*. Der Umhang in Abb. 14 in leuchtenden Rottönen über mattgelber Kleidung. (JPN)
15 Ankündigung der internationalen Schuhmesse in Düsseldorf. (GER)
17 Plakat für die Image-Werbung des Kaufhauses *Central Park*, das jeden Tag geöffnet ist. Mehrfarbige Aufnahme. (JPN)
18 Weihnachtliche Plakatwerbung für das Kaufhaus *Central Park*. (JPN)
19 Weiteres Beispiel aus der Plakatwerbung für Damenmode des Kaufhauses *Matsuya* (s. auch Abb. 14 und 16). (JPN)

13 Affiche d'un fabricant de substances odorantes servant à la prospection directe d'une clientèle internationale. On y trouve un tableau des différentes nuances et de leur utilisation. (USA)
14, 16 Exemples d'une série d'affiches réalisées pour le dixième anniversaire des grands magasins *Matsuya*. La cape rouge vif de la fig. 14 est drapée sur un habit jaune mat. (JPN)
15 Annonce du Salon international de la chaussure à Düsseldorf. (GER)
17 Affiche pour l'image globale de marque des grands magasins *Central Park* ouverts tous les jours. Photo polychrome. (JPN)
18 Affiche de Noël pour les grands magasins *Central Park*. (JPN)
19 Un autre exemple de la publicité par voie d'affiche pour la mode féminine des grands magasins *Matsuya* (cf. également les fig. 14 et 16). (JPN)

20

21

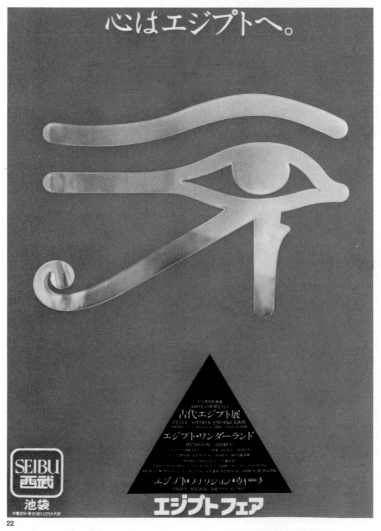

22

23

Varia

ARTIST / KÜNSTLER / ARTISTE:

20 Christian Coigny
21, 22, 24 Ikko Tanaka/Katsuhiro Kinoshita
23 RKM

DESIGNER / GESTALTER / MAQUETTISTE:

21, 22, 24 Ikko Tanaka/Katsuhiro Kinoshita
23 Julien van der Wal

ART DIRECTOR / DIRECTEUR ARTISTIQUE:

21, 22, 24 Ikko Tanaka
23 Julien van der Wal

AGENCY / AGENTUR / AGENCE – STUDIO:

23 VDW

20 Poster for the *Bon Génie* fashion store in Geneva. Model in black and white on a background of beige and grey shades. (SWI)
21 Poster advertising a picture book by the illustrator Yoshitaro Isaka (Péro) and published by *Parco*. Full-colour figures. (JPN)
22 Poster of the *Seibu* department store for an exhibition of ancient Egyptian art held there. Gold eye on a brilliant blue background, white lettering, triangle in black. (JPN)
23 From a series of posters for a jeweller's. White, black and three pale green pearls which are divided by gold buffers. (SWI)
24 Fool in cap and bells—detail from the poster shown in Fig. 21 for the book with illustrations by Yoshitaro Isaka (Péro). (JPN)

20 Plakat für das Modehaus *Bon Génie* in Genf. Modell in Schwarz und Weiss auf einem Hintergrund in Beige- und Grautönen. (SWI)
21 Plakat für ein von *Parco* herausgegebenes Bilderbuch des Illustrators Yoshitaro Isaka (Péro) mit farbenfrohen Figuren. (JPN)
22 Ankündigung einer Ausstellung alter ägyptischer Kunst im Kaufhaus *Seibu*. Auge gold auf leuchtend blauem Hintergrund, Schrift weiss, Dreieck schwarz. (JPN)
23 Werbung für einen Juwelier. Weisse, schwarze und drei blassgrüne Perlen mit goldenen Zwischengliedern. (SWI)
24 Narrenfigur, Detail aus dem in Abb. 21 gezeigten Plakat für das Buch mit Zeichnungen von Yoshitaro Isaka (Péro). (JPN)

20 Affiche pour le magasin de mode *Bon Génie* à Genève. Modèle noir et blanc sur fond composé de tons beiges et gris. (SWI)
21 Pour un livre d'images de l'illustrateur Yoshitaro Isaka (Péro) agrémenté de personnages hauts en couleur, ouvrage paru aux Editions *Parco*. (JPN)
22 Affiche des grands magasins *Seibu* pour une exposition d'art égyptien organisée dans leurs locaux. Œil doré sur fond bleu lumineux, texte blanc, triangle noir. (JPN)
23 Affiche pour un joaillier suisse. Perles blanches, noires, trois perles vert pâle, reliées par des éléments dorés. (SWI)
24 Personnage de bouffon, détail de l'affiche de la fig. 21 pour le livre illustré des dessins de Yoshitaro Isaka (Péro). (JPN)

FINLAND PINE

フィンランド パイン

25

FINLAND PINE

フィンランド パイン

26

THE BMW LUXURY SPORTS COUPE. THE EPITOME OF TRUTH IN PACKAGING.

27

THE BMW 733i. IT DOESN'T SCREAM WEALTH. IT JUST QUIETLY REWARDS INSIGHT.

28

25, 26 Two complementary posters for furniture made with Finnish pine-wood. Full-colour photographs. (JPN)
27, 28 From a sophisticated poster campaign for BMW cars. (USA)
29 Poster inspired by Oskar Schlemmer's works, for the Japanese departement store *Seiyu*. (JPN)
30 A *Mac* (jeans) poster for the retail trade. (GER)

25, 26 Zwei zusammengehörende Plakate für Möbel aus finnischer Kiefer. Farbaufnahmen. (JPN)
27, 28 Aus einer Plakatkampagne für BMW. Beim Sport-Coupé geht es um die Formschönheit, beim BMW 733i um das unaufdringliche Äussere und den angenehmen Luxus der Innenausstattung. (USA)
29 Vom Werk Oskar Schlemmers inspiriertes Plakat für das japanische Kaufhaus *Seiyu*. (JPN)
30 Für den Einzelhandel bestimmtes Plakat für *Mac*-Jeans. (GER)

25, 26 Deux affiches groupées, pour des ameublements en pin de Finlande. Photos couleur. (JPN)
27, 28 Eléments d'une campagne d'affiches pour BMW. Le coupé sport est vanté pour son élégance, la BMW 733i pour son extérieur sans prétention et le luxe de son confort intérieur. (USA)
29 Affiche inspirée par l'œuvre d'Oskar Schlemmer, pour les grands magasins japonais *Seiyu*. (JPN)
30 Affiche d'une campagne de publicité pour les jeans *Mac* destinée au commerce de détail allemand. (GER)

面白がるから、人間なんだ。西友土浦店、ファッションボックス・ウォーク　11月23日[火]、同時オープン

SEIYU
Fashion Box
WALK

地球人、夢中人。

29

30

Varia

31

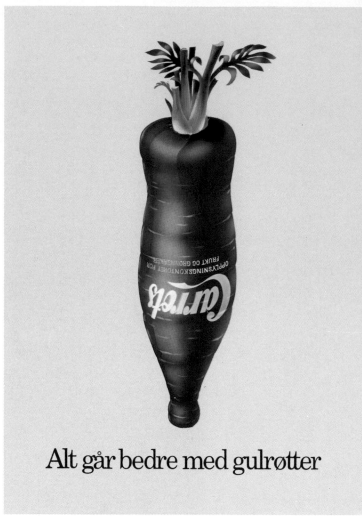

Alt går bedre med gulrøtter

32

33

Sun! Sun! Sun! (Burn! Burn! Burn!)

34

35

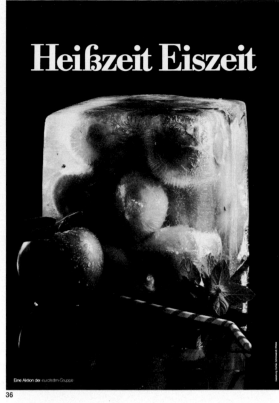

36

37

38

31 Poster advertising a drink containing vitamin C. Pink fridge and ground, yellow background. (JPN)
32 From a campaign for Norwegian carrots, referring to the classic *Cola* bottle. (NOR)
33 "Careful packaging." Poster advertising aluminium foil. In full colour. (JPN)
34 Sporting holidays on the sunny Okinawa island are the subject of this poster. (JPN)
35 "Gas heating for your winter comfort." Cap in warm colours, blue gas flames. (SWI)
36 Poster for a special sale of drinking glasses by the *Euroteam* group, in shops and windows. (GER)
37 "Poland invites you." Full-colour silkscreen poster of the Polish tourism and information office. (POL)
38 Mexico City's opera-house is the focal point of this poster advertising the city's attractions. (MEX)

31 Plakat für ein Getränk mit Vitamin C. Eisschrank und Boden rosa, Hintergrund gelb. (JPN)
32 Aus einer Kampagne für norwegische Karotten; Anspielung auf die klassische *Cola* Flasche. (NOR)
33 «Liebevolle Verpackung.» Plakatwerbung für Aluminiumfolie. In Farbe. (JPN)
34 Sportferien auf der sonnigen Okinawa-Insel sind Thema dieses Plakates. (JPN)
35 «Gasheizung für Ihren winterlichen Komfort.» Mütze in warmen Farben, blaue Gasflammen. (SWI)
36 Plakat für eine Trinkglasaktion der *Euroteam*-Gruppe, in Schaufenstern und Läden. (GER)
37 «Polen lädt ein.» Farbiges Siebdruckplakat des polnischen Touristik- und Informationsbüros. (POL)
38 Das Opernhaus von Mexiko-City ist Mittelpunkt des Plakates, das für diese Stadt wirbt. (MEX)

31 Affiche pour une boisson à la vitamine C. Frigo et sol rose, fond jaune. (JPN)
32 Campagne pour les carottes norvégiennes; allusion à la bouteille *Cola* classique. (NOR)
33 «Emballé avec amour.» Affiche pour les feuilles d'aluminium. En couleurs. (JPN)
34 Affiche vantant les charmes de vacances sportives aux îles Ryūkyū, notamment Okinawa. (JPN)
35 «Le chauffage au gaz pour votre confort hivernal.» Bonnet aux couleurs chaudes, gaz bleu. (SWI)
36 Affiche pour une vente promotionnelle de verres du groupe *Euroteam*, pour vitrines et magasins. (GER)
37 Affiche sérigraphique en couleurs publiée par l'Office polonais du tourisme et de l'information. (POL)
38 Affiche pour la ville de Mexico, avec l'Opéra comme centre de l'image. (MEX)

Varia

39 Point-of-sale poster for *Jeandenimes*, a make of jeans. (FRA)
40 "Dream Jeans." Three-part poster taken from an advertising campaign for *Rifle* jeans. (SWI)
41 From a series of posters on the occasion of the fifteenth anniversary of the *Kamata-Tokyo Plaza* department store, here for summer fashions. (JPN)
42 Example from a campaign for elegant women's fashions by *Sistiene*. Silvery trousers with a black waistcoat and a white blouse. (JPN)
43 From an advertising campaign for *Chesterfield* socks and stockings. (FRA)

39 Für den Innenaushang in Läden bestimmtes Plakat für eine Jeans-Marke. (FRA)
40 Dreiteiliges Plakat aus einer Werbekampagne für *Rifle*-Jeans. (SWI)
41 Aus einer Serie von Plakaten, hier speziell für Sommermode, anlässlich des fünfzehnjährigen Bestehens eines japanischen Kaufhauses. (JPN)
42 Beispiel aus einer Kampagne für elegante Damenmode von *Sistiene*. Silbrige Hosen mit schwarzer Weste und weisser Bluse. (JPN)
43 Aus einer Werbekampagne für Strümpfe und Socken von *Chesterfield*. (FRA)

39 Affiche intérieure pour une marque de jeans. (FRA)
40 Affiche tripartite utilisée dans une campagne pour les jeans *Rifle*. (SWI)
41 Exemple d'une série d'affiches, ici particulièrement consacrées à la mode estivale, à l'occasion du 15e anniversaire d'un grand magasin japonais. (JPN)
42 Exemple d'affiche dans une campagne en faveur des modes *Sistiene* incarnant l'élégance féminine. Pantalon argenté, veste noire, blouse blanche. (JPN)
43 Elément d'une campagne en faveur des bas et chaussettes *Chesterfield*. (FRA)

ARTIST / KÜNSTLER / ARTISTE:

40 Bruno Bisang
41 Toru Kogure
42 Koichi Inakoshi
43 Pierre Peyrolles

DESIGNER / GESTALTER:

39 Nicole Widmer
40 Ch. Hitz
41 Masaki Hirate
42 Jun Yoshida/Toshinori Nozaki

ART DIRECTOR:

39 Jean Widmer
40 R. Lacher
41 Masaki Hirate
42 Shozo Murase
43 J. Claude Lachery

AGENCY / AGENTUR / AGENCE:

39 Visuel Design
40 Marti Werbung
41 C. C. Les Mains
42 Kasugai Co., Ltd.
43 Greener Grass

39

41

42

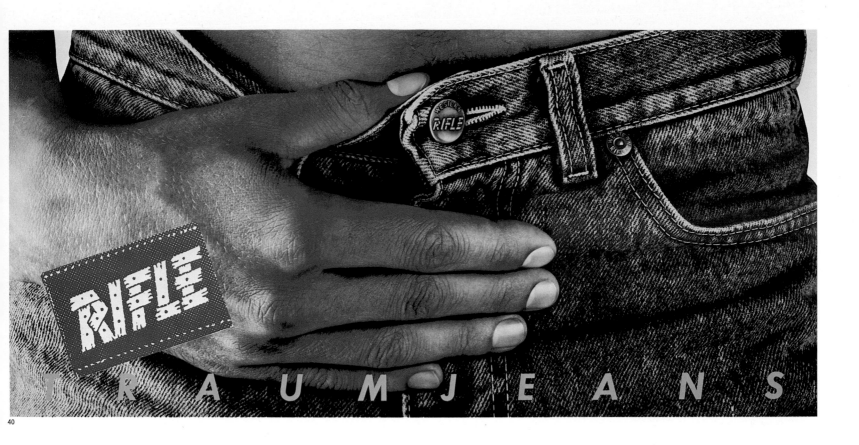

T R A U M J E A N S

40

43

un monde à partager

44

Stimulants/Genussmittel

44 "A world to be shared." Three-part poster for *Gauloises* cigarettes. Blue and white. (SWI)
45 An Italian restaurant's poster, used as a gift and also as table decoration. (USA)
46 Poster for *Roland* biscuit-bread, recommended here for hot and cold meals. (SWI)
47 A slogan in the Swiss-German language ("Come on, we've deserved it") advertises *Feldschlösschen* beer on a three-part poster. (SWI)
48 "Have you already had your *Ovo*?" Large-format poster taken from an advertising campaign for *Ovomaltine* breakfast drink. (SWI)

45

Roland Biscottes

46

CHUMM, MER HÄNDS VERDIENT.

FELDSCHLÖSSCHEN BIER

EIN SCHLUCK VOM BESTEN

47

Déjà eu ton Ovo aujourd'hui?

Ovomaltine – une valeur sûre.

48

49

50

53

42

51

S'isch guat, ds Valsarwasser.

Grand Marnier
Grandeur oblige...

52

49 For a Japanese milk drink. The figure in the yellow area is an approximately hundred years old "classic" of Japanese advertising graphics. (JPN)
50 Poster for a *Lipton* ice-tea drink. The text refers to the tea tradition as well as to how famous *Lipton* teas have become over the years. (SWI)
51 Three-part poster for a Swiss mineral water. In shades of grey and green. (SWI)
52 "Greatness obliges." Tripartite poster for *Grand Marnier*. White lettering on a yellow ground. (SWI)
53 Example from a campaign with woodcut posters for *Schweppes*. Tripartite poster. (SWI)
54 Full-colour poster for a seafood restaurant. (USA)

49 Plakat für ein japanisches Milchgetränk. Die Figur im gelben Feld ist ein ca. hundert Jahre alter «Klassiker» der japanischen Werbegraphik. (JPN)
50 Plakat für ein Eistee-Getränk von *Lipton*. Englischer Text als Anspielung auf die Tee-Tradition und die Bekanntheit des *Lipton*-Tees. (SWI)
51 Dreiteiliges Plakat für *Valser*-Wasser, ein Schweizer Mineralwasser. In Grau- und Grüntönen. (SWI)
52 «Grösse verpflichtet.» Dreiteiliges Plakat für *Grand-Marnier*-Likör. Weisse Schrift auf Gelb. (SWI)
53 Beispiel aus einer Kampagne mit Holzschnittplakaten für *Schweppes*. Dreiteiliges Plakat. (SWI)
54 Mehrfarbiges Plakat für ein Fischrestaurant. (USA)

49 Pour une boisson japonaise à base de lait. Le personnage inscrit dans le rectangle jaune est un classique déjà centenaire de la publicité. (JPN)
50 Affiche pour l'ice-tea *Lipton*. Le texte anglais fait allusion au flegme britannique et à la réputation des thés *Lipton*. (SWI)
51 Affiche tripartite pour l'eau minérale suisse *Valser*. Divers tons gris et verts. (SWI)
52 Affiche tripartite pour la liqueur *Grand Marnier*. (SWI)
53 Exemple d'une campagne de gravures sur bois pour *Schweppes*. Affiche tripartite. (SWI)
54 Affiche d'un restaurant de poissons. (USA)

ARTIST / KÜNSTLER / ARTISTE:
49 Shigeo Fukuda
50 A. & P. Schudel
51 Henry-Pierre Schultz
52 Christoph Markwalder
53 Jeannette Vuillemin
54 Warren Lynch

DESIGNER / GESTALTER / MAQUETTISTE:
49 Shigeo Fukuda
50 Bep SA
51 Felix Zimmermann
52 Stephan Kaister
53 Jeannette Vuillemin
54 Julius Friedman

ART DIRECTOR / DIRECTEUR ARTISTIQUE:
49 Shigeo Fukuda
51 Felix Zimmermann
52 Urs Tschan
53 Atelier Jaquet
54 Julius Friedman

AGENCY / AGENTUR / AGENCE – STUDIO:
50 BEP SA
51 Gisler & Gisler
52 Urs Tschan AG
53 Atelier Jaquet
54 Images

54

ook voor
uitzendkrachten
recht op vakantie
vakantiebijslag
geld voor feestdagen
en voor kort verzuim

55

je zit goed
bij randstad

56

GEO

58

McCoy Limited, Screenprint Serigraphie Siebdruck

96 Wolcott Avenue, Torrington, Connecticut 06790

59

55, 56 From an advertising campaign for *Randstad*, an employment agency. Fig. 55: "Part-time personnel also have the right to holidays and special bonuses"; Fig. 56: "You are in the right place with *Randstad*." (NLD)
57 Small-format poster with a stocking pattern, for the *New York Times*: the success story of an advertising campaign for *Dim* stockings. (USA)
58 Poster which appeared in a limited edition for the American *Geo* magazine. In full colour. (USA)
59 Part of a letterform- and type-poster alphabet, promoting quality commercial and fine art silkscreen printing. (USA)
60 Poster as invitation to a ladies' brunch during the ICSC (International Council of Shopping Centers) Convention in New Orleans. (USA)
61 New Year greetings of the graphic designer Tom Eckersley. (GBR)

55, 56 Aus einer Werbekampagne für das Stellenvermittlungsbüro *Randsta* Abb. 55: «Auch für Teilzeit-Personal das Recht auf Ferien und Sonderzulager Abb. 56: «Bei *Randstad* sitzen Sie richtig.» (NLD)
57 Kleinformatiges Plakat mit Strumpfmuster für die *New York Times*: c Erfolgsgeschichte einer Werbekampagne für *Dim*-Strümpfe. (USA)
58 In beschränkter Auflage erschienenes Plakat für das amerikanische *Ge* Magazin. Mehrfarbig. (USA)
59 Teil einer Schrifttypen-Alphabet-Plakatserie als Werbung für einen Sie drucker. (USA)
60 Einladung zu einem Damen-Brunch, veranstaltet während einer Tagung zu Thema Einkaufszentren. (USA)
61 Neujahrsgruss des Graphikers Tom Eckersley. (GBR)

Varia

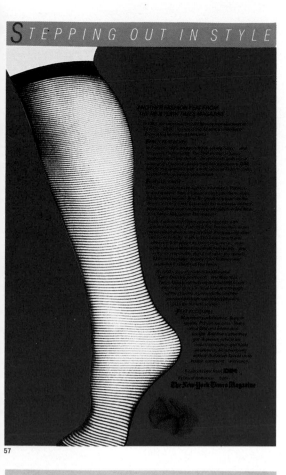

STEPPING OUT IN STYLE

57

60

ARTIST / KÜNSTLER / ARTISTE:

55, 56 Ben Bos
57 Bill Aller
58 Nicholas Gaetano
59 Walter Allner
60 Don Sibley
61 Tom Eckersley

DESIGNER / GESTALTER / MAQUETTISTE:

55, 56 Ben Bos
57 Ellen Kier
58 Nicholas Gaetano
59 Walter Allner
60 Don Sibley
61 Tom Eckersley

ART DIRECTOR / DIRECTEUR ARTISTIQUE:

57 Andrew Kner
59 Walter Allner
60 Bob Dennard/Don Sibley

AGENCY / AGENTUR / AGENCE – STUDIO:

55, 56 Total Design
60 Dennard Creative, Inc.

55, 56 Campagne publicitaire pour l'agence de placement *Randstad.*
Fig. 55: «Le droit aux vacances et indemnités aussi pour les intéri-
maires»; fig. 56: «Vous êtes bien chez *Randstad.*» (NLD)
57 Affichette avec échantillon de bas, pour le *New York Times:* histoire
du succès d'une campagne pour les bas *Dim.* (USA)
58 Affiche au tirage limité pour le magazine américain *Geo.* En polychromie. (USA)
59 Elément d'une série d'affiches présentant une famille de caractères.
Publicité pour un sérigraphe. (USA)
60 Affiche d'invitation à un brunch réunissant des dames lors d'un
congrès sur le thème des centres commerciaux. (USA)
61 Carte de vœux de Nouvel An du graphiste Tom Eckersley. (GER)

Greetings 1983 Tom Eckersley

ECKERSLEY

61

45

Der beste Gastgeber ist die Natur. Hirschquelle.

M Mineralbrunnen AG, Bad Teinach

Das große stille Heilwasser aus dem Schwarzwald. *Heilanzeige: Fördert die Funktion von Nieren, Blase, Magen und Darm. Harntreibend.*

62

ARTIST / KÜNSTLER / ARTISTE:

62 Rupert Schneider
63 Teresa Fasolino
64 Aldo Fallai
65 Gregory King
66 Bob Boyd

DESIGNER / GESTALTER / MAQUETTISTE:

62 Hans-Joachim Sommer
65, 66 Laurie Sillay-Lahr

ART DIRECTOR / DIRECTEUR ARTISTIQUE:

62 Hans-Joachim Sommer
63 Milton Glaser
64 Jan v. d. Ven
65, 66 Laurie Sillay-Lahr

AGENCY / AGENTUR / AGENCE – STUDIO:

62 Leonhardt & Kern
63 Milton Glaser, Inc.
64 Prad B. V.
65, 66 Umphenour & Martin

62 "Nature is the best host." Poster advertising *Hirschquelle* table water. The canvas texture of the still-life painted in classic style is clearly visible. (GER)
63 *Grand Union's* fine fowl is the subject of this poster which was displayed throughout the branches of this supermarket chain. (USA)
64 Two-part poster for *Caballero* cigarettes: "Taste for two." Photograph in warm brown shades corresponding with the packet's orange-brown colour. (NLD)
65, 66 Examples from a series of full-colour posters in which different milkshakes are featured monthly. Used as a milk-shake promotional in point-of-sale displays in *Arby's* restaurants. (USA)

Caballero Filter. Smaak voor twee.

64

Stimulants/Genussmittel

63

62 Plakatwerbung für das Mineralwasser *Hirschquelle*. Die Leinwandstruktur des dafür im klassischen Stil gemalten Stillebens wird deutlich sichtbar. (GER)
63 *Grand Unions* feines Geflügel ist Thema dieses Plakates, das für den Aushang in den Filialen dieser Supermarkt-Kette bestimmt ist. (USA)
64 Zweiteiliges Plakat für *Caballero*-Zigaretten: «Geschmack für zwei.» Aufnahme in warmen Brauntönen, der orangebraunen Farbe der Packung entsprechend. (NLD)
65, 66 Beispiele aus einer Serie von mehrfarbigen Plakaten, die im monatlichen Wechsel für verschiedene Milch-Shakes in *Arby's* Restaurants werben. (USA)

62 Publicité par voie d'affiche pour l'eau minérale *Hirschquelle*. La structure de la toile de cette nature morte peinte dans le style classique est apparente. (GER)
63 Les volailles de choix de la marque *Grand Union* illustrent cette affiche destinée aux succursales de cette chaîne de supermarchés. (USA)
64 Affiche bipartite pour les cigarettes *Caballero*: «Du goût pour deux.» Photo aux tons brun chaud correspondant au brun orangé du paquet. (NLD)
65, 66 Exemples d'une série d'affiches polychromes remplacées chaque mois pour la promotion des milk-shakes du restaurant *Arby's*. (USA)

65

66

Das Höchste an Kommunikation: Nixdorf 8818
Das erste digitale Telefon-Vermittlungssystem

NIXDORF COMPUTER

67

In the United Kingdom...

Mobil Oil Company, Ltd. employs more than 2,500 people, and has operated in the U.K. since 1886. Its Coryton refinery has the capacity to process 175,000 barrels of crude oil a day into a full range of petroleum products. MOCL markets these to a variety of industrial and commercial customers, through over 1,000 retail outlets.

In the British North Sea, Mobil North Sea, Ltd. produces about 100,000 barrels of oil a day. The affiliate is having the Beryl field's second production platform built, with startup scheduled for 1984. By 1985, production from the field is expected to be more than 200,000 barrels a day.

The need for energy is worldwide. So are Mobil's efforts to help meet it.

Mobil

68

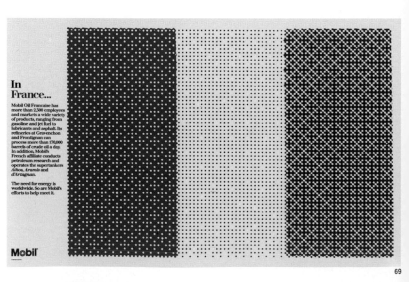

In France...

Mobil Oil Française has more than 2,500 employees and markets a wide variety of products, ranging from gasoline and jet fuel to lubricants and asphalt. Its refineries at Gravenchon and Frontignan can process more than 170,000 barrels of crude oil a day. In addition, Mobil's French affiliate conducts petroleum research and operates the supertankers *Aïbos, Aramis* and *d'Artagnan*.

The need for energy is worldwide. So are Mobil's efforts to help meet it.

Mobil

69

Industry/Industrie

70

71

67, 70 Examples from an advertising campaign with humorous illustrations, for *Nixdorf* computers. Both posters are in full colour. (GER)
68, 69 Posters taken form an image campaign for *Mobil.* The illustrations refer to this oil company's activities in France and Great Britain. (USA)
71, 72 "The end of the typewriting era begins with *Nixdorf* text processing" and "How you can clean up your administration with *Nixdorf* computers". From a series of posters with photographic illustrations for *Nixdorf.* (GER)

67, 70 Beispiele aus einer Werbekampagne mit humorvollen Illustrationen für *Nixdorf*-Computer. Beide Plakate in Farbe. (GER)
68, 69 Plakate aus einer Image-Kampagne für *Mobil.* Sie beziehen sich auf die Unternehmungen des Ölkonzerns in Grossbritannien und Frankreich, wie auch deutlich aus den Illustrationen ersichtlich ist. (USA)
71, 72 Aus einer Serie von Plakaten mit photographischen Illustrationen für *Nixdorf*-Computer (s. auch Abb. 67, 70). (GER)

67, 70 Eléments d'une campagne publicitaire utilisant des illustrations pleines d'humour pour promouvoir la cause des ordinateurs *Nixdorf.* Les deux affiches sont en couleurs. (GER)
68, 69 Affiches utilisées pour une campagne de prestige de *Mobil.* On s'y réfère aux entreprises du groupe pétrolier en France et au Royaume-Uni, comme le montrent clairement les illustrations. (USA)
71, 72 Exemples d'une série d'affiches illustrées de photos pour les ordinateurs *Nixdorf* (cf. aussi les fig. 67, 70). (GER)

72

73

74

Publishers Publicity
Verlagswerbung
Publicité d'éditeurs

ARTIST / KÜNSTLER / ARTISTE:

73, 74 Barbara Nessim
75 Alan E. Cober
76–79 Seymour Chwast

DESIGNER / GESTALTER / MAQUETTISTE:

73 Barbara Nessim
74 Irene Ramp
76–79 Seymour Chwast

ART DIRECTOR / DIRECTEUR ARTISTIQUE:

73 Barbara Nessim/Mare Earley
74 Irene Ramp/Rudolph Hoglund
75 Suzanne Nelson
76 Greg Davis
77–79 Warren Watwood

AGENCY / AGENTUR / AGENCE – STUDIO:

73, 74 Nessim & Associates
76 Pushpin Lubalin Peckolick/
Tracey-Locke Advertising
77–79 Doremus & Co.

76

77

50

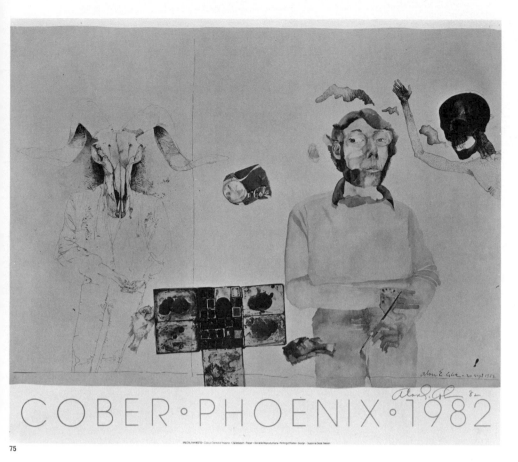

73 Poster for *Scarlett-Letters*, which introduces this firm's new typefaces. The purpose was to do a type poster that did not look like a typical type poster. Because of its popularity, 30 000 copies had to be printed to date. (USA)
74 Poster for *Time*, taken from a cover of this magazine. The image expresses all women's struggle towards equality. (USA)
75 Promotion for the artist Alan E. Cober on the occasion of an exhibition at the Art Directors Club in Phoenix, Arizona. (USA)
76 Poster of a telephone company appealing to its employees to excell by means of eliminating unnecessary mistakes. (USA)
77–79 Examples from a series of posters recommending *Forbes* business magazine as the up-and-coming executive's aid to success. (USA)

73 Plakat für *Scarlett-Letters*, das die neuen Schrifttypen dieser Firma vorstellen, aber trotzdem nicht wie ein Schrifttypen-Plakat aussehen sollte. Es wurde von der Doppelbedeutung des Wortes «face» ausgegangen, das sowohl Gesicht als auch Schrifttyp («type face») bedeutet. Wegen seiner Popularität wurden bereits 30 000 Exemplare des Plakats gedruckt. (USA)
74 Plakat für *Time*, das auch Umschlag einer Ausgabe des Magazins war. Thema ist der beschwerliche Weg zur Gleichberechtigung der Frau, gleich welcher Hautfarbe. (USA)
75 Werbung für den Künstler Alan E. Cober anlässlich einer Ausstellung im Art Directors Club von Phoenix. (USA)
76 Plakat einer Telephongesellschaft als Aufruf an die Angestellten, sich durch das Aufspüren und Beheben von Fehlern hervorzutun. (USA)
77–79 Beispiele aus einer Serie von Plakaten, die dem Geschäftsmann das Wirtschaftsmagazin *Forbes* als sichere Leiter zum Erfolg empfehlen. (USA)

73 Affiche pour un nouveau caractère de *Scarlett Letters*. Il s'agissait de présenter une information complète aux typographes tout en évitant l'affiche professionnelle ennuyeuse. Le mot «caractère» en anglais, «face», signifie aussi la face, le visage, d'où la solution adoptée. L'affiche devenue populaire en est déjà à 30 000 exemplaires. (USA)
74 Affiche pour *Time*, utilisée aussi comme couverture du magazine. Le sujet en est la douloureuse ascension des femmes vers l'égalité, quelle que soit la couleur de leur peau. (USA)
75 Autopromotion de l'artiste Alan E. Cober à l'occasion d'un exposition à l'Art Directors Club de Phoenix. (USA)
76 Affiche d'une société du téléphone invitant ses employés à rivaliser de zèle pour la détection et la réparation de défauts. (USA)
77–79 Exemples d'une série d'affiches où le jeune cadre et patron se voit recommander la lecture du magazine *Forbes* sur la voie du succès. (USA)

80

81

82

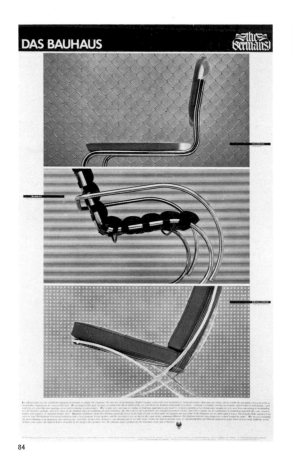

84

85

86

80–82 From the poster campaign of a telephone company, showing various models of telephones. (JPN)
83 Point-of-sale poster for *Bridgestone* tyres. Tyres and landscape in shades of brown, blue sky. (USA)
84, 85 Examples from a series of posters for *Phoenix Imperial*, a new quality of German paper. Fig. 84: Bauhaus and the enduring idea of combining art and technology are the theme of this poster which shows three Bauhaus "classics"; Fig. 85: this poster deals with communication from the artist through an instrument, or on paper, to the listener or viewer, by means of perfect reproduction. Both posters are in full colour. (USA)
86 Poster printed on both sides, for *Knoll* furniture. (USA)
87 Small-format poster for *Mitsubishi* music decks. (GER)

80–82 Aus einer Plakatkampagne für eine Telephongesellschaft, mit verschiedenen Modellen von Telephonapparaten. (JPN)
83 Für den Innenaushang bestimmtes Plakat für *Bridgestone*-Reifen. Reifen und Landschaft in Brauntönen, Himmel blau. (USA)
84, 85 Beispiele aus einer Plakatserie für *Phoenix Imperial*, eine neue deutsche Papierqualität. Abb. 84: Das Bauhaus und die These der Verbindung von Kunst und Technik sind Gegenstand dieses Plakates, das drei Bauhaus-Klassiker zeigt; Abb. 85: die grossen deutschen Komponisten (hier Bach) und die Wichtigkeit des Mediums (Instrumente und auch Papier) für die Reproduktion sind das Thema. Beide Plakate mehrfarbig. (USA)
86 Beidseitig bedrucktes Plakat für *Knoll*-Möbeldesign. (USA)
87 Kleinformatiges Plakat für *Mitsubishi*-Musikanlagen. (GER)

80–82 Affiches figurant dans une campagne pour une société de téléphone, avec divers modèles d'appareils. (JPN)
83 Affiche intérieure pour les pneus *Bridgestone*. Pneus et paysage en divers bruns, ciel bleu. (USA)
84, 85 Exemples d'une série d'affiches pour *Phoenix Imperial*, une nouvelle qualité allemande de papier. Fig. 84: Le Bauhaus et l'idée d'une interrelation entre l'art et la technique dominent cette affiche illustrée de trois classiques du Bauhaus; fig. 85: les grands compositeurs allemands (ici, Bach) et l'importance du média (les instruments, et aussi le papier) pour la reproduction. Les deux affiches en polychromie. (USA)
86 Affiche imprimée des deux côtés pour les meubles *Knoll*. (USA)
87 Affichette pour les chaînes hi-fi *Mitsubishi*. (GER)

"Got your Bridgestones on?"

83

Industry/Industrie

ARTIST / KÜNSTLER / ARTISTE:

80–82 Yamazaki Akira
83 D. Millsap
84 Joe Baraban
85 John Collier
86 Milton Glaser
87 Gerhard Vormwald

DESIGNER / GESTALTER / MAQUETTISTE:

80–82 Kameyama Yoshifumi
83 Jim Doyle
84, 85 C. Randall Sherman
86 Milton Glaser

ART DIRECTOR / DIRECTEUR ARTISTIQUE:

80–82 Nakajo Iwao
83 Jim Doyle/Paul Nelson
84, 85 Jay Loucks
86 Milton Glaser
87 Robert Pütz

AGENCY / AGENTUR / AGENCE – STUDIO:

80–82 Hakuhodo Nagoya Shisha
83 Dancer Fitzgerald Sample, Inc.
84, 85 Loucks Atelier, Inc.
86 Milton Glaser, Inc.
87 Robert Pütz GmbH

MITSUBISHI OHRWERK ── ECHT SENKRECHT

87

Aa Bb Cc Dd Ee Ff Gg Hh Ii Jj Kk Ll Mm Nn Oo Pp Qc

alligator   butterfly   cat   dog   elephant   frog   giraffe   hippo   ibis   jaguar   kangaroo   lion   mouse   nightingale   orangutan   parrot   quail

88

The Xerox 630 Memorywriter

XEROX

89

OLIVETTI ELECTRONIC CALCULATOR

olivetti

90

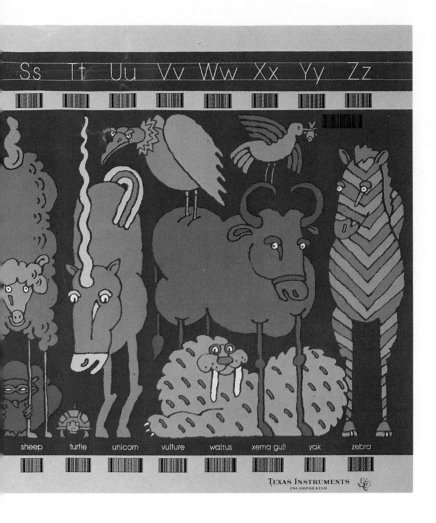

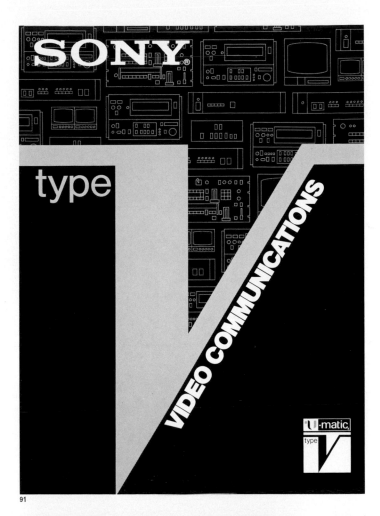

91

Industry/Industrie

ARTIST / KÜNSTLER / ARTISTE:

88 Nancy Hoefig
89 Peter Steiner
90 Fabio Simion
92 Charly Franklin

ART DIRECTOR / DIRECTEUR ARTISTIQUE:

88 Steve Gibbs
89 James L. Selak
90 Roberto Pieraccini
92 M. Lees

DESIGNER / GESTALTER / MAQUETTISTE:

88 Steve Gibbs/Nancy Hoefig
89 James L. Selak
90 Giulio Milanesi
91 Michael Tedesco
92 Michael Patrick Cronan

AGENCY / AGENTUR / AGENCE – STUDIO:

88 Richards, Sullivan, Brock & Associates
89 Xerox Corporation
90 Direzione Pubblicità Olivetti
91 Michael Tedesco

88 Poster accompanying a *Texas Instruments'* computer toy for children which reads bar codes and speaks the alphabet and animal names aloud. (USA)
89 Poster for a *Xerox* memory-writer typewriter. Full-colour shot, silver background. (USA)
90 Small-format poster for an *Olivetti* electronic calculator. (ITA)
91 Point-of-sale poster for *Sony* video comunications apparatus. (USA)
92 Full-colour poster taken from an American advertising campaign for *Apple* computers. (USA)

88 Dieses Plakat begleitet ein Computer-Spielzeug, das die Strich-Codes lesen und das Alphabet und die Tiernamen laut aussprechen kann. (USA)
89 Plakat für eine Speicherschreibmaschine von *Xerox*. Die Margerite ist die ursprüngliche Bezeichnung für das Typenrad. Mehrfarbige Aufnahmen, Hintergrund silber. (USA)
90 Kleinformatiges Plakat für eine elektronische Rechenmaschine von *Olivetti*. (ITA)
91 Für den Verkaufsort bestimmtes Plakat für die *Sony*-Videoproduktfamilie. (USA)
92 Mehrfarbiges Plakat aus einer US-Kampagne für *Apple*-Computer, hier für das Modell «Lisa». (USA)

88 Cette affiche accompagne un ordinateur-jouet qui sait déchiffrer les codes en barres et énoncer à voix haute les lettres de l'alphabet et les noms d'animaux. (USA)
89 Affiche pour une machine à écrire électronique *Xerox* à mémoire. La marguerite est en même temps le nom du support de caractères dans ce type de machine. Photos polychromes sur argent. (USA)
90 Affichette pour une calculatrice électronique *Olivetti*. (ITA)
91 Affiche point de vente pour la famille des produits vidéo *Sony*. (USA)
92 Affiche polychrome dans une campagne américaine pour les ordinateurs *Apple*, ici pour «Lisa». (USA)

92

93

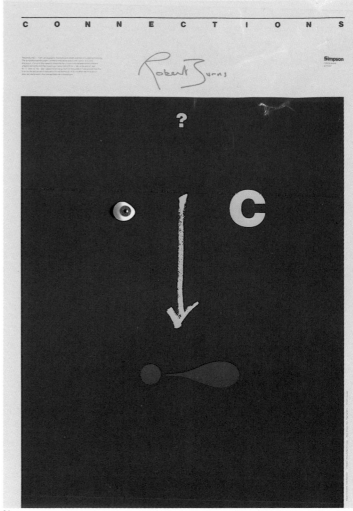

94

96

97

95

ARTIST / KÜNSTLER / ARTISTE:

93 Heather Cooper
94 Robert Burns
95 Michael Vanderbyl
96 Ivan Chermayeff
97 Tony DiSpigna
98 James Cross
99 Seymour Chwast

DESIGNER / GESTALTER / MAQUETTISTE:

93 Heather Cooper
94 Robert Burns
95, 98 Woody Pirtle
96 Ivan Chermayeff
97 Alan Peckolick
99 Seymour Chwast

ART DIRECTOR / DIRECTEUR ARTISTIQUE:

93–99 James Cross

AGENCY / AGENTUR / AGENCE – STUDIO:

93–95, 98 Cross Associates
96 Cross Associates/
    Chermayeff & Geismar Assoc.
97, 99 Cross Associates/
    Pushpin Lubalin Peckolick

93–99 Taken from a series of posters for *Simpson* paper, illustrating "connections" as seen by various graphic designers: Heather Cooper depicts perception of beauty, discovery and comedy as connecting facets of human experience; Robert Burns chooses simple graphic symbols and a play upon words; Michael Vanderbyl shows the designer going back for inspiration from the modern to the classical; Ivan Chermayeff chooses paper as a bridge between idea and communication; Alan Peckolick uses typography (Goudy Old Style) as the purest symbol for connections; James Cross combines fingerprints and computer language and Seymour Chwast shows the things that connect him to the reality of life. (USA)

93–99 Aus einer Serie von Plakaten für *Simpson*-Papier, die «Zusammenhänge» illustrieren, wie sie von Graphikern gesehen werden: Heather Cooper stellt das Empfinden des Schönen, das Entdecken und die Komödie als verbindende menschliche Erfahrungen dar; Robert Burns wählt einfache graphische Symbole und ein Wortspiel, die besagen, dass Kommunikation nur möglich ist, wenn man denkt bevor man spricht; Michael Vanderbyl zeigt den Designer, der für seine Inspiration von modernen zu klassischen Vorbildern übergeht; Ivan Chermayeff wählt Papier als Brücke zwischen Vorstellung und Kommunikation; Alan Peckolick verwendet Typographie als reinstes Symbol für Zusammenhänge; James Cross kombiniert Fingerabdrücke und Computersprache; Seymour Chwast zeigt die Dinge, die ihn mit der Realität des Lebens verbinden. (USA)

93–99 Exemples d'affiches réalisées pour les papiers *Simpson* dans une série illustrant les «connexions» telles que les voient les graphistes: Heather Cooper représente le sentiment du beau, la découverte et la comédie comme expériences humaines unifiantes. Robert Burns opte pour de simples symboles graphiques; Michael Vanderbyl montre un designer abandonnant ses sources d'inspiration modernes pour retrouver les classiques; Ivan Chermayeff choisit le papier comme pont jeté entre l'idée et la communication; Alan Peckolick fait appel à la typo, pur symbole des connexions recherchées; James Cross combine les empreintes digitales et le langage de l'ordinateur; quant à Seymour Chwast, il présente les choses qui le relient à la réalité de la vie. (USA)

98

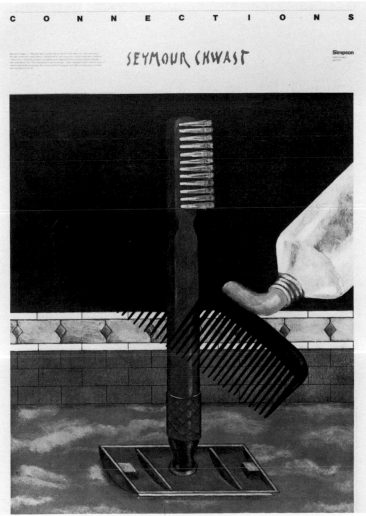

99

57

XEROX
1020
MARATHON COPIER

100

ARTIST / KÜNSTLER / ARTISTE:

100 Peter Steiner
101, 102 Focus on Sports
103 Sally Andersen-Bruce
104 Stephen Tarantal/Saul Bass/
     Peter Garfield (Photo)

DESIGNER / GESTALTER / MAQUETTISTE:

100 James L. Selak
101, 102 David van Blarcom
103 Frank Armstrong
104 David Foote

ART DIRECTOR / DIRECTEUR ARTISTIQUE:

100 James L. Selak
101, 102 David van Blarcom
103 Frank Armstrong
104 David Foote

AGENCY / AGENTUR / AGENCE – STUDIO:

100 Xerox Corporation
101, 102 IBM Design
103 Armstrong Design Consultants
104 U.S. Postal Service Headquarters

100 Poster advertising a model from the *Xerox Marathon* series of copying machines, in which the main point of communication is the product name. (USA)
101, 102 Poster taken from a series employed as motivation for IBM representatives, which was issued and printed in July, September and November 1981. The theme is that of commitment and the will to win. Full-colour photographs, white lettering on red. (USA)
103 Poster for ITT computer programmes. The P of productivity (green and yellow) and the Q of quality (greyish-brown and red) are emphasized. White lettering and grey on a black ground. (USA)
104 Science and industry are the theme of this poster and the postage stamp shown here. The poster was issued by the United States Mail and aimed at encouraging stamp collecting. In full colour. (USA)

100 Plakatwerbung für ein Modell aus der *Xerox-Marathon*-Serie von Kopiergeräten, wobei das Hauptgewicht der Aussage eindeutig auf dem Produktnamen liegt. (USA)
101, 102 Als Motivation für das IBM-Aussendienstpersonal herausgegebene Plakate aus einer Serie, die im Juli, September und November 1981 veröffentlicht wurde. Thema sind Einsatz und Siegeswille. Mehrfarbige Aufnahmen, Schrift weiss auf Rot. (USA)
103 Plakat für ITT-Computerprogramme. Das P von Produktivität (grün und gelb) und das Q von Qualität (grau-braun und rot) bilden den Schwerpunkt. Schrift weiss und grau auf schwarzem Grund. (USA)
104 Wissenschaft und Industrie sind Thema dieses Plakates und der abgebildeten Briefmarke. Herausgeber ist die Post der Vereinigten Staaten, die hier für das Briefmarkensammeln wirbt. In Farbe. (USA)

100 Affiche publicitaire pour un modèle de photocopieur de la série *Xerox Marathon*. L'accent est mis sur le nom du produit. (USA)
101, 102 Affiches publiées à l'intention de la force de vente IBM, dans une série diffusée en juillet, septembre et novembre 1981. Le thème: la combativité, le désir de vaincre à tout prix. Photos polychromes, texte blanc sur rouge. (USA)
103 Affiche d'une campagne publicitaire pour le logiciel ITT. Le P de Productivité (vert, jaune) et le Q de Qualité (tons vert olive et jaune chaud) sont mis en vedette. Texte blanc et gris sur fond noir. (USA)
104 La science et l'industrie constituent le sujet de cette affiche et du timbre-poste qui y est reproduit. Publication des P.T.T. américains pour inciter les usagers à collectionner les timbres. En couleurs. (USA)

Industry/Industrie

IBM

OPD...
Committed
to
Win

COMMITMENT'81

101

IBM

OPD...
Committed
to
Win

COMMITMENT'81

102

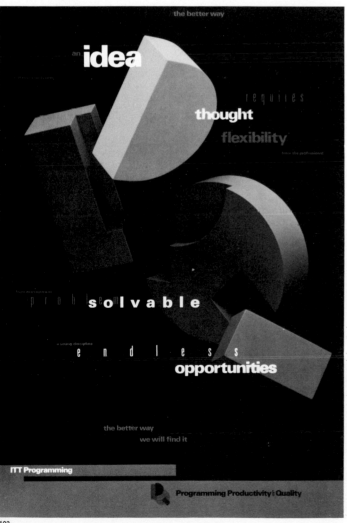

the better way

an **idea**

requires

thought

flexibility

from the professional

prob **solvable**

a vising discipline

e n d l e s s

opportunities

the better way

we will find it

ITT Programming

Programming Productivity & Quality

103

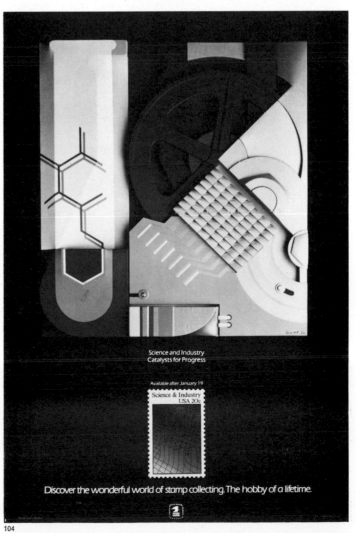

Science and Industry
Catalysts for Progress

Available after January 19

Science & Industry
USA 20c

Discover the wonderful world of stamp collecting. The hobby of a lifetime.

104

105 Full-colour poster advertising a book of anecdotes concerning presidents of the United States. (USA)
106 "The White Rose." Self-promotional poster by André François. Crayon and water-colour. (FRA)
107 Self-promotional poster of Nakahara, a Japanese design studio. Pastel colours, mainly pink. (JPN)
108 Poster sent as direct-mail advertising in the United States for *Design-Tex* cloth. Cloth samples in full colour. (USA)
109 Poster advertising a book with illustrations. (JPN)

105 Mehrfarbiges Plakat für ein Buch mit Anekdoten über die Präsidenten der Vereinigten Staaten. (USA)
106 «Die weisse Rose.» Eigenwerbungsplakat des Franzosen André François. Zeichenstift und Aquarell. (FRA)
107 Eigenwerbungsplakat des japanischen Design-Studios Nakahara. Pastellfarben, vorwiegend Rosa. (JPN)
108 Als Direktwerbung in den Vereinigten Staaten versandtes Plakat für *Design-Tex*-Stoffe. Stoffmuster mehrfarbig. (USA)
109 Plakatwerbung für ein Buch mit Illustrationen. (JPN)

105 Affiche polychrome pour un livre d'anecdotes sur les présidents des Etats-Unis. (USA)
106 «La Rose blanche.» Affiche autopromotionnelle du Français André François. Crayon et aquarelle. (FRA)
107 Affiche autopromotionnelle du studio de design japonais Nakahara. Tons pastel, le rose prédominant. (JPN)
108 Affiche de publicité directe aux Etats-Unis pour les tissus *Design-Tex*. Echantillons polychromes. (USA)
109 Affiche publicitaire pour un livre illustré. (JPN)

Publishers Publicity
Verlagswerbung
Publicité d'éditeurs

ARTIST / KÜNSTLER / ARTISTE:

105 Edward Sorel
106 André François
107 Kenji Nakahara
108 Harry & Marion Zelenko
109 Hitoshi Sawano

DESIGNER / GESTALTER / MAQUETTISTE:

105 Edward Sorel
107 Kenji Nakahara
109 Tokiyoshi Tsubouchi

ART DIRECTOR / DIRECTEUR ARTISTIQUE:

105 Edward Sorel
108 Harry & Marion Zelenko
109 Tokiyoshi Tsubouchi

AGENCY / AGENTUR / AGENCE – STUDIO:

107 Design Office Nakahara

105

106

107

108

スーパーエッセイ

かつをぶしの時代なのだ

イラストレーション・沢野ひとし

椎名 誠

定価＝830円

情報センター出版局
東京都新宿区四谷2-1 四谷ヒル 〒160 注文 03-358-0231

110 Poster advertising a book with ten cut-out paper kites. (USA)
111 Poster advertising editions of the Mirage gallery in Santa Monica, California. (USA)
112 Poster for *Atlanta Weekly*, the weekend magazine of the *Atlanta Journal and Constitution* newspaper: "Atlanta's the uppitiest of the urban up-and-comers." (USA)
113 Self-promotional poster for the printing firm *Stephenson*. Full-colour photograph, black ground. (USA)
114 Poster series for a financial institution, for display in offices. (USA)

110 Plakatwerbung für ein Buch mit zehn Papierdrachen zum Ausschneiden. (USA)
111 Werbeplakat für die Editionen der Galerie Mirage in Santa Monica, Kalifornien. (USA)
112 «Keine Prahlerei, Tatsachen.» Hier werden einige der «hervorragenden» Dinge der Stadt Atlanta aufgeführt, darunter *Atlanta Weekly*, das Wochenendmagazin der Zeitung *Atlanta Journal and Constitution*, für das dieses Plakat wirbt. (USA)
113 Eigenwerbungsplakat der Druckerei Stephenson Inc. Mehrfarbige Aufnahme, schwarzer Grund. (USA)
114 Aus einer als Aushang in Büros gedachten Plakatserie für eine Finanzierungsgesellschaft. (USA)

110 Affiche publicitaire pour un ouvrage contenant dix cerfs-volants à découper. (USA)
111 Affiche pour les Editions de la Galerie Mirage de Santa Monica (Californie). (USA)
112 «Pas de vantardise, juste des faits.» Sous cette devise, on énumère ici certains traits saillants de la ville d'Atlanta, dont l'*Atlanta Weekly*, le magazine dominical du quotidien *Atlanta Journal and Constitution*, qui publie cette affiche. (USA)
113 Affiche autopromotionnelle de l'imprimerie Stephenson Inc. Photo polychrome sur noir. (USA)
114 L'une des affiches d'une société de financement destinée à l'affichage dans les bureaux. (USA)

110

111

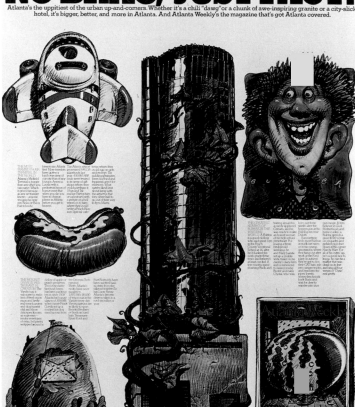

112

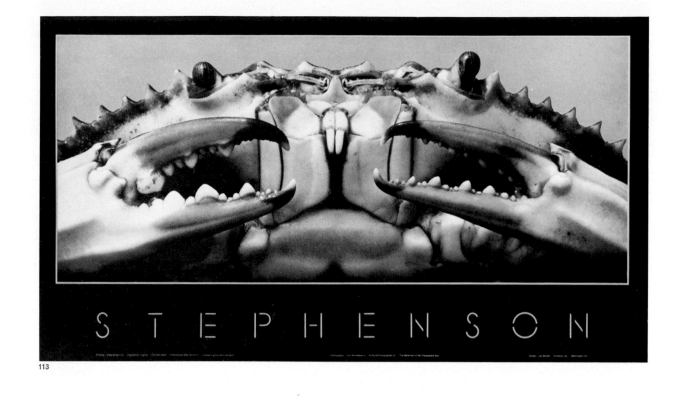

113

114

WashingtonHill

115

119

Direct Mail/Direktwerbung
Publicité directe

115 Poster for an area in the city of Baltimore. Brilliant pink, strong green, blue sky. (USA)
116 Small-format poster as an invitation to a party in conjunction with the construction of a new building. (USA)
117 Self promotion of a Swedish graphic designer. (Reference is made to a popular Scandinavian book that deals with intolerance and narrowmindedness.) Black and grey on silver. (SWE)
118 Poster of the Royal Insurance company. (AUS)
119 Poster advertising a private television channel. Some advantages, all beginning with C, are listed. (CAN)
120 Self-promotional poster with a photograph that was also used in a campaign for children's fashions, employing fairy-tales. (GER)

115 Plakat für ein Gebiet der Stadt Baltimore. Leuchtendes Pink, kräftiges Grün, blauer Himmel. (USA)
116 Kleinplakat als Einladung zu einer Party, die im Zusammenhang mit einem Bauvorhaben veranstaltet wird. (USA)
117 Eigenwerbung für einen schwedischen Graphiker. (Es wird auf ein skandinavisches Buch angespielt, in dem es um Intoleranz und Engstirnigkeit geht.) Schwarz und Grau auf Silber. (SWE)
118 Plakat der Royal Insurance für Gebäudeversicherungen. (AUS)
119 Plakatwerbung für einen privaten Fernsehsender, Kanal C. Es werden einige mit C beginnende Vorteile aufgeführt. (CAN)
120 Eigenwerbungsplakat mit einer Aufnahme, die auch als Werbung für Kindermode verwendet wurde, präsentiert im Rahmen eines Märchens. (GER)

115 Affiche pour un quartier de la ville de Baltimore. Rose lumineux, vert savoureux, ciel bleu. (USA)
116 Affichette d'invitation à une fête organisée en rapport avec un projet de construction. (USA)
117 Autopromotion d'un graphiste suédois. Noir et gris sur fond argent. (SWE)
118 Affiche de la Royal Insurance (assurance immobilière). (AUS)
119 Publicité par voie d'affiche pour une chaîne de télévision privée, le «canal C». On y énumère certains avantages commençant par la lettre C. (CAN)
120 Affiche autopromotionnelle du photographe Ross Feltus. La photo a été utilisée aussi pour la promotion de modes enfantines présentées dans le cadre d'un conte de fées. (GER)

116

117

118

120

122

121

ARTIST / KÜNSTLER / ARTISTE:

121, 122 Marvin Rubin
124 Jim Jacobs
125 Jözef Sumichrast

DESIGNER / GESTALTER / MAQUETTISTE:

121, 122 Marvin Rubin
123 Willi Bühler
124 Michael Campbell
125 Jözef Sumichrast

ART DIRECTOR / DIRECTEUR ARTISTIQUE:

121, 122 Elin Waite
123 Willi Bühler
124 Michael Campbell
125 Jözef Sumichrast

AGENCY / AGENTUR / AGENCE – STUDIO:

123 Adolf Wirz AG
124 Jim Jacobs' Studio, Inc.

Lassen Sie sich nichts vormachen. NZZ

123

Anne McGilvray Delights!

124

121, 122 Illustration and complete poster for the magazine *Westways*. The motif was originally used for an edition about the Osaka Expo. (USA)
123 "Don't let yourself be taken in." Three-part poster for the *Neue Zürcher Zeitung*. Black, white and blue. (SWI)
124 Poster as an invitation to a preview of various products. (USA)
125 Self-promotional poster of Jözef Sumichrast, with illustrations in the form of Hebraic characters. (USA)

121, 122 Illustration und vollständiges Plakat für die Zeitschrift *Westways*, die das Motiv ursprünglich als Umschlag einer Ausgabe über die Expo in Osaka verwendet hat. (USA)
123 Dreiteiliges Plakat der *Neuen Zürcher Zeitung*. In Schwarzweiss, Zeitungsname blau. (SWI)
124 Plakat als Einladung zu einer Kollektionsvorschau. (USA)
125 Eigenwerbungsplakat von Jözef Sumichrast mit Illustrationen in Form von hebräischen Schriftzeichen. (USA)

121, 122 Illustration et affiche complète pour le magazine *Westways*, qui a utilisé à l'origine ce sujet pour la couverture d'un numéro consacré à l'Expo d'Osaka. (USA)
123 Affiche tripartite de la *Neue Zürcher Zeitung*: «Ne vous en laissez pas accroire.» Noir-blanc, titre du journal bleu. (SWI)
124 Affiche servant d'invitation à l'avant-première d'un défilé de mode. (USA)
125 Affiche autopromotionnelle de Jözef Sumichrast. Illustrations en forme de lettres hébraïques. (USA)

125

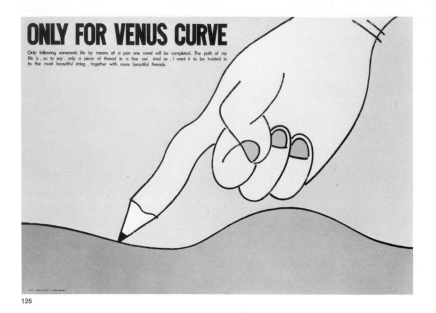

126

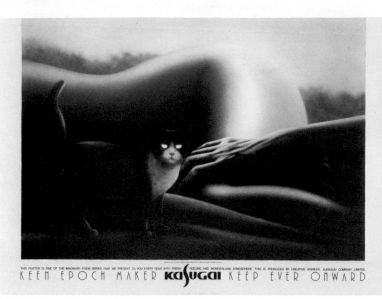

127

Direct Mail
Direktwerbung
Publicité directe

126 Self-promotional poster of a graphic designer. Violet, grey, skin-coloured "hand" with pink. (JPN)
127, 128 From a series of self-promotional posters of a design studio. Fig. 127: dark shades of green and grey, pale blue sky; Fig. 128: violet and brown shades, with red. (JPN)
129 Poster advertising a magazine. Beige shades with black and white. (JPN)
130 Poster used for Christmas greetings and for self-promotional purposes. (JPN)
131 "From classical to modern Ikebana." Poster for an Ikebana school. (JPN)
132 Poster of the transport organization Teito Rapid Transit Authority, drawing attention to the non-smoking times. Mainly in shades of blue and white. (JPN)

128

129

130

ARTIST / KÜNSTLER / ARTISTE:

126 Shigeyuki Hattori
127, 128 Masahiko Fuji
129 Masakazu Tanabe
130 Bob Coonts
131 Yoshikatsu Kosakai
132 Atsushi Yoshioka

DESIGNER / GESTALTER / MAQUETTISTE:

126 Shigeyuki Hattori/Makiko Hisamatsu
127, 128 Jun Yoshida/Toshinori Nozaki
129 Masakazu Tanabe
130 Bob Coonts
131 Yoshikatsu Kosakai
132 Hisao Hayakawa

ART DIRECTOR / DIRECTEUR ARTISTIQUE:

126 Shigeyuki Hattori
127, 128 Shozo Murase
129 Masakazu Tanabe
130 Bob Coonts
131 Yoshikatsu Kosakai
132 Nobuo Sugimoto/Hiroshi Izumi

AGENCY / AGENTUR / AGENCE – STUDIO:

127, 128 Kasugai Co., Ltd.
129 Media Co., Ltd.
130 Bob Coonts Graphic Design
131 Ad. Brain Center
132 F. Eight & Co. Ltd.

131

132

126 Eigenwerbungsplakat eines japanischen Graphikers, mit einem poetischen Text. Violett und Grau, «Hand» hautfarben mit Rosa. (JPN)
127, 128 Aus einer Serie von Eigenwerbungsplakaten eines Design-Studios. Abb. 127: Dunkle Grün- und Grautöne, blassblauer Himmel; Abb. 128: Violett- und Brauntöne, mit Rot. (JPN)
129 Plakatwerbung für das X-Magazin. Beigetöne und Schwarzweiss. (JPN)
130 Als Weihnachtsgruss und Eigenwerbung verwendetes Plakat. (JPN)
131 «Vom klassischen zum modernen Ikebana.» Für eine Schule. (JPN)
132 Plakat der Verkehrsbetriebe Teito Rapid Transit Authority, mit Angabe der Nichtraucher-Zelten. Vorwiegend Blautöne und Weiss. (JPN)

126 Affiche autopromotionnelle d'un graphiste japonais. Texte poétique. Violet et gris, «main» couleur chair, avec du rose. (JPN)
127, 128 Affiches autopromotionnelles dans une série créée par un studio de design. Fig. 127: verts et gris sombres, ciel bleu clair; fig. 128: violets et bruns, avec du rouge. (JPN)
129 Affiche publicitaire pour le magazine X. Beiges, noir-blanc. (JPN)
130 Affiche autopromotionnelle utilisée pour les vœux de Noël. (JPN)
131 «Ikebana: du classique au moderne.» Pour une école d'ikebana. (JPN)
132 Affiche des transports métropolitains Teito Rapid Transit Authority, avec indication des heures «non-fumeurs». Surtout bleus e blanc. (JPN)

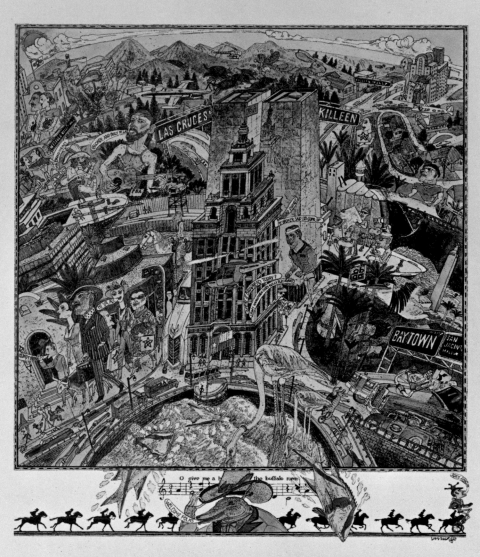

It's Willie, western boots and white-collared executives. It's long necks, longhorns and loads of new activity. It's cowboys, Cadillacs and construction galore. It's the west. The new west. Full of new people, new ideas and new retail opportunities. A place Paul Broadhead and Associates thinks you should be. How? It's easy. Join us during the ICSC Convention in New Orleans, May 17-21. We'll tell you about three of the biggest, most beautiful shopping malls west of the Mississippi. All to open in 1981. So drop by and see us at the New Orleans Marriott, Suite 3630, and we'll introduce you to a west that was never wilder. ▣ **Paul Broadhead and Associates, Inc.**

133 Poster issued by Paul Broadhead & Assoc., shopping mall developers, as an invitation to informational talks about new shopping centres in the western states of America. In full colour. (USA)
134 "Telecommunications encourage contact." Poster for the telegraphic services of the Swiss Post Office. Various shades of blue and red. (SWI)
135 Poster advertising a private railway company, referring here to the railway as a way to the discovery of the romance of landscape. (JPN)
136 Reproduction of a painted portrait of Miwa, one of Japan's most popular singers, used as an advertising poster. (JPN)
137 Self-promotional poster of *Helico Graphics* in Toronto, showing all those who contributed to it. Full-colour shot, yellow letters. (CAN)

133 Von Planern für Einkaufszentren herausgegebenes Plakat als Einladung zu Informationsgesprächen über neue Einkaufszentren im Westen der Vereinigten Staaten. Mehrfarbige Illustration. (USA)
134 «Telekommunikation fördert Kontakte.» Plakat für die Schweizerischen PTT-Betriebe. Verschiedene Blau- und Rottöne. (SWI)
135 Plakatwerbung einer privaten Eisenbahngesellschaft, die hier das romantische Erleben der Landschaft durch eine Bahnfahrt anspricht. (JPN)
136 Reproduktion eines gemalten Porträts der in Japan populären Sängerin Miwa, als Plakatwerbung für ihre Platten und Konzerte verwendet. (JPN)
137 Eigenwerbungsplakat von *Helico Graphics* in Toronto, mit Angabe aller am Plakat Beteiligten. Mehrfarbige Aufnahme, Schrift gelb. (CAN)

133 Affiche diffusée par un promoteur de centres commerciaux, invitant à se renseigner au sujet des nouveaux centres commerciaux implantés dans l'ouest des Etats-Unis. Illustration polychrome. (USA)
134 Affiche réalisée pour les P.T.T. suisses. Divers bleus et rouges. (SWI)
135 Publicité par voie d'affiche pour une société de chemins de fer privés. L'accent est mis ici sur le contact romantique avec la campagne que procurent les trajets sur cette ligne. (JPN)
136 Reproduction d'un portrait de peintre de la cantatrice Miwa populaire au Japon, utilisée pour la publicité par voie d'affiche. (JPN)
137 Affiche autopromotionnelle de *Helico Graphics* à Toronto, avec les noms de tous ceux qui y ont collaboré. Photo polychrome, texte jaune. (CAN)

133

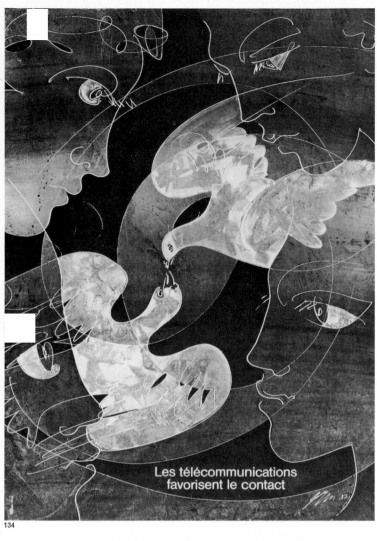

Les télécommunications
favorisent le contact

134

シティから、パリの春が見えます。ニューヨークの春も見えます。パステルトーンがまぶしいです。——

気分は、最高。

なんば
CITY 南海電鉄

感性と情報の333店〈共感の街〉

135

Mima

136

THE TARTS OF TORONTO

137

Varia

ARTIST / KÜNSTLER / ARTISTE:

138 Judd Pilossof
139 Clint Clemens
140, 141 Peter Bailey

DESIGNER / GESTALTER / MAQUETTISTE:

138 Norman D. Hulme
139 Bruce McGaw

ART DIRECTOR / DIRECTEUR ARTISTIQUE:

138 Norman D. Hulme
140, 141 Stuart Byfield

AGENCY / AGENTUR / AGENCE – STUDIO:

138 Automatic Data Processing, Inc.
139 Clint Clemens Studio
140, 141 Hayes Cowcher Dailey

138 Poster advertising automatic data processing. Full-colour photograph. (USA)
139 Self-promotional poster of the photographer Clint Clemens. In full colour. (USA)
140, 141 From a series of image posters of the State Bank of Victoria, using the signet as the main element. (AUS)

138 «Stelle Dein eigenes Ticket aus.» Plakatwerbung für automatische Datenverarbeitung. Farbaufnahme. (USA)
139 «Eine Tonne mit Lachen.» Eigenwerbungsplakat des Photographen Clint Clemens. In Farbe. (USA)
140, 141 Aus einer Reihe von Image-Plakaten der State Bank of Victoria, mit dem Signet als Hauptelement. «Wir sind stolz auf unsere Bank.» (AUS)

138 «Etablissez votre propre billet.» Affiche pour la diffusion de l'informatique. Photo couleur. (USA)
139 «Une masse de rires»: affiche autopromotionnelle du photographe Clint Clemens. En couleur. (USA)
140, 141 «Nous sommes fiers de notre banque»: exemples d'une série d'affiches de prestige destinées à cimenter l'image de marque de la State Bank of Victoria. Les sujets sont centrés sur l'emblème de l'établissement. (AUS)

138

139

140

May the Spirit of the Season Decorate Your Life During 1983

BOB COONTS DESIGN

142

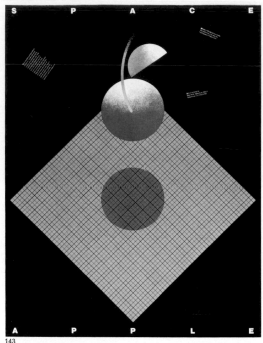

SPACE

APPLE

143

WINDY

SPACE

144

Con l'augurio cordiale per un millenovecentottantuno felice e pieno di cose da festeggiare, una serigrafia portafortuna da PROSPERO

145

La mela ti aspetta al varco. Ti sei cacciato in un labirinto. Hai detto: "Perché sempre il Prospero? Cambiamo un pò". Ma poi, l'anguilla affumicata non l'hai trovata e neanche le sedie-poltrone così accoglienti e neppure il Prospero che fa il flambé e allora torni e la mela vorrebbe farti una scenata invece si scioglie nel caramello e corre in forno a cuocere d'amore per te. PROSPERO

146

Nei discorsi dei buongustai, la cucina del Prospero è sempre al centro dell'attenzione: la mela dice che è tutto merito suo e aumenta le pretese. Per Natale, invece dei soliti biglietti, ho voluto un manifesto per fare gli auguri agli amici. Il Prospero scuote la testa e prepara la sua rivincita con un menu natalizio d'eccezione: staremo a vedere se è merito è della mela... PROSPERO

147

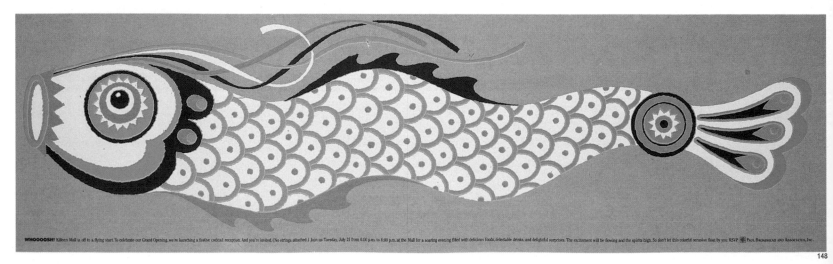

WHOOOSH! Killeen Mall is off to a flying start. To celebrate our Grand Opening, we're launching a festive cocktail reception. And you're invited. (No strings attached.) Join us Tuesday, July 21 from 6.00 p.m. to 8.00 p.m. at the Mall for a soaring evening filled with delicious foods, delectable drinks, and delightful surprises. The excitement will be flowing and the spirits high. So don't let this colorful occasion float by you. RSVP PAUL BROADHEAD AND ASSOCIATES, Inc.

148

Varia

149

142 Christmas- and New-Year-greetings poster of the graphic designer Bob Coonts. Brilliant red ball on blue background. (USA)
143, 144 Posters from a series for the Californian company *Modern Mode*, manufacturers of office furniture, announcing here the opening of showrooms in New York and Chicago. (USA)
145–147 From a series of posters for Prospero, a Milanese restaurant. The apple (symbol of Prospero) and the labyrinth are employed throughout in order to support the copy that points out the restaurant's advantages over the competition. (ITA)
148 Poster printed on thick wrapping paper as an invitation to the opening ceremony of a shopping centre. (USA)
149 Poster advertising the magazine *Tenri*, published by a religious organization of the same name. (JPN)

142 Weihnachts- und Neujahrsplakat des Graphikers Bob Coonts. Leuchtend rote Kugel auf blauem Hintergrund. (USA)
143, 144 Plakate aus einer Serie für den kalifornischen Büromöbelhersteller *Modern Mode*, hier mit Ankündigung der Eröffnung von Schauräumen in New York und Chicago. (USA)
145–147 Aus einer Serie von Plakaten für Prospero, ein Mailänder Restaurant. Mit dem Apfel und dem Labyrinth als Gestaltungsmittel und Symbole werden die Vorteile des Restaurants gegenüber der Konkurrenz hervorgehoben. (ITA)
148 Auf festes Packpapier gedrucktes Plakat als Einladung zu der Eröffnungsfeier eines Einkaufszentrums. (USA)
149 Plakatwerbung für die Zeitschrift *Tenri*, die von einer religiösen Organisation gleichen Namens herausgegeben wird. (JPN)

142 Affiche de Noël et de Nouvel An du graphiste Bob Coonts. Boule rouge vif sur fond bleu. (USA)
143, 144 Affiches figurant dans une série réalisée pour le fabricant de meubles de bureau californien *Modern Mode*: annonce de l'inauguration de halls d'exposition à New York et Chicago. (USA)
145–147 Exemples d'une série d'affiches pour le restaurant milanais Prospero. La pomme (symbole de Prospero) et le labyrinthe sont utilisés pour souligner les avantages dont le restaurant bénéficie face à la concurrence. (ITA)
148 Affiche imprimée sur du papier d'emballage épais: invitation à l'inauguration d'un centre commercial. (USA)
149 Affiche pour le magazine *Tenri* publié par une organisation religieuse du même nom. (JPN)

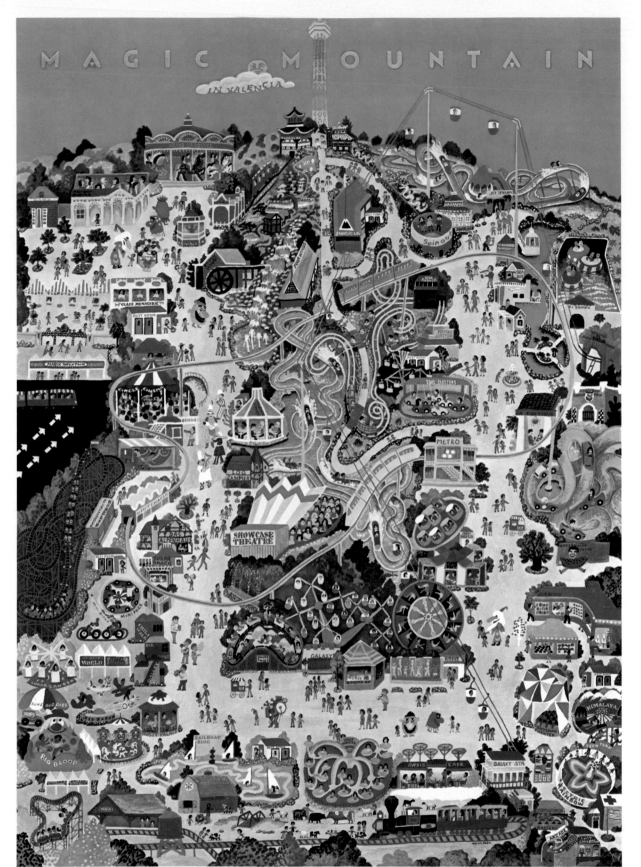

150

ARTIST / KÜNSTLER / ARTISTE:

150 Marvin Rubin
151, 152 Milton Glaser
153 Charles White
154 Fred Cornelissen

DESIGNER / GESTALTER / MAQUETTISTE:

150 Jerry Braude & Assoc.
151, 152 Milton Glaser
154 Hans Goedicke

ART DIRECTOR / DIRECTEUR ARTISTIQUE:

151, 152 Milton Glaser
153 Keith Bright
154 Hans Goedicke

AGENCY / AGENTUR / AGENCE – STUDIO:

151, 152 Milton Glaser, Inc.
153 Bright & Associates
154 KVH/GGK International

150 Poster used as an advertisement for an American amusement park. (USA)
151, 152 Examples from a series of tourist posters issued by New York State. Fig. 151 advertises summer holidays on the Hudson, Fig. 152 advertises a summer festival in another region of the state. (USA)
153 Announcement of a cruise around the world with the "SS Rotterdam", that began in January, 1983. Ship in silvery metal shades, background in deep blue. (USA)
154 Poster employed for advertising organized guided tours from Amsterdam to various places in England. Black lettering on white, Amsterdam in blue-white, the bus destination indicator in red, grey and white. (NLD)

150 Plakatwerbung für einen amerikanischen Vergnügungspark. (USA)
151, 152 Beispiele aus einer Serie von Touristikplakaten des Staates New York. Abb. 151 wirbt für Sommerferien am Hudson, Abb. 152 für eine Region im nördlichen Teil des Staates New York, die sogenannte «Lederstrumpf»-Gegend. (USA)
153 Ankündigung einer Schiffsreise um die Welt mit der «SS Rotterdam», die im Januar 1983 auslief. Schiff in silbrigen Metalltönen (der Bezeichnung «Silberne Kreuzfahrt» entsprechend), Hintergrund tiefblau. (USA)
154 Plakat für organisierte Reisen von Amsterdam nach verschiedenen Orten in England. Schwarze Schrift auf Weiss, Amsterdam blauweiss, Bus-Anzeige rot, grau und weiss. (NLD)

150 Publicité par voie d'affiche pour un parc d'attractions américain. (USA)
151, 152 Exemples puisés dans une série d'affiches touristiques de l'Etat de New York: fig. 151 pour des vacances d'été au bord du Hudson, fig. 152 pour une région au nord de l'Etat, celle du «dernier des Mohicans». (USA)
153 Annonce d'une croisière autour du monde à bord du paquebot Rotterdam, débutant en janvier 1983. Navire aux tons métalliques argentés (c'est la «Croisière d'argent») sur fond bleu profond. (USA)
154 Affiche pour des voyages organisés d'Amsterdam à différentes destinations anglaises. Texte noir sur blanc, Amsterdam blanc-bleu, plaque d'autobus rouge, gris, blanc. (NLD)

Tourism/Tourismus/Toursime

151

152

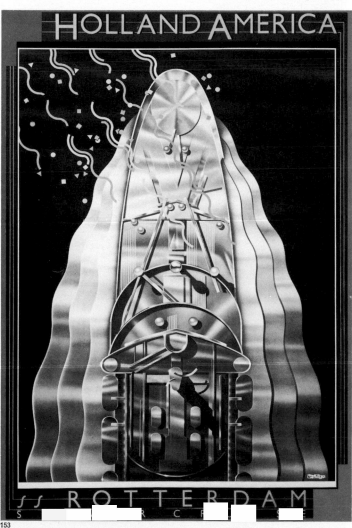

153

154

155

155 Example from a series of posters for *Lee Cooper*, with photographs by well-known photographers; here a shot by Hans Feurer. (SWI)
156 Poster advertising the *Tecno Collection*, makers of technical furniture designs. (SWI)
157 "So that the attic can become a warm room." Full-colour poster for *SarnaRoof* insulation. (SWI)
158 Full-colour poster sent as direct-mail advertising for carpets in the USA. (USA)
159 Poster advertising woolen carpets manufactured by *Weston Imperial*. Carpet and trees in warm red, lettering in white. (DEN)

155 Beispiel aus einer Serie von Plakaten für *Lee Cooper*, mit Aufnahmen bekannter Photographen; hier von Hans Feurer. (SWI)
156 Plakat für technisches Möbel-Design der *Tecno Collection*. (SWI)
157 Mehrfarbiges Plakat für *SarnaRoof*, Unterdachisolation aus Kunststoff. (SWI)
158 Als Direktwerbung für Teppiche in den USA versandtes Plakat, in bunten Farben. (USA)
159 Plakatwerbung für Wollteppiche von *Weston Imperial*. Teppich und Bäume in warmem Rot, Schrift weiss. (DEN)

155 Exemple d'une série d'affiches pour *Lee Cooper*, avec des photos de photographes réputés, ici de Hans Feurer. (SWI)
156 Affiche pour le design technique d'ameublements de la *Tecno Collection*. (SWI)
157 Affiche polychrome pour *SarnaRoof*, une isolation de toit en matériau synthétique. (SWI)
158 Affiche de publicité directe aux Etats-Unis, pour des tapis. Couleurs vives. (USA)
159 Affiche publicitaire pour les tapis pure laine *Weston Imperial*. Tapis et arbres rouge chaud, texte blanc. (DEN)

Industry
Industrie

Damit der Dachstock eine gute Stube wird.

⋮☰ Sarna

Unser Unterdachsystem für Steildächer. *SarnaRoof* aus Kunststoff.

157

Tecno
Tecno Collection Milano

Roma Genova Napoli Torino Catania Firenze Paris Amsterdam Bruxelles München Düsseldorf Wien Stockholm Athens Buenos Aires Genève

156

MOHAIR PLUSH + MOHAIR PLUSH ULTIMO/100% ANGORA PILE

158

Weston Imperial IC.

PURE NEW WOOL

159

160 Small-format poster for a printer's, in which a play upon words combining a mildly rude expression with a printing term is used to advertise a new type-face. (USA)
161 For a children's books publisher. Blue and green. (SWI)
162, 163 Examples from a public-relations series of six posters entitled "German Fairy-Tale Street". The company's headquarters is situated in this area. (GER)
164 Poster for the *New York Times*, stressing the heavier demands made on the modern citizen. (USA)
165 Invitation in poster form for a competition of the Art Directors Club in Salt Lake City. (USA)
166 "It will arrive shortly!" For a collectors' journal. (FRA)
167 From a series of decorative posters. (JPN)

160 Kleinformatiges Plakat für eine Setzerei, die u.a. für eine neue Schrift wirbt. Das englische Wort für Gesicht, «face», wird auch für Schrifttypen (hier fett) gebraucht. (USA)
161 Für einen Kinderbuchverlag. Blau- und Grüntöne. (SWI)
162, 163 Beispiele aus einer PR-Serie von sechs Plakaten unter dem Titel «Deutsche Märchenstrasse». Der Sitz der Firma befindet sich in der betroffenen Gegend. (GER)
164 Plakat für die *New York Times*: Die Zeiten verlangen nach der *Times*. (USA)
165 Einladung in Plakatform, für einen Wettbewerb des Art Directors Club von Salt Lake City. (USA)
166 Plakatwerbung für ein Sammler-Journal. (FRA)
167 Aus einer Serie von dekorativen Plakaten. (JPN)

160 Affichette pour un atelier de composition faisant entre autres la publicité pour un nouveau caractère. Le mot anglais «face» signifie visage et caractère (ici, gras, «fat»). (USA)
161 Pour un éditeur de livres d'enfants. Bleus et verts. (SWI)
162, 163 Examples d'une série de relations publiques de six affiches, «La Route des contes de fées allemands» – qui se trouve traverser la région où est implantée l'entreprise. (GER)
164 Affiche pour le *New York Times*, dont on dit la configuration du temps présent le rend indispensable. (USA)
165 Invitation sous forme d'affiche à un concours de l'Art Directors Club de Salt Lake City. (USA)
166 Affiche pour un journal de collectionneurs. (FRA)
167 Exemple d'une série de posters décoratifs. (JPN)

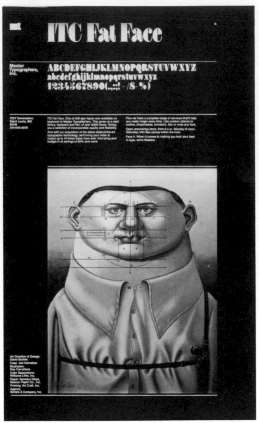

160

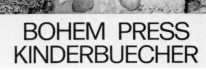

BOHEM PRESS
KINDERBUECHER

161

ARTIST / KÜNSTLER / ARTISTE:

160 Roy Carruthers
161 Ivan Gantschev
162, 163 Fritz Henry Oerter
164 R.O. Blechman
165 McRay Magleby
166 Bruno Caillat
167 Kenzo Tama

DESIGNER / GESTALTER / MAQUETTISTE:

160 David Bartels
161 O. Bozejovsky
162, 163 Fritz Henry Oerter
164 R.O. Blechman
165 McRay Magleby
167 Masakazu Tanabe

ART DIRECTOR / DIRECTEUR ARTISTIQUE:

160 David Bartels
161 S. Zavrel
162, 163 Lothar F. Kümper
164 R.O. Blechman
165 McRay Magleby
167 Masakazu Tanabe

AGENCY / AGENTUR / AGENCE – STUDIO:

160 Bartels & Company
161 Bohem Press
165 Graphic Communications
166 Atelier 00
167 Gifu Graphic Designers Club/
    Gifu Seihan Co., Ltd.

Publishers Publicity

Verlagswerbung

Publicité d'éditeurs

162

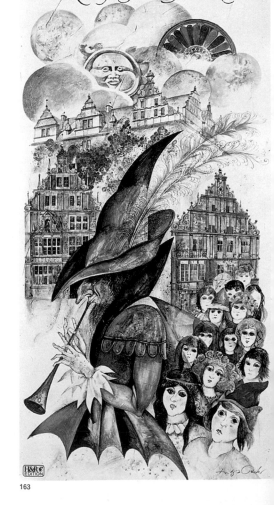

163

164

165

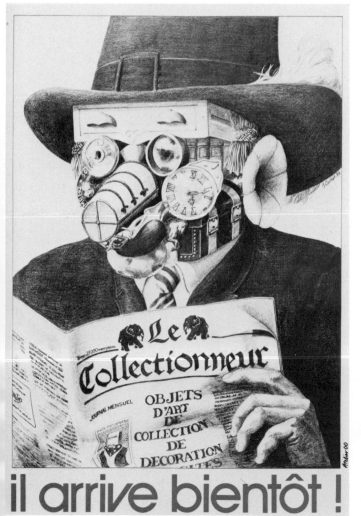

166

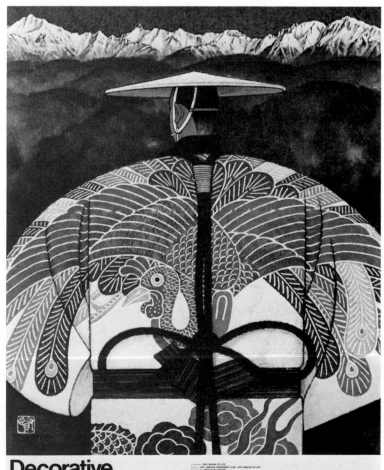

167

ARTIST / KÜNSTLER:

168, 172 Clint Clemens
169–171 Peter Chou

DESIGNER / GESTALTER:

168 Tyler Smith
169–171 Carverhill,
        Russell & Timmerman
172 Clint Clemens

ART DIRECTOR:

168 Tyler Smith
169–171 Peter Chou/
        Bob Russell
172 Carmen Timpanelli

AGENCY / AGENTUR:

172 Insight, Inc.

168

169   170   171

168 Poster taken from a series that can be collected, used for self-promotional purposes by a lithographer. The 1935 *Mercedes 500*K is used here as an example of how more performance than necessary is a positive factor in professional life, an attitude which is also valid for the lithographer. Full-colour shot. (USA)
169–171 From a series of self-promotional posters of the photographer Peter Chou, also available in stores. (CAN)
172 Self-promotion by the photographer Clint Clemens. Black with warm red and silvery white. (USA)

168 Plakat aus einer Serie zum Sammeln, als Eigenwerbung eines Lithographen. Das *Mercedes*-Modell aus dem Jahre 1935 dient als Beispiel für mehr Leistung als unbedingt erforderlich ist, eine Einstellung, welche auch für den Lithographen Gültigkeit hat. Farbaufnahme. (USA)
169–171 Aus einer Reihe von Eigenwerbungsplakaten des Photographen Peter Chou, die jetzt auch im Handel erhältlich sind. (CAN)
172 Eigenwerbung des Photographen Clint Clemens. Schwarz mit warmem Rot und Silberweiss. (USA)

168 Exemple d'une série d'affiches de collection servant à l'auto-promotion d'un lithographe. Le modèle *Mercedes* 500 K de l'année 1935 incarne la performance au-delà de ce qui est absolument nécessaire – une attitude que le lithographe fait volontiers la sienne. Photo couleur. (USA)
169–171 Exemples d'une série d'affiches autopromotionnelles du photographe Peter Chou, également mises en vente. (CAN)
172 Autopromotion du photographe Clint Clemens. Noir, avec du rouge chaud et du blanc argenté. (USA)

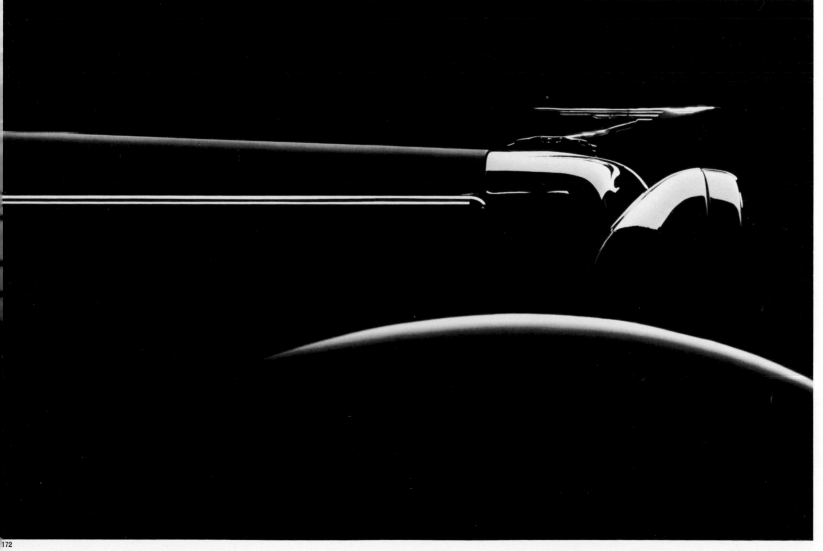

172

173

174

175

173–175 Posters issued on the occasion of the 325th anniversary of the Royal Danish Life Guards.(DEN)
176 Large-format outdoor poster of the Swiss Federal Railways, advertising for transporting goods by rail. (SWI)
177 Poster issued by SAS, the Scandinavian airlines company; here for Copenhagen airport. (DEN)

173–175 Anlässlich des 325jährigen Bestehens der königlich-dänischen Leibgarde veröffentlichte Plakate.(DEN)
176 Grossformatiges Aussenplakat der Schweizer Bundesbahnen als Werbung für den Gütertransport mit der Bahn. (SWI)
177 Von der skandinavischen Luftverkehrsgesellschaft SAS herausgegebenes Plakat. (DEN)

173–175 Affiches publiées à l'occasion du 325e anniversaire de la garde royale danoise.(DEN)
176 Affiche extérieure des Chemins de Fer Fédéraux, au grand format, pour le transport des marchandises par le rail. (SWI)
177 Affiche publiée par la compagnie aérienne scandinave SAS, pour l'aéroport de Copenhague-Kastrup. (DEN)

Tourism
Tourismus
Tourisme

ARTIST / KÜNSTLER / ARTISTE:

173–175, 177 Per Arnoldi
176 Christian Küenzi

DESIGNER / GESTALTER / MAQUETTISTE:

176 Mathias Babst

ART DIRECTOR / DIRECTEUR ARTISTIQUE:

176 Mathias Babst

AGENCY / AGENTUR / AGENCE – STUDIO:

173–175 Mogens Raffel
176 Young & Rubicam

Ein Laster mit 42 Anhängern.

Für Güter die Bahn.   ⊕ Ihre SBB

176

KASTRUP

COPENHAGEN AIRPORT

178–185 The posters by the graphic designer Gerhard Preiss that are shown on this double spread are part of the advertising-, cultural- and public-works of the cities of Nuremberg, Erlangen and Ingolstadt. Fig. 178 announces an exhibition dedicated to Ingolstadt, with photographs, slides and plans; Figs. 179, 180 refer to two lecture series in Erlangen: "Regionalism and Counter Culture", "Courage for the Future"; Fig. 181 deals with a comic-strips exhibition in Nuremberg; Fig. 182 announces an exhibition with drawings and sculptures, in Erlangen's municipal gallery; Fig. 183 appeals for participation in a commemorative hour organized by the evangelical church: the infamous "Crystal Night" in Nuremberg; Fig. 184: for the 70th anniversary of Nuremberg's zoological gardens; Fig. 185: the opening of an underground line.(GER)

178–185 Die auf dieser Doppelseite gezeigten Plakate des Graphikers Gerhard Preiss sind im Rahmen der Werbe-, Kultur- und Öffentlichkeitsarbeit der Städte Nürnberg, Erlangen und Ingolstadt entstanden. Abb. 178 kündigt eine Ingolstadt gewidmete Ausstellung mit Photos, Dias und Plänen an; Abb. 179, 180 betreffen zwei Vortragsreihen in Erlangen; Abb. 181 bezieht sich auf eine Comic-Strips-Ausstellung in der Kunsthalle Nürnberg, Abb. 182 kündigt eine Ausstellung mit Zeichnungen und Skulpturen niederländischer Bildhauer in der Städtischen Galerie Erlangen an; Abb. 183 ruft zur Teilnahme an einer von der evangelischen Kirche organisierten Gedenkstunde auf; Abb. 184: zum siebzigjährigen Bestehen des Tiergartens Nürnberg; Abb. 185 als Erinnerung an die Eröffnung einer wichtigen U-Bahn-Strecke.(GER)

178–185 Les affiches du graphiste Gerhard Preiss présentées sur cette double page proviennent de commandes des municipalités de Nuremberg, Erlangen et Ingolstadt dans les secteurs publicité, affaires culturelles et relations publiques. La fig. 178 annonce une exposition sur Ingolstadt agrémentée de photos, de diapos, de plans; les fig. 179 et 180 concernent deux séries de conférences à Erlangen, la fig. 181 une exposition de bandes dessinées à la Kunsthalle de Nuremberg. La fig. 182 annonce une exposition de l'œuvre dessiné et sculpté de sculpteurs hollandais à la Galerie municipale d'Erlangen; la fig. 183 appelle à une réunion protestante du souvenir; fig. 184: pour les 70 ans du zoo de Nuremberg; fig. 185: en mémoire de l'inauguration d'une ligne de métro importante. Toute ces affiches sont polychromes. (GER)

178

179

180

181

182

183

70 Jahre Tiergarten Nürnberg

184

U-BAHN NÜRNBERG-FÜRTH

185

Tourism/Tourismus/Toursime

ARTIST / KÜNSTLER / ARTISTE:

178 Gerhard Preiss/
     Helmut Bauer (Photo)
179–183, 185 Gerhard Preiss
184 Fritz Henry Oerter

DESIGNER / GESTALTER / MAQUETTISTE:

178–183, 185 Gerhard Preiss
184 Fritz Henry Oerter

ART DIRECTOR / DIRECTEUR ARTISTIQUE:

170–183, 185 Gerhard Preiss
184 Fritz Henry Oerter

2

Cultural Posters

Kulturelle Plakate

Affiches culturelles

186

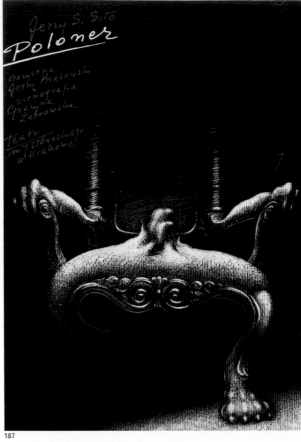

187

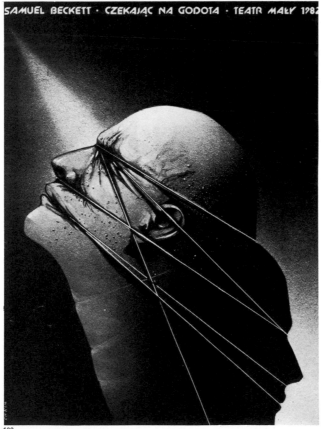

189

190

ARTIST / KÜNSTLER / ARTISTE:

186, 187 M. Gorowski
188 Wrosocha
189 Irena Chrul
190 Hanna Zalewska
191 Andrzej Pagowski

ART DIRECTOR:

190 Bohdan Hussakowski

188

186 Announcement of the performance of a play entitled "Police" by Sławomir Mrożek. (POL)
187 Poster announcing performances of a play entitled "Polonaise" by Jerzy S. Sito. (POL)
188 For the stage performance of a play in Warsaw. ("Phantasies"). (POL)
189 Poster for the performance of Samuel Beckett's *Waiting for Godot*, held in Warsaw. (POL)
190 For a play held at the Jaracza theatre in Lódź. Black and white with blue. (POL)
191 Poster for a play entitled "The Wolf's Smile", performed in Warsaw. (POL)

186 Ankündigung der Aufführung eines Stückes mit dem Titel «Polizei» von S. Mrożek. (POL)
187 Plakat für die Ankündigung eines Stückes mit dem Titel «Polonaise» von Jerzy S. Sito. (POL)
188 Für eine Theateraufführung in Warschau («Phantasien»). (POL)
189 Plakat für die Aufführung von Becketts *Warten auf Godot* in Warschau. (POL)
190 Für eine Aufführung des Theaters Jaracza in Lódź. Schwarzweiss mit Blau. (POL)
191 Plakat für ein in Warschau aufgeführtes Stück mit dem Titel «Das Lächeln des Wolfes». (POL)

186 Annonce de la représentation d'une pièce de théâtre intitulée «Police» par S. Mrożek. (POL)
187 Affiche annonçant la représentation d'une pièce intitulée «Polonaise» par Jerzy S. Sito. (POL)
188 Pour une représentation théâtrale à Varsovie («Fantaisies»). (POL)
189 Affiche pour *En attendant Godot*, par Samuel Beckett, mis en scène à Varsovie. (POL)
190 Pour une pièce jouée au Théâtre Jaracza de Lódź. Noir et blanc, avec du bleu. (POL)
191 Affiche pour une pièce jouée à Varsovie sous le titre de «Le Sourire du loup». (POL)

191

Films/Filme

192

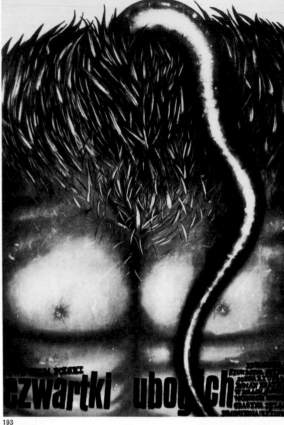

193

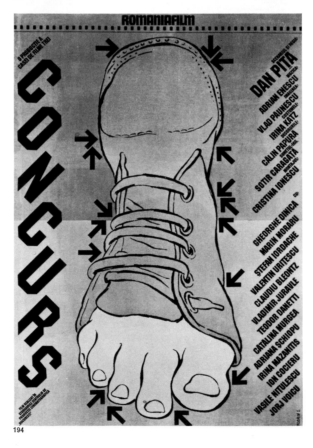

194

195

192 Full-colour poster announcing the showing of a film. (BUL)
193 Poster in light brown and olive-green announcing the release of a new Polish film. (POL)
194 Poster for a Rumanian film entitled "Bankruptcy". Light brown and pink, background in two shades of green, black lettering. (RUM)
195 Poster for "The Small Wasp", a French film. (HUN)
196 Poster announcing a film festival in Japan, showing films from South Asia. Green "mouth", red and violet. (JPN)
197 For a Rumanian film entitled "The Man in the Raincoat". (POL)
198 Poster used as an invitation to a festival in Hongkong for experimental films and other independent short films. (HKG)
199 For a *Macbeth* performance by the Royal Shakespeare Theatre. Dirty dun, orange, yellow and pink. (GBR)

192 Mehrfarbiges Plakat für die Ankündigung eines Spielfilms. (BUL)
193 In Hellbraun und Olivgrün gehaltenes Plakat für die Ankündigung eines neuen polnischen Films. (POL)
194 Plakat für einen rumänischen Film mit dem Titel «Konkurs». Hellbraun und Rosa, Hintergrund in zwei Grüntönen, Schrift schwarz. (RUM)
195 Für die Vorführung eines französischen Films. (HUN)
196 Plakat für die Ankündigung eines Film-Festivals in Japan mit südasiatischen Filmen. «Mund» grün, rot und violett. (JPN)
197 Für einen rumänischen Film («Der Mann im Regenmantel»). (POL)
198 Plakat als Einladung zur Teilnahme an einem Festival für experimentelle und andere unabhängige Kurzfilme, in Hongkong. (HKG)
199 Für eine *Macbeth*-Inszenierung des Royal Shakespeare Theatre in Stratford-upon-Avon. Schmutziges Graubraun, Orange, Gelb und Rosa. (GBR)

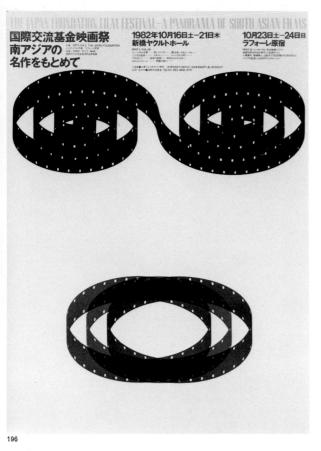

196

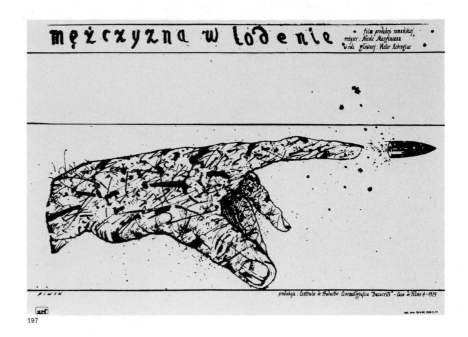

197

198

192 Affiche polychrome pour un long métrage. (BUL)
193 Affiche en couleurs brun clair et olive annonçant la sortie d'un nouveau film polonais. (POL)
194 Affiche pour un film roumain intitulé «Faillite». Brun clair et rose, fond en deux verts différents, texte en noir. (RUM)
195 Pour la sortie d'un film français («Petite Guêpe»). (HUN)
196 Affiche pour un festival du cinéma sud-asiatique au Japon. «Bouche» vert, rouge, violet. (JPN)
197 Pour un film roumain («L'Homme à l'imperméable»). (POL)
198 Affiche invitant à participer à un festival du cinéma d'expérimentation et du court métrage indépendant, organisé à Hong Kong. (HKG)
199 Pour une mise en scène de *Macbeth* au Royal Shakespeare Theatre de Stratford-upon-Avon. Brun grisâtre sale, orange, jaune, rose. (GBR)

199

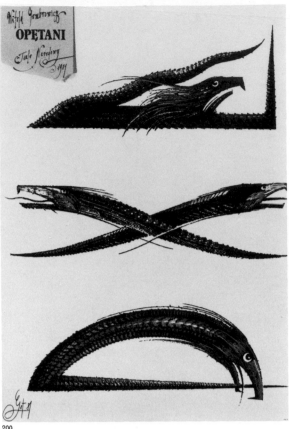

200

201

ARTIST / KÜNSTLER / ARTISTE:

200 Eugeniusz Stankiewicz
201 Olle Frankzen
202, 205 Gancho St. Ganev
203 Klára Tamás Blaier
204 Erhard Grüttner
206, 207 Waldemar Swierzy

ART DIRECTOR:

201 Olle Frankzen
203 Andrei Alexandru
206 Anna Mieczyńska

AGENCY / AGENTUR / AGENCE:

201 Design 2001

202

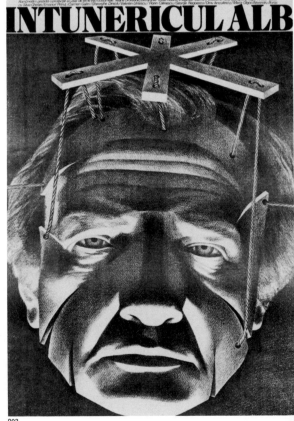

203

200 For the performance in Warsaw of a Gombrowicz play entitled "The Obsessed". Green "snakes", red, blue and violet. (POL)
201 Poster announcing a Finnish film to be shown in Sweden. Illustration in brown shades with gold and red, outer edge in grey. (SWE)
202 Poster for a play performed by the Haskovo dramatic-theatre group, entitled "A toast to today". Black and white and light brown. (BUL)
203 For a Rumanian film production. Pale yellow and violet. (RUM)
204 Announcement of an Edward Albee play's premiere in East Germany, in Magdeburg. Black and white with red luminous lettering. (GDR)
205 Poster for a Françoise Sagan play performed in Bulgaria. Black and white with green, pink and yellow. (BUL)
206 Portrait of the dramatist Sławomir Mrożek to announce an exhibition devoted to him in a Warsaw theatre. (POL)
207 Poster for the release of a Polish film. (POL)

200 Für die Warschauer Aufführung eines Stückes von Gombrowicz («Die Besessenen»). «Schlangen» in Grün, Rot, Blau und Violett. (POL)
201 Für die Ankündigung eines finnischen Films («Milka») in Schweden. Illustration in Brauntönen mit Gold und Rot, äusserer Rahmen grau. (SWE)
202 Plakat für eine Inszenierung des Dramatischen Theaters Haskovo: «Ein Toast auf heute.» Schwarzweiss und Hellbraun. (BUL)
203 Für eine rumänische Filmproduktion. Taue gelb und violett. (RUM)
204 Ankündigung der DDR-Erstaufführung eines Stückes von Edward Albee in Magdeburg. Schwarzweiss mit roter Leuchtschrift. (GDR)
205 Für eine bulgarische Françoise-Sagan-Inszenierung. Schwarzweiss mit Grün, Rosa und Gelb. (BUL)
206 Porträt des Theaterautors Sławomir Mrożek für die Ankündigung einer ihm gewidmeten Ausstellung in einem Warschauer Theater. (POL)
207 Plakat für eine polnische Filmproduktion. (POL)

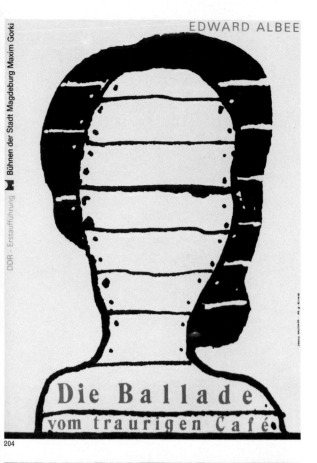

204

205

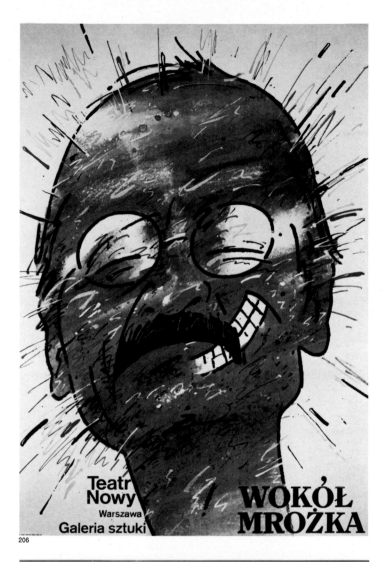

206

207

200 Pour la représentation à Varsovie d'une pièce de Gombrowicz («Les Fous»). «Serpents» en tons verts, rouges, bleus, violets. (POL)
201 Pour la sortie d'un film finlandais («Milka») en Suède. Illustration en divers bruns avec de l'or et du rouge, cadre extérieur gris. (SWE)
202 Affiche pour une mise en scène du Théâtre dramatique de Haskovo: «Un toast à aujourd'hui.» Noir et blanc, brun clair. (BUL)
203 Pour un film roumain. Cordages jaune et violet. (RUM)
204 Affiche pour la première d'une pièce d'Edward Albee jouée à Magdeburg. Noir et blanc, texte rouge lumineux. (GDR)
205 Pour une mise en scène bulgare d'une pièce de Françoise Sagan. Noir et blanc avec du vert, du rose et du jaune. (BUL)
206 Portrait de l'auteur dramatique Sławomir Mrożek pour annoncer une exposition consacrée à son oeuvre dans un théâtre de Varsovie. (POL)
207 Affiche pour la sortie d'un film polonais. (POL)

208

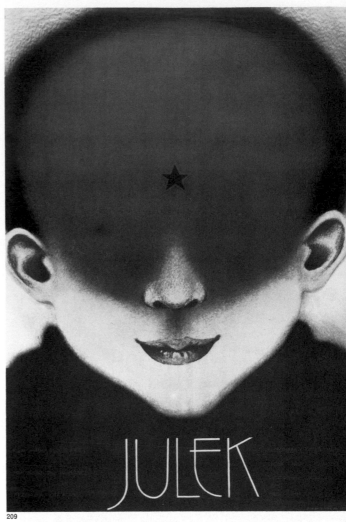

209

211

212

210

ARTIST / KÜNSTLER / ARTISTE:

208 Andrzej Pagowski
209 Dana Andreyev
210 Jerzy Cerniawsky
211 Jerzy Nowosielski
212 Waldemar Swierzy
213 Henryk Tomaszewski

Cultural Events
Veranstaltungen
Evénements culturels

213

208 For a Polish film: "Rise in the Mountains Like an Eagle." (POL)
209 Announcement of a film. Face in beige-pink and tomato red. (POL)
210 Poster announcing the performance of an Anton Chekhov play, held in the Warsaw theatre Maly. (POL)
211 Poster for an *Antigone* performance in Warsaw. (POL)
212 For a performance of Shakespeare's *A Midsummer Night's Dream.* (POL)
213 Poster for a play performed in Warsaw at the Powszechny theatre. Black bird, olive-grey dots. (POL)

208 Für einen polnischen Film: «Sich in die Berge erheben wie ein Adler.» (POL)
209 Ankündigung eines Films. Gesicht beigerosa und tomatenrot. (POL)
210 Plakat für die Ankündigung eines Stückes von Anton Tschechow, aufgeführt von einem Warschauer Theater. (POL)
211 Plakat für eine *Antigone*-Inszenierung in Warschau. (POL)
212 Für eine Aufführung von Shakespeares *Ein Sommernachtstraum.* (POL)
213 Für eine Aufführung des Theaters Powszechny in Warschau. Schwarze Vögel, olivgraue Punkte. (POL)

208 Pour un film: «Prends ton essor dans les montagnes comme un aigle.» (POL)
209 Annonce de film. Visage rose beige et rouge tomate. (POL)
210 Affiche pour la représentation d'une pièce d'Anton Tchekhov sur une scène de Varsovie. (POL)
211 Affiche pour une interprétation d'*Antigone* jouée à Varsovie. (POL)
212 Pour une interprétation du *Songe d'une nuit d'été,* de Shakespeare. (POL)
213 Affiche pour une soirée du Théâtre Powszechny de Varsovie. Oiseaux noirs, points gris olive. (POL)

214

215

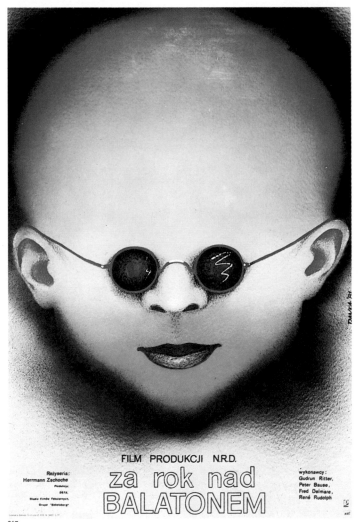

217

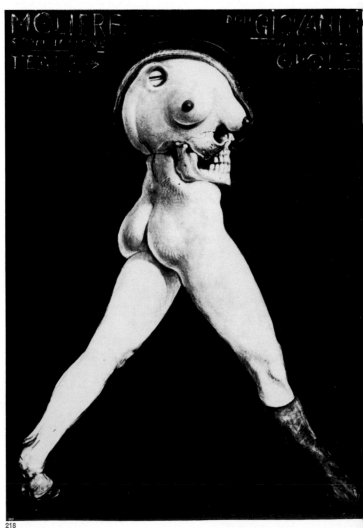

218

216

ARTIST / KÜNSTLER / ARTISTE:

214 Henryk Waniek
215, 216, 218, 219 Franciszek
        Starowieyski
217 Dana Andreyev
220 Lech Majewski

214 Poster for a Polish film entitled "Valley of Issa", based on a novel. The landscape can be viewed from any side. (POL)
215 For a Polish film ("The Quack"). Grey shades with blue. (POL)
216 Monochrome poster for a Polish film entitled "Nightmares". (POL)
217 For an East German film shown in Poland: "In a Year over Lake Balaton". (POL)
218 Poster for Molière's *Don Juan*. In black and white. (POL)
219 Announcement of a poster fair in Warsaw. (POL)
220 Poster for a French film ("Feelings Have Turned Up") shown in Polish cinemas. (POL)

214 Für einen Film («Das Tal der Issa»), der auf einem Roman basiert. Die Landschaft kann von allen Seiten her betrachtet werden. (POL)
215 Ankündigung eines polnischen Films («Der Kurpfuscher»). Grautöne mit Blau. (POL)
216 Einfarbiges Plakat für einen polnischen Film mit dem Titel «Alpträume». (POL)
217 Für einen in Polen gezeigten DDR-Film: «In einem Jahr über dem Balaton-See.» (POL)
218 Plakat für eine Aufführung von Molières *Don Juan*. In Schwarzweiss. (POL)
219 Ankündigung einer Plakatmesse in Warschau. (POL)
220 Für einen französischen Film, der in polnischen Kinos gezeigt wurde. (POL)

214 Pour un film («La Vallée de l'Issa») basé sur un roman. Le paysage s'étage sur les quatre côtés de l'illustration. (POL)
215 Annonce d'un film polonais («Le Charlatan»). Divers gris, avec du bleu. (POL)
216 Affiche monochrome pour un film polonais intitulé «Cauchemars». (POL)
217 Pour un film est-allemand joué en Pologne: «Dans un an sur le lac Balaton.» (POL)
218 Affiche pour une représentation du *Don Juan* de Molière. Noir et blanc. (POL)
219 Annonce d'un festival de l'affiche à Varsovie. (POL)
220 Pour un film français («Les sentiments sont parvenus») à l'affiche en Pologne. (POL)

219

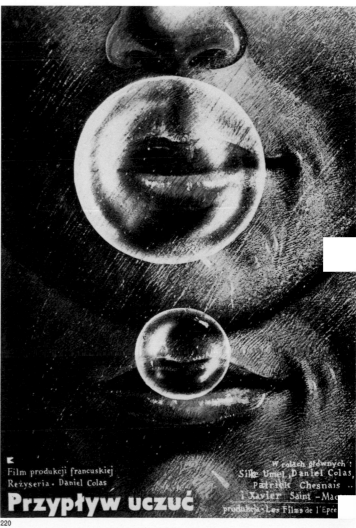

220

99

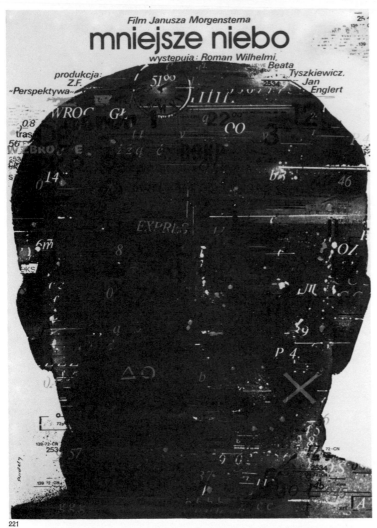

221

222

224

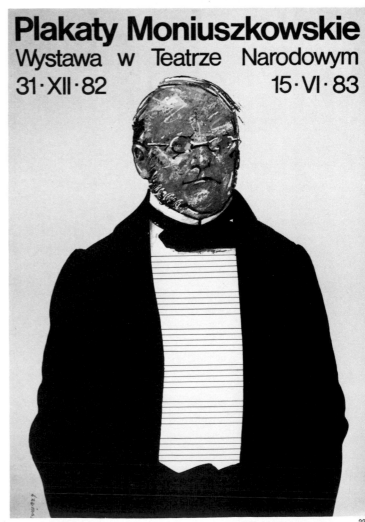

225

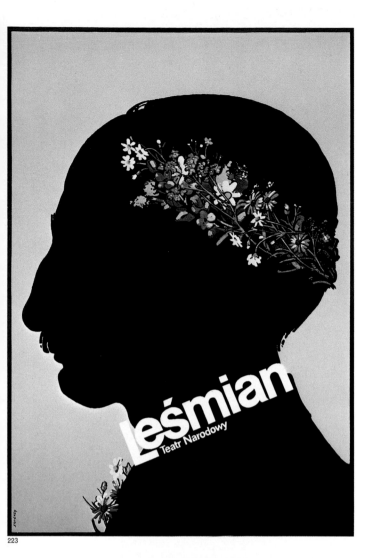

223

Films/Filme

ARTIST/KÜNSTLER/ARTISTE:
221–227 Waldemar Swierzy

221 Poster for a Polish film entitled "The Smaller Sky". Red, white and black on a dark red-brown head. (POL)
222 Announcement of a concert given by the Polish Chamber Orchestra, conducted by Jerzy Maksymiuk who is portrayed here. Violet-blue and brown. (POL)
223 For lectures given by the writer Leśmian at Warsaw's National Theatre. (POL)
224 For a film ("The Chance") set in the world of football. Full colour. (POL)
225 Announcement of an exhibition of posters devoted to Moniuszkowskie, composer and father of the Polish National Opera. (POL)
226 For a performance of *A Midsummer Night's Dream*. Black and white, blue. (POL)
227 For "Double", a Japanese film shown in Polish cinemas. (POL)

221 Plakat für einen polnischen Film mit dem Titel «Der kleinere Himmel». Rot, weiss und schwarz auf rot-braunem Kopf. (POL)
222 Ankündigung eines Konzertes des Polnischen Kammerorchesters, dirigiert von Jerzy Maksymiuk, der hier porträtiert ist. Violettblau und Braun. (POL)
223 Für Lesungen des Dichters Leśmian im National Theater, Warschau. (POL)
224 Für einen Film, der in der Welt des Fussballs spielt («Die Chance»). (POL)
225 Ankündigung einer Ausstellung von Plakaten, die dem Komponisten und Vater der polnischen Nationaloper, Moniuszkowskie, gewidmet sind. (POL)
226 Für Shakespeares *Ein Sommernachtstraum*. Schwarzweiss, Blau. (POL)
227 Ankündigung eines japanischen Films («Doppelgänger») in polnischen Kinos. (POL)

221 Affiche pour un film polonais intitulé «Le ciel plus petit». Rouge, blanc, noir sur tête brun rougeâtre. (POL)
222 Annonce d'un concert de l'Orchestre de chambre polonais sous la direction de Jerzy Maksymiuk représenté ici. Bleu violet et brun. (POL)
223 Pour le poète Leśmian donnant lecture de ses œuvres au Théâtre National. (POL)
224 Pour un film qui joue dans le monde du football («La Chance»). (POL)
225 Annonce d'une exposition d'affiches consacrées au compositeur Moniuszkowskie, le père de l'opéra national polonais. (POL)
226 Pour le *Songe d'une nuit d'été* de Shakespeare. Noir et blanc, bleu. (POL)
227 Annonce d'un film japonais («Sosie») à l'affiche en Pologne. (POL)

226

227

228 Poster for a play based on a story by Gottfried Keller and performed at Willisau near Lucerne. (SWI)
229 For a production at Colorado State University. Black illustration, background in grey and blue, white title. (USA)
230 "Programmed." Announcement of a cabaret at the Kasematten Theatre in Luxemburg. Black and white on silvery-grey ground, red flower. (LUX)
231 For a production of a play by Jean-Paul Wenzel at the Wireworks Theatre in Edinburgh. (GBR)
232 Poster for the production of a comedy. In full colour. (FIN)
233 For a cooperative production of the Théâtre Ouvert with the Kasematten Theatre in Luxembourg. (LUX)
234 Poster for the production of a Gilbert & Sullivan play on the occasion of the Stratford Festival in Canada. (CAN)

228 Plakat für ein Stück nach Gottfried Kellers *Romeo und Julia auf dem Lande*, uraufgeführt im luzernischen Willisau. (SWI)
229 Für eine Theaterproduktion der Colorado State University. Illustration schwarz, Hintergrund grau und blau, Titel weiss. (USA)
230 Ankündigung einer Kabarettvorstellung im Kasemattentheater Luxemburg. Schwarzweiss auf silbergrauem Grund, rote Blume. (LUX)
231 «Weit von der Stadt.» Für eine Theaterproduktion des Wireworks Theatre, Edinburg. (GBR)
232 Plakat für die Aufführung einer Komödie. Mehrfarbig. (FIN)
233 Für eine Gemeinschaftsproduktion des Théâtre Ouvert und des Kasematten-Theaters in Luxemburg. (LUX)
234 Plakat für die Inszenierung eines Theaterstücks von Gilbert & Sullivan anlässlich des Stratford-Festivals in Kanada. (CAN)

ARTIST / KÜNSTLER / ARTISTE:

228 Niklaus Troxler
229 Phil Risbeck
230, 233 Pit Weyer
231 Nicholas Jenkins
232 Kari Piippo
234 Heather Cooper

DESIGNER / GESTALTER / MAQUETTISTE:

228 Niklaus Troxler
229 Phil Risbeck
231 Nicholas Jenkins
232 Kari Piippo
234 Heather Cooper

ART DIRECTOR / DIRECTEUR ARTISTIQUE:

228 Niklaus Troxler
229 Phil Risbeck
231 Nicholas Jenkins
232 Kari Piippo
234 Heather Cooper

AGENCY / AGENTUR / AGENCE – STUDIO:

228 Niklaus Troxler Grafik-Studio
229 CSU Art Dept.
231 The Jenkins Group
232 Kari Piippo
234 Burns, Cooper, Hynes Ltd.

228

229

230

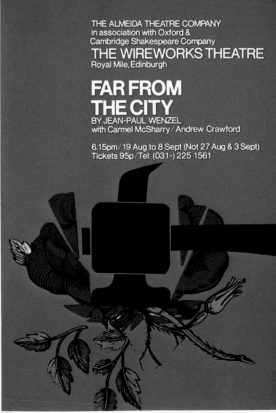

231

228 Affiche pour une pièce tirée du roman de Gottffried Keller *Romco und Julia auf dem Lande*; première mondiale à Willisau/Lucerne. (SWI)
229 Pour une pièce de théâtre montée par la Colorado State University. Illustration en noir, fond gris et bleu, titre blanc. (USA)
230 Annonce d'un programme de chansonniers au Théâtre des Casemattes de Luxembourg. Noir et blanc sur fond gris argenté, fleur rouge. (LUX)
231 «Loin de la ville.» Affiche pour une mise en scène du Wireworks Theatre d'Edinbourg. (GBR)
232 Affiche pour la représentation d'une comédie. En polychromie. (FIN)
233 Pour une production commune du Théâtre Ouvert et du Théâtre des Casemattes de Luxembourg. (LUX)
234 Affiche pour la mise en scène du *Mikado* de Gilbert & Sullivan dans le cadre du festival de Stratford au Canada. (CAN)

232

233

234

235

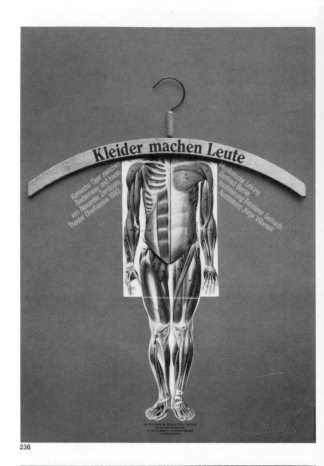

236

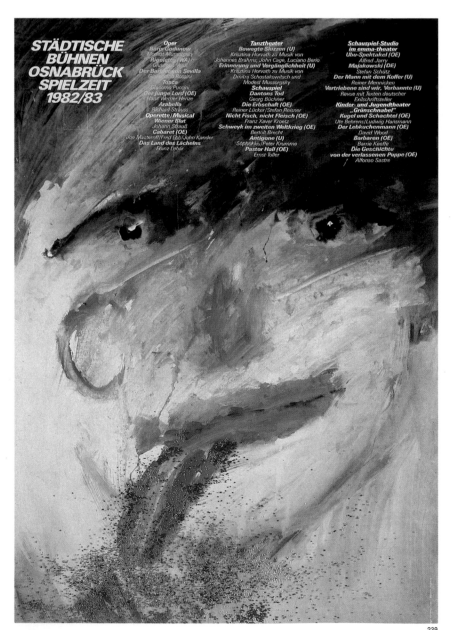

239

240

235 Poster for Smetana's comic opera *The Secret*, performed by Hagen's municipal theatre group. (GER)
236 "Clothes Make People." Poster for the performance of a comic opera at the Oberhausen theatre. Brown shades on luminous violet background. (GER)
237 Silkscreen poster for a production of Aristophanes' *Peace*. Brown shades with white lettering. (GER)
238 "The Principle of Loneliness." Announcement of a production at the Théâtre de l'Etoile in Paris. (FRA)
239 Poster showing the programme of Osnabrück's municipal theatre group for the 1982/83 season. (GER)
240 Mr. Pickwick himself is the subject of this poster announcing a performance of Charles Dickens' famous play in Toronto. (CAN)
241 Announcement of two one-act operas. Black and white on a red and pink background. (USA)
242 Poster for a *Hamlet* production on the occasion of a Shakespeare Festival in New York. (USA)

237

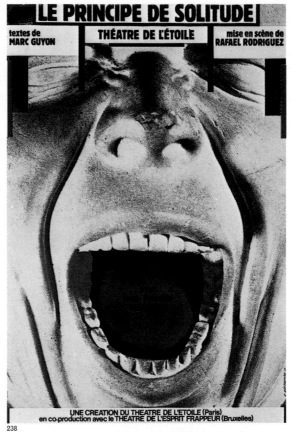

238

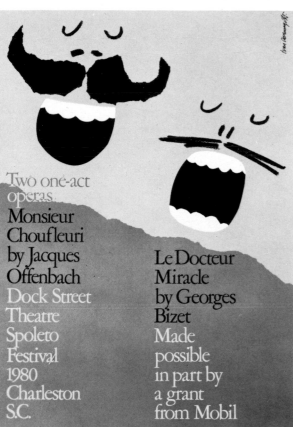

241

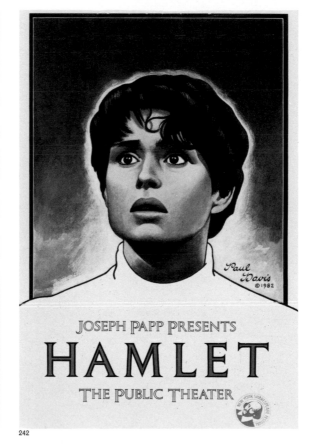

242

ARTIST / KÜNSTLER / ARTISTE:

235 Günter Schmidt
236, 239 Holger Matthies
237 Charles de Paeuw
238 Roman Cieslewicz
240 Theo Dimson
241 Ivan Chermayeff
242 Paul Davis

DESIGNER / GESTALTER / MAQUETTISTE:

235 Günter Schmidt
236, 239 Holger Matthies
237 Charles de Paeuw
238 Roman Cieslewicz
240 Theo Dimson
241 Ivan Chermayeff
242 Paul Davis

ART DIRECTOR / DIRECTEUR ARTISTIQUE:

236, 239 Holger Matthies
237 Charles de Paeuw
238 Rafael Rodriguez
240 Theo Dimson
241 Ivan Chermayeff

AGENCY / AGENTUR / AGENCE – STUDIO:

240 Dimson & Smith
241 Chermayeff & Geismar Assoc.

235 Plakat für Smetanas komische Oper *Das Geheimnis*, aufgeführt von der Städtischen Bühne Hagen. (GER)
236 Für die Aufführung einer komischen Oper am Theater Oberhausen. Brauntöne auf leuchtend violettem Hintergrund. (GER)
237 Siebdruck-Plakat für eine Inszenierung von Aristophanes' *Der Frieden*. Brauntöne mit weisser Schrift. (GER)
238 «Das Prinzip der Einsamkeit.» Ankündigung einer Aufführung am Théâtre de l'Etoile, Paris. (FRA)
239 Plakat mit dem Programm der Städtischen Bühnen Osnabrück für die Spielzeit 1982/83. (GER)
240 Mr. Pickwick aus Charles Dickens' *Pickwickier* ist Gegenstand dieses Plakates für eine Aufführung in Toronto. (CAN)
241 Ankündigung von zwei Ein-Akt-Opern. Schwarzweiss auf rotem und rosa Hintergrund. (USA)
242 Plakat für eine *Hamlet*-Inszenierung im Rahmen des New Yorker Shakespeare Festivals. (USA)

235 Affiche pour l'opéra comique *Le Secret* de Smetana, dans une mise en scène du Théâtre municipal de Hagen. (GER)
236 Pour la représentation d'un opéra bouffe au Théâtre d'Oberhausen. Divers bruns sur fond violet lumineux. (GER)
237 Affiche sérigraphique pour une représentation de *La Paix* d'Aristophane. Divers bruns, texte blanc. (GER)
238 Annonce d'une mise en scène au Théâtre de l'Etoile de Paris. (FRA)
239 Affiche-programme des Théâtres municipaux d'Osnabrück pour la saison 1982/83. (GER)
240 Mr. Pickwick, le personnage de *Pickwickier* de Charles Dickens, fournit le thème de cette affiche annonçant une représentation dans la ville de Toronto. (CAN)
241 Annonce de deux opéras en un acte. Noir et blanc sur fond rouge et rose. (USA)
242 Affiche pour un *Hamlet* présenté sur une scène newyorkaise dans le cadre du Festival Shakespeare de New York. (USA)

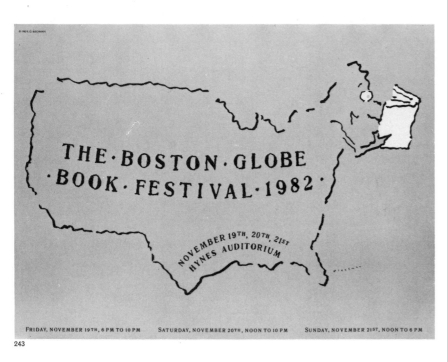

243

244

ARTIST / KÜNSTLER / ARTISTE:

243 R.O. Blechman
244 Bälz Baechi
245 Heather Cooper
246 Andrzej Dudzinski
247 Gottfried Helnwein
248 V. Courtlandt Johnson
249 Gabriele Burde

DESIGNER / GESTALTER / MAQUETTISTE:

243 Stephen J. Pena
244 Balz Baechi
245 Diane Mellor
246 Cipe Pineles
247 Gottfried Helnwein
248 Marty Neumeier/
     Byron Glaser
249 Gabriele Burde

ART DIRECTOR / DIRECTEUR ARTISTIQUE:

243 Stephen J. Pena
244 Balz Baechi
245 Heather Cooper
248 Marty Neumeier
249 Gabriele Burde

AGENCY / AGENTUR / AGENCE – STUDIO:

243 The Boston Globe
245 Burns, Cooper, Hynes Ltd.
248 Neumeier Design Team
249 Gabriele Burde

243 *The Boston Globe* makes an announcement. Black and white on strong light blue, red pupil. (USA)
244 Large-format poster for a Nô play performed at Zurich's Theatre 11. (SWI)
245 Announcement of a production on the occasion of the Stratford Festival in Canada. (CAN)
246 Poster for an art school situated in Paris, New York and Los Angeles. (USA)
247 Announcement of a lecture series at Graz University. (AUT)
248 Poster for schools and libraries, to encourage the reading of classical short stories. (USA)
249 Poster issued within the framework of the Berlin Festival for the Gustav Mahler cycle on the occasion of the 100th anniversary of the Berlin Philharmonic Orchestra. (GER)

243 Ankündigung der Zeitung *The Boston Globe* für eine Buchausstellung. Schwarzweiss auf kräftigem Hellblau, rote Pupille. (USA)
244 Grossformatiges Plakat für ein Nô-Spiel, aufgeführt am Theater 11 in Zürich. (SWI)
245 Ankündigung einer Theateraufführung im Rahmen des kanadischen Stratford-Festivals. (CAN)
246 Plakat für eine Kunstschule, mit Sitz in Paris, New York und Los Angeles. (USA)
247 Ankündigung einer Vortragsreihe an der Universität Graz. (AUT)
248 Plakat für Bibliotheken und Schulen, als Ansporn zum Lesen klassischer Kurzgeschichten. (USA)
249 Im Rahmen der Berliner Festspiele veröffentlichtes Plakat für den Gustav-Mahler-Zyklus zum 100jährigen Jubiläum des Berliner Philharmonischen Orchesters. (GER)

243 Annonce du quotidien *The Boston Globe* pour une exposition de livres. Noir et blanc sur bleu clair vigoureux, pupille rouge. (USA)
244 Affiche au grand format pour un drame nô joué au Théâtre 11 de Zurich. (SWI)
245 Annonce d'une représentation de théâtre au Festival de Stratford au Canada. (CAN)
246 Affiche pour une école d'art à Paris, New York et Los Angeles. (USA)
247 Annonce d'une série de conférences à l'Université de Graz. (AUT)
248 Affiche pour les écoles et les bibliothèques: lecture de nouvelles classiques. (USA)
249 Affiche pour le cycle Gustav Mahler exécuté à l'occasion du 100e anniversaire de l'Orchestre Philharmonique de Berlin dans le cadre du Festival de Berlin. (GER)

247

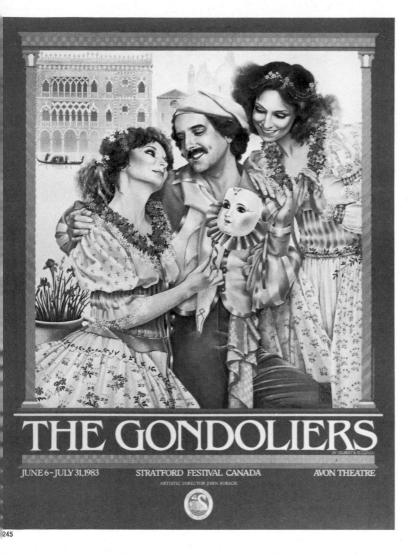

245

246

248

249

250

251

250 For a music festival on the island of Crete. (GRE)
251 Poster announcing a performance in a theatre. (POL)
252 For a Rumanian production of Shakespeare's famous play. Brown and black on light grey. (RUM)
253 Black-and-white poster for a performance by the Polish State Theatre for puppets and actors. (POL)
254 "Drama and the Stage" is the title of the exhibition announced here for décors and costumes of the Hungarian theatre and television covering the period 1979–83. In black and white. (HUN)
255 For the performance of a play by Aristophanes. Yellow and brown shades, red mouth. (POL)
256 Poster for a theatre centre in Wroclaw. Brown shades on a dark ground, white and red eye. (POL)
257 Poster for a Bulgarian production of Shakespeare's *The Twelfth Night or What You will*. Yellow and brown on black, white lettering. (BUL)

252

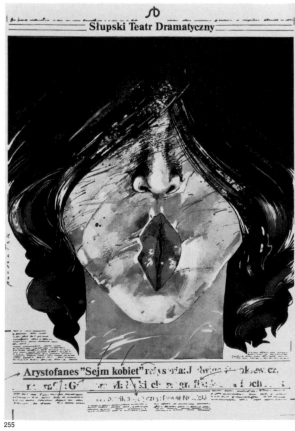

255

250 Für ein auf Kreta stattfindendes Musik-Festival. (GRE)
251 Plakat für die Ankündigung einer Theateraufführung. (POL)
252 Für eine rumänische Inszenierung von Shakespeares *Richard III*. Braun und Schwarz auf Hellgrau. (RUM)
253 Plakat in Schwarzweiss für eine Aufführung des polnischen Staatstheaters für Marionetten und Schauspieler. (POL)
254 «Drama und Bühne» ist der Titel der hier angekündigten Ausstellung mit Bühnenbildern und Kostümen des ungarischen Theaters und Fernsehens aus der Zeit von 1979–83. Schwarzweiss. (HUN)
255 Für eine Aufführung von Aristophanes' *Die Weibervolksversammlung*. Gelb und Brauntöne, roter Mund. (POL)
256 Plakat für ein Theaterzentrum in Wroclaw. Brauntöne auf dunklem Grund, Auge weiss und rot. (POL)
257 Für eine bulgarische Inszenierung von Shakespeares *Was ihr wollt*. Gelb und Braun auf Schwarz, weisse Schrift. (BUL)

250 Pour un festival de la musique organisé en Crète. (GRE)
251 Affiche annonçant une reprise théâtrale. (POL)
252 Pour un *Richard III* de Shakespeare mis en scène par les Roumains. Brun et noir sur gris clair. (RUM)
253 Affiche noir et blanc pour une représentation au Théâtre d'Etat polonais de marionnettes. (POL)
254 «Drame et scène», ainsi est intitulée l'exposition de décors et costumes du théâtre et de la télévision hongrois de la période 1979–1983 annoncée par cette affiche. Noir et blanc. (HUN)
255 Pour une représentation de *L'Assemblée des femmes* d'Aristophane. Jaune et divers bruns, bouche rouge. (POL)
256 Affiche pour un centre du théâtre à Wroclaw. Divers bruns sur fond sombre, œil blanc et rouge. (POL)
257 Pour une mise en scène bulgare de *La Nuit des Rois*, par William Shakespeare. Jaune et brun sur noir, texte blanc. (BUL)

253

254

ARTIST / KÜNSTLER / ARTISTE:

250 Michael Katzourakis
251, 253 Tadeusz Grabowski
252 Klára Tamás Blaier
254 György Kemény
255 Grzegorz Marszalek
256 Jacek Cwikla
257 Gancho St. Ganev

ART DIRECTOR / DIRECTEUR ARTISTIQUE:

250 Michael Katzourakis
254 Krisztina Jerger

AGENCY / AGENTUR / AGENCE – STUDIO:

250 A & M Katzourakis

256

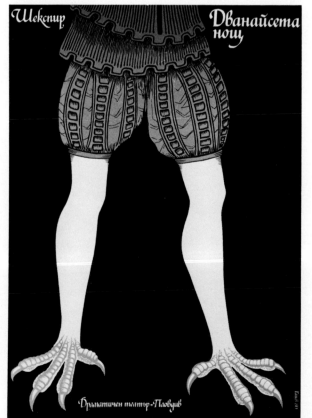

257

Theatre
Theater
Théâtre

ARTIST / KÜNSTLER / ARTISTE:

258 Romuald Socha
259 Mieczyslaw Gorowski
260, 261 Dana Andreyev
262 Marcin Stadewski
263 Roslaw Szaybo
264 Maria Ekier
265 Grzegorz Marszalek

258

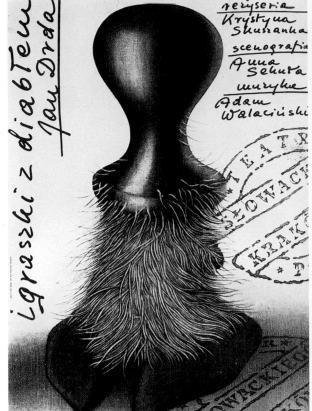

259

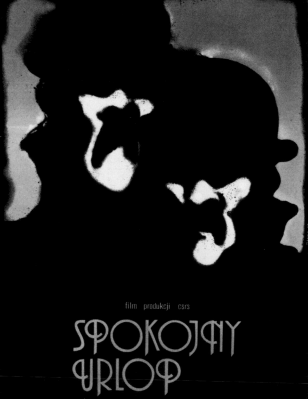

261

262

Theatre
Films

258 Affiche polychrome annonçant la sortie d'un film. (POL)
259 «Jeux avec le Diable», tel est le titre d'une pièce de Słowacki annoncée par cette affiche. Jaune et brun. (POL)
260 Annonce d'un film mongol au titre de «Légende de l'oasis». Noir et blanc, étoile rouge, sur gris beige. (POL)
261 Pour la projection d'un film tchèque en Pologne. Noir, jaune lumineux et rouge. (POL)
262 Pour une pièce tirée du roman *Guerre et Paix* de Tolstoï. Noir et blanc, sang rouge. (POL)
263 Annonce d'une adaptation de *Roméo et Juliette* de Shakespeare par un théâtre de Varsovie. Blanc sur vert gris. (POL)
264 «Bonne chance, Marilyn!» Pour un film hongrois joué en Pologne. (POL)
265 Pour un film italien à l'affiche en Pologne. (POL)

260

263

264

265

ARTIST / KÜNSTLER / ARTISTE:

266 Seymour Chwast
267 Andrea Mancini
268 Finn Nygaard
269 Joseph Sellars
270 Elso Schiavo

DESIGNER / GESTALTER / MAQUETTISTE:

266 Seymour Chwast
267 Daniele Cavari/
    Stefano Rovai
268 Finn Nygaard
269 Joseph Sellars
270 Elso Schiavo

ART DIRECTOR / DIRECTEUR ARTISTIQUE:

266 Sandra Ruch
267 Andrea Rauch
269 Joseph Sellars
270 Elso Schiavo

AGENCY / AGENTUR / AGENCE – STUDIO:

266 Pushpin Lubalin Peckolick
267 Graphiti
269 Joseph Sellars
270 Elso Schiavo

266 Poster announcing a television recording in four episodes of a theatre production of Charles Dickens' *Nicholas Nickleby*. The series was financed by *Mobil*. (USA)
267 "The Land of the Toy." Full-colour poster for a performance within the framework of a Pinocchio Festival in Florence. (ITA)
268 Poster in red and yellow with black and white for a play entitled "Fleamarket". (DEN)
269 Collage composed of old masters as well as classics from the spheres of children's books and advertising illustrations, for a theatre of fantasy in the United States. (USA)
270 The history of the provincial town of Zug in Switzerland is the subject of the "ironically amusing spectacle" announced here. (SWI)

266 Plakat für die Ankündigung der von *Mobil* finanzierten, vierteiligen Fernsehaufzeichnung einer Theaterproduktion von Charles Dickens' *Nicholas Nickleby*. (USA)
267 «Das Land des Spielzeugs.» Mehrfarbiges Plakat für eine Aufführung im Rahmen eines Pinocchio-Festivals in Florenz. (ITA)
268 In Rot und Gelb (mit Schwarzweiss) gehaltenes Plakat für ein Theaterstück mit dem Titel «Flohmarkt». (DEN)
269 Collage mit Anleihen bei alten Meistern sowie Klassikern der Kinderbuch- und Werbeillustration für ein phantastisches Theater. (USA)
270 Die Geschichte der schweizerischen Kleinstadt Zug ist Gegenstand des hier angekündigten «amüsant-ironischen Spektakels». (SWI)

266 Affiche annonçant une dramatique en quatre épisodes d'après le *Nicholas Nickleby* de Charles Dickens, émission patronnée par *Mobil*. (USA)
267 «Le Pays des jouets»: affiche polychrome pour une représentation dans le cadre d'un festival Pinocchio organisé dans la ville de Florence. (ITA)
268 Affiche rouge et jaune (avec du noir-blanc) pour une pièce de théâtre intitulée «Marché aux puces». (DEN)
269 Collage pour un théâtre fantastique, inspiré de vieux maîtres et de classiques du livre d'enfants et de la publicité. (USA)
270 «Un spectacle ironique et amusant», voici ce que promet sur cette affiche une revue satirique de l'histoire de Zoug en Suisse. (SWI)

Theatre
Theater
Théâtre

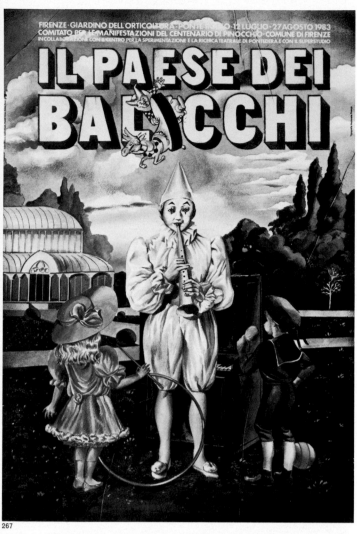

267

268

269

270

271

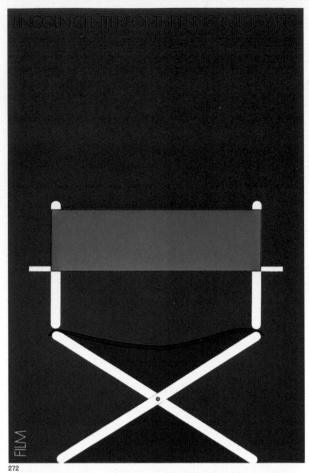

272

273

274

ARTIST / KÜNSTLER / ARTISTE:

271, 272 Per Arnoldi
273 Theo Dimson
274 Pit Weyer
275 Boris Bućan

DESIGNER / GESTALTER / MAQUETTISTE:

271, 272 Per Arnoldi
273 Theo Dimson
275 Boris Bućan

ART DIRECTOR / DIRECTEUR ARTISTIQUE:

273 Doug Eliuk
275 Boris Bućan

AGENCY / AGENTUR / AGENCE – STUDIO:

273 Dimson & Smith

271, 272 Examples from a series of five posters for the Lincoln Center in New York. (USA)
273 Poster for a Canadian film about the aftermaths of being fired. In mat shades of red, beige and brown with black and white. (CAN)
274 For a performance of a Fassbinder play, held in Luxemburg. Pink and black and white. (LUX)
275 Large-format, six-part poster for a performance of Aristophanes' *Lysistrata*. In black and white with light brown. (YUG)

271, 272 Exemples d'une série de cinq affiches créées pour le Lincoln Center newyorkais. (USA)
273 Pour un film canadien où il est question de cadres d'entreprise dont on sape le poste. Rouge mat, beige et brun, avec du noir et blanc. (CAN)
274 Pour la représentation à Luxembourg d'une pièce de Fassbinder. Rose, noir et blanc. (LUX)
275 Affiche hexapartite au grand format pour une représentation de la *Lysistrata* d'Aristophane. Noir et blanc, avec du brun clair. (YUG)

271, 272 Beispiele aus einer Reihe von fünf Plakaten für das New Yorker Lincoln Center. (USA)
273 Für einen kanadischen Film, in dem es um das «Absägen» von leitenden Angestellten geht. In mattem Rotton, Beige und Braun mit Schwarzweiss. (CAN)
274 Für die Luxemburger Aufführung eines Stücks von Fassbinder. Pink und Schwarzweiss. (LUX)
275 Grossformatiges (sechsteiliges) Plakat für eine Aufführung von Aristophanes' *Lysistrata*. In Schwarzweiss mit Hellbraun. (YUG)

275

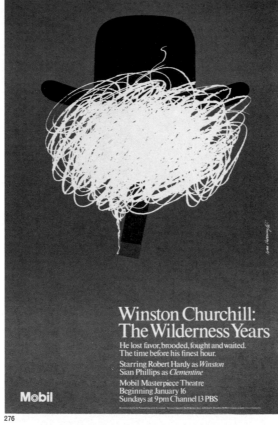

276

277

276–279 For performances within the framework of the televised Masterpiece Theatre programme financed by *Mobil*. Fig. 276: a production about the years when Winston Churchill kept a low profile; Fig. 277: a series of Agatha Christie stories; Fig. 278: *On Approval*, a play; Fig. 279: a play by Ford Madox Ford. All posters are in full colour. (USA)
280 Announcement of performances on the occasion of the New York Shakespeare Festival. Collage with canvas strips on canvas. (USA)
281–283 More posters taken from the series of televised theatre programmes financed by *Mobil*, here for two thrillers. (USA)

276–279 Für Aufführungen im Rahmen eines von *Mobil* finanzierten Fernseh-Theaterprogramms. Abb. 276: Bearbeitung eines Buches von Churchill über sein Leben; Abb. 277: eine Agatha-Christie-Reihe; Abb. 278: ein Stück mit dem Titel «Zur Ansicht»; Abb. 279: ein Stück des amerikanischen Autors Ford Madox Ford. Alle Plakate mehrfarbig. (USA)
280 Ankündigung von Aufführungen im Rahmen des New Yorker Shakespeare-Festivals. Collage mit Leinwandstreifen auf Leinwand. (USA)
281–283 Weitere Plakate aus der Reihe für *Mobil*-Theaterpräsentationen im Fernsehen, hier für zwei Kriminalstücke. (USA)

276–279 Affiches annonçant une série de dramatiques financées par *Mobil*. Fig. 276: d'après une autobiographie de Churchill; fig. 277: une série inspirée d'Agatha Christie; fig. 278: une pièce intitulée «A l'essai»; fig. 279: une pièce de l'auteur américain Ford Madox Ford. En polychromie. (USA)
280 Annonce de représentations données dans le cadre du Festival Shakespeare de New York. Collage de bandes de toile sur toile. (USA)
281–283 Autres exemples d'affiches de présentation de dramatiques patronnées par *Mobil*. Il s'agit ici de deux émissions consacrées à des pièces policières. Toutes les deux en polychromie. (USA)

278

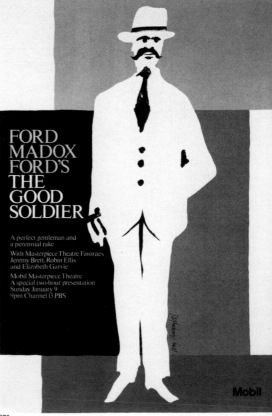

279

280

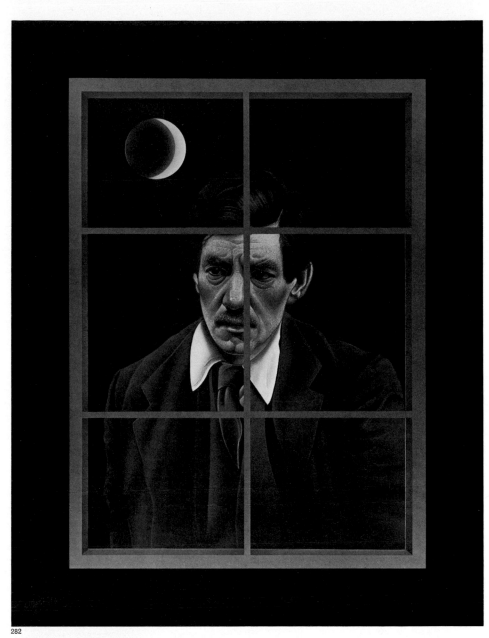

282

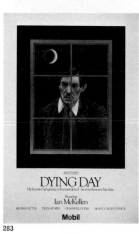

283

281

284

285

287

288

284 Poster for an annual flower exhibition that takes place in the state of Massachusetts. In mat shades. (USA)
285 Poster for an international conference of ITT computer-programme specialists. Lettering in bright blue and red on black. (USA)
286 "Youth Protest and Official Reaction." For a series of lectures held at the Berlin school of administration and justice. In full colour. (GER)
287 Poster showing work by students in the graduation class for architecture at the Cranbrook Academy. Black and white with red. (USA)
288 Announcement of an architecture and building exhibition. In full colour. (GBR)
289 "Fullfilled Living." Small-format poster for a series of lectures organised by various church bodies. Shades of green, brown and red. (SWI)
290 Announcement of international festivals of television and radio programmes, in which the "Prix Italia" is awarded. Water-colour. (ITA)
291 For an exhibition entitled "One Italy talking about another Italy", organised by the city of Turin. (ITA)

284 Plakat für eine jährlich stattfindende Blumenausstellung in Massachusetts. In matten Farbtönen. (USA)
285 Für eine internationale Konferenz der ITT-Programmierer. Schrift in leuchtendem Blau und Rot auf Schwarz. (USA)
286 Ankündigung einer Vortragsreihe der Berliner Fachhochschule für Verwaltung und Rechtspflege. In Farbe. (GER)
287 Vergrösserung eines Projekts von Studenten der Abschlussklasse für Architektur an der Cranbrook-Akademie. Schwarzweiss mit Rot. (USA)
288 Ankündigung einer Bau-Fachmesse in Birmingham. In Farbe. (GBR)
289 Kleinformatiges Plakat für eine Vortragsreihe, von kirchlichen Organisationen veranstaltet. Grün-, Braun- und Rottöne. (SWI)
290 Ankündigung von internationalen Festspielen für TV- und Radioprogramme, bei denen der «Prix Italia» verliehen wird. Aquarell. (ITA)
291 Für eine von der Stadt Turin organisierte Ausstellung: «Von einem Italien zu einem anderen Italien sprechend.» (ITA)

Jugendprotest und Beamtenreaktion

Verwaltung in verschärften Konflikten

Hochschultage der Fachhochschule für Verwaltung und Rechtspflege
Kurfürstendamm 207/208 · 20. und 21. Oktober 1981
Bitte Programm anfordern · Tel. 318 34 40

286

Arbeitsgemeinschaft für Kirchliche Schulung (AKS)
Amt für Gesamtstädtische Kirchliche Aufgaben
Röm.-kath. Amt für Erwachsenenbildung

GANZHEITLICH LEBEN

Ein Vortragskurs im Grossen Saal des Kirchlichen Zentrums Bürenpark, Bern

Dienstag, 11. Januar 1983
Prof. Dr. Herbert Haag
Du hast mich verzaubert
Liebe und Sexualität in der Bibel

Dienstag, 18. Januar 1983
Dr. Marga Bührig
Ganzheitlich glauben
Leben und Glauben aus der Sicht
der feministischen Theologie

Donnerstag, 27. Januar 1983
Prof. Dr. med. Rolf Adler,
Chefarzt des Lory Spitals,
und **Willi Hemmeler**
dipl. Psychologe
Ganzheitlicher Zugang zum
Patienten

Dienstag, 1. Februar 1983
Dr. August E. Hohler
Wie werde ich ganz?
Wir Menschen zwischen
Anonymität und Intimität

jeweils 20 Uhr

Kursbeitrag: Fr. 20.–
Einzeleintritt: Fr. 6.–

289

284 Affiche pour des floralies organisées annuellement au Massachusetts. Couleurs mates. (USA)
285 Pour une conférence internationale des programmeurs ITT. Texte bleu et rouge lumineux sur noir. (USA)
286 Annonce d'une série de conférences organisées à l'Ecole supérieure d'administration et de droit administratif de Berlin. En couleurs. (GER)
287 Agrandissement d'un projet des étudiants de la classe terminale d'architecture de la Cranbrook Academy. Noir-blanc, avec du rouge. (USA)
288 Annonce d'une Foire du Bâtiment à Birmingham. En couleurs. (GBR)
289 Affichette pour une série de conférences organisées par des organisations religieuses. Divers verts, bruns et rouges. (SWI)
290 Annonce d'un festival international de programmes TV et radio au cours duquel un «Prix Italia» vient d'être décerné. Aquarelle. (ITA)
291 Pour une exposition organisée par la municipalité de Turin sur le thème «Parler de l'Italie à une autre Italie.» (ITA)

290

PARLANDO DELL'ITALIA A UN'ALTRA ITALIA

CITTA' DI TORINO ASSESSORATO PER LA CULTURA – FONDAZIONE GIOVANNI AGNELLI
ROTONDA E SALA CONFERENZE GALLERIA CIVICA D'ARTE MODERNA 23 GENNAIO 18 FEBBRAIO

291

292

293

296

297

292 Poster for a Yugoslav film entitled "Occupation in 26 Pictures". Black and white, red mouth. (POL)
293 For a Belgian production of Shakespeare's *Macbeth*. (BEL)
294 Preview of New York's Lincoln Center programme for the 1982/83 season. Colourful hats on a black ground. (USA)
295 For a series of war films. In black and white. (USA)
296 Poster for an annual festival held in Perth, Australia. (AUS)
297 "The Testament of a Dog." Full-colour poster for a Brazilian play performed in France. (FRA)
298 Poster for an American thriller film. (HUN)
299 Invitation to a small event held on election day in the USA. Cases were enacted there in which one single vote turned out to be the deciding factor. (USA)

294

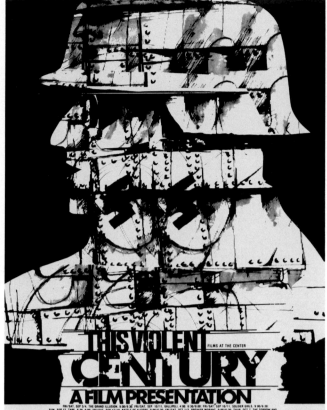

295

298

299

ARTIST / KÜNSTLER / ARTISTE:

292 M. Wasilewski
293 Jacques Richez
294 Bob Coonts
295 John J. Sorbie
296 Fritz Kos
297 Alain Le Quernec
298 Katalin Rényi
299 Bill Mayer

DESIGNER / GESTALTER / MAQUETTISTE:

293 Jacques Richez
294 Bob Coonts
295 John J. Sorbie
296 Mandy Browne
297 Alain Le Quernec
299 Bill Mayer

ART DIRECTOR / DIRECTEUR ARTISTIQUE:

293 Jacques Richez
294 Bob Coonts
295 John J. Sorbie
297 Alain Le Quernec
299 Bill Mayer

AGENCY / AGENTUR / AGENCE – STUDIO:

294 Bob Coonts Graphic Design
295 Sorbie Roche
298 Magyar Hirdetö
299 Graphicsgroup, Inc.

292 Für einen jugoslawischen Film mit dem Titel «Okkupation in 26 Bildern». Schwarzweiss, roter Mund. (POL)
293 Für eine belgische Aufführung von Shakespeares *Macbeth*. (BEL)
294 «Hut ab» – vor dem Spielplan des New Yorker Lincoln Centers für die Saison 1982/83. Farbige Hüte auf schwarzem Grund. (USA)
295 Für eine Reihe von Kriegsfilmen. In Schwarzweiss. (USA)
296 Plakat für jährlich stattfindende Festwochen in Perth. (AUS)
297 «Das Testament des Hundes.» Mehrfarbiges Plakat für ein brasilianisches Theaterstück. (FRA)
298 Für einen amerikanischen Kriminalfilm. (HUN)
299 Einladung zu einer kleinen Veranstaltung am Wahltag in den USA, Es werden Fälle aufgeführt, bei denen eine Stimme den Ausschlag gab. (USA)

292 Pour un film yougoslave intitulé «Occupation en 26 tableaux». Noir et blanc, bouche rouge. (POL)
293 Pour un *Macbeth* de Shakespeare mis en scène en Belgique. (BEL)
294 «Tirez votre chapeau» – au programme du Lincoln Center de New York pour la saison 1982/83. Chapeaux polychromes sur fond noir. (USA)
295 Pour une série de films de guerre. Noir et blanc. (USA)
296 Affiche pour le Festival annuel de Perth. (AUS)
297 Affiche polychrome pour une pièce de théâtre brésilienne. (FRA)
298 Pour un film policier américain. (HUN)
299 Invitation à une mini-manifestation le jour des élections présidentielles aux Etats-Unis. On y cite des cas dans l'Histoire où la voix d'un seul électeur fit pencher la balance en faveur d'un candidat ou de l'autre. Appel au vote patriotique. (USA)

300

301

304

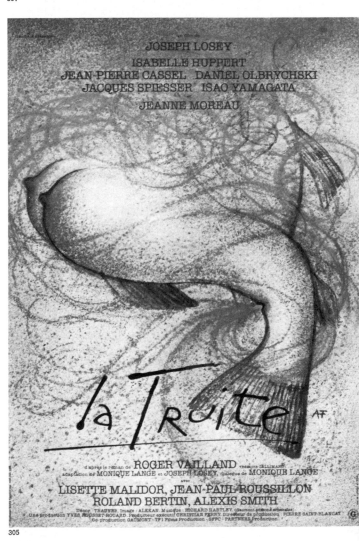

305

302

ARTIST / KÜNSTLER / ARTISTE:

300 Holger Matthies
301 Frank Oriach
302 Paul Brühwiler
303 Elzbieta Procka
304, 305 André François
306 Piwon

DESIGNER / GESTALTER / MAQUETTISTE:

300 Holger Matthies
301 Santiago Pol
302 Paul Brühwiler

303

ART DIRECTOR / DIRECTEUR ARTISTIQUE:

300 Holger Matthies
301 Santiago Pol
302 Paul Brühwiler

AGENCY / AGENTUR / AGENCE – STUDIO:

301 Vision 3

306

300 Poster for the Hamburg Museum of Arts and Crafts, announcing an exhibition devoted to tales and masks concerning the Commedia dell'Arte as well as a theatre production. (GER)
301 "Cinema for World Peace." Poster issued on the occasion of a film festival in Leipzig. (VEN)
302 Edward G. Robinson graces the poster for a Zurich retrospective of the American gangster film. (SWI)
303 Black-and-white poster for a Polish film. (POL)
304 Cinema poster for a production entitled "Yoyo". Black and white with red. (FRA)
305 "The Trout." Full-colour poster for the film version of a novel. (FRA)
306 Black-and-white poster for a Russian film called "Portrait of the Artist's Wife". (POL)

300 Für das Hamburger Museum für Kunst und Gewerbe mit Ankündigung einer Ausstellung über Geschichte und Masken der Commedia dell'Arte und einer Theatervorführung. (GER)
301 «Kino für den Frieden der Welt.» Zum Filmfestival in Leipzig veröffentlichtes Plakat. (VEN)
302 Edward G. Robinson auf dem Plakat für eine Retrospektive des amerikanischen Gangster-Films. (SWI)
303 Schwarzweisses Plakat für einen polnischen Film. (POL)
304 Kinoplakat für eine Produktion mit dem Titel «Yoyo». Schwarzweiss mit Rot. (FRA)
305 «Die Forelle.» Mehrfarbiges Plakat für die Verfilmung eines Romans. (FRA)
306 Schwarzweisses Plakat für einen russischen Film: «Porträt der Frau des Künstlers.» (POL)

300 Pour le Musée des arts et métiers de Hambourg, qui organise une exposition sur l'histoire et les masques de la Commedia dell'Arte, ainsi qu'une représentation de théâtre. (GER)
301 «Le cinéma pour la paix dans le monde.» Affiche pour le festival du cinéma de Leipzig. (VEN)
302 Edward G. Robinson tête d'affiche pour une rétrospective du film de gangsters américain. (SWI)
303 Affiche noir et blanc pour un film polonais. (POL)
304 Affiche de cinéma pour une production intitulée «Yoyo». Noir et blanc, avec du rouge. (FRA)
305 Affiche polychrome pour un film tiré d'un roman. (FRA)
306 Affiche noir et blanc pour le film russe «Portrait de la femme de l'artiste.» (POL)

307

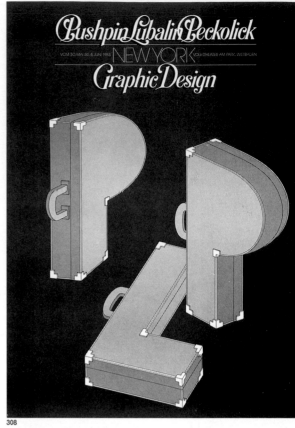

308

310

311

307 Announcement of a lecture at Penn State University, dealing with the current state of graphic design and applied arts. Black on beige. (USA)
308 For an exhibition of the New York graphic design studio Pushpin Lubalin Peckolick, in Wiesbaden, West Germany. Bright yellow on grey. (GER)
309 Dance masks of Mexican and Guatemalan Indians are the subject of an exhibition in a New York museum announced here. (USA)
310 For an exhibition with pictures, films and lectures concerning America in the 30's. Yellow, red and grey on a white ground. (USA)
311 Car tyres and their structures, a favourite theme of the artist whose exhibition is announced on this poster. Red on pale yellow. (SWI)
312 Poster for an exhibition of contemporary illustrators in the Rizzoli Galleries, New York. Hands in many bright colours on black. (USA)
313 Poster issued by the state of Pennsylvania in which "friends" of Pennsylvania's past are shown. (USA)

307 Ankündigung einer Vorlesung an der Penn State University, über den gegenwärtigen Stand der Graphik und angewandten Kunst. (USA)
308 Für eine Ausstellung des New Yorker Graphik-Studios Pushpin Lubalin Peckolick in Wiesbaden. Leuchtendes Gelb auf Grau. (GER)
309 Tanzmasken mexikanischer und guatemaltekischer Indianer sind Gegenstand der hier angekündigten Ausstellung in New York. (USA)
310 Für eine Ausstellung mit Bildern, Filmen und Vorträgen über das Amerika der dreissiger Jahre. Gelb, Rot und Grau auf weissem Grund. (USA)
311 Autoreifen und deren Strukturen, ein bevorzugtes Thema des Künstlers, dessen Ausstellung hier angezeigt wird. Rot auf blassem Gelb. (SWI)
312 In vielen Farben leuchtende Hände auf Schwarz, für eine Ausstellung zeitgenössischer Illustratoren in den Rizzoli Galleries, New York. (USA)
313 «Freunde aus Pennsylvaniens Vergangenheit» sind Gegenstand dieses Plakates des amerikanischen Bundesstaates Pennsylvanien. (USA)

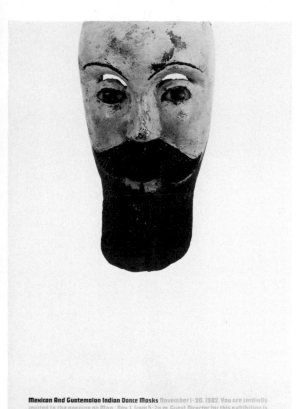

Mexican And Guatemalan Indian Dance Masks November 1-20, 1982. You are cordially invited to the opening on Mon., Nov.1, from 5-7 p.m. Guest Director for this exhibition is Garry Rich. Visual Arts Museum, 209 East 23rd St., New York City, 10010. (212) 679-7350 The Museum is open Mon. thru Thurs., from 12-8 p.m. Fri., 11a.m.-4:30p.m. Sat., 9a.m.-4p.m.

309

RIZZOLI GALLERIES: 712 FIFTH AVENUE, NEW YORK, OCTOBER 5, 1982
835 NORTH MICHIGAN AVENUE, CHICAGO, NOVEMBER 12, 1982

Great Illustrators of Our Time

312

307 Annonce d'une conférence sur l'état des arts graphiques et appliqués organisée à la Penn State University. Noir sur beige. (USA)
308 Pour une exposition des œuvres du studio d'art publicitaire newyorkais Pushpin Lubalin Peckolick à Wiesbaden. Jaune éclatant sur gris. (GER)
309 Les masques de danse des Indiens du Mexique et du Guatemala sont le thème de l'exposition d'un musée newyorkais annoncée ici. (USA)
310 Pour une exposition agrémentée de films, photos et conférences sur l'Amérique des années 30. Jaune, rouge, gris sur fond blanc. (USA)
311 Les pneus et leur texture sont le sujet préféré de l'artiste dont on annonce ici l'exposition. Rouge sur jaune pâle. (SWI)
312 Mains multicolores sur noir, pour une exposition des œuvres d'illustrateurs contemporains aux Rizzoli Galleries de New York. (USA)
313 «Les amis venus du passé de la Pennsylvanie», voici le thème de cette affiche réalisée pour l'Etat américain de Pennsylvanie. (USA)

313

125

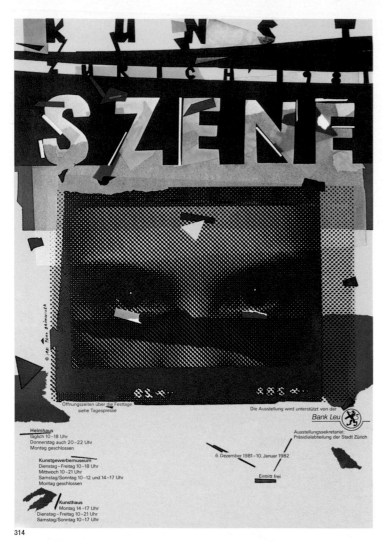

314

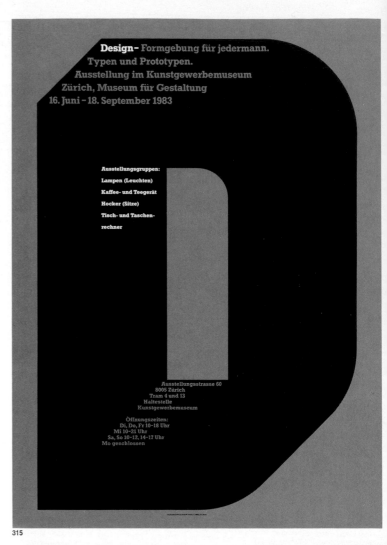

315

316

317

Exhibitions/Ausstellungen
Expositions

ARTIST/KÜNSTLER/ARTISTE:

314 Paul Brühwiler
317 Marc Garanger
318, 319 Hélène Majera

DESIGNER/GESTALTER/MAQUETTISTE:

314 Paul Brühwiler
315 Jörg Hamburger/Georg Staehelin
316 Siegfried Odermatt
317 Werner Jeker
318, 319 Patrick Couratin

ART DIRECTOR/DIRECTEUR ARTISTIQUE:

314 Paul Brühwiler
317 Werner Jeker
318, 319 Hélène Majera

AGENCY/AGENTUR/AGENCE:

317 Werner Jeker

318

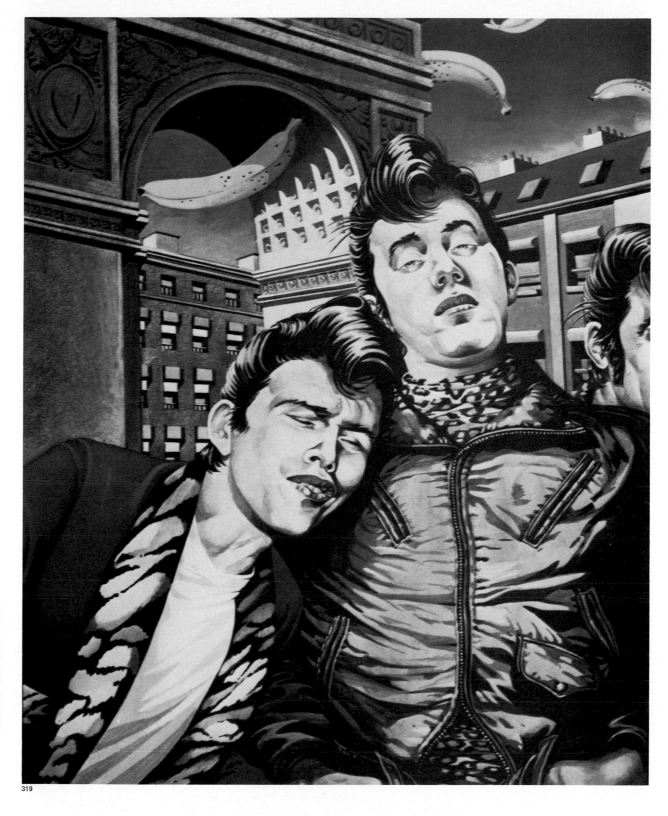

319

314 Poster for the exhibition "Art Scene, Zurich", shown in three Zurich museums and for which all artists in Zurich and environs are welcome to enter their work. (SWI)
315 Poster for a design exhibition held at the Zurich Museum of Arts and Crafts. Black D on cold red, red and white lettering. (SWI)
316 For an exhibition, "Design from Holland", at the Zurich Museum of Arts and Crafts. (SWI)
317 "The Power of the Moment." Black-and-white poster with yellow for a photo exhibition. (SWI)
318, 319 Complete poster and illustration for an exhibition within the framework of a Comic-Strips "fair" (Salon International de la Bande Dessinée). (FRA)

314 Für die Ausstellung «Kunstszene Zürich», die in drei Zürcher Museen präsentiert wurde, und für die alle Künstler aus Zürich und Umgebung ihre Arbeiten einreichen können. (SWI)
315 Plakat für eine Design-Ausstellung im Zürcher Kunstgewerbemuseum. Schwarzes D auf kaltem Rot, Schrift rot und weiss. (SWI)
316 Ankündigung einer Ausstellung im Zürcher Kunstgewerbemuseum. (SWI)
317 Schwarzweisses Plakat mit gelbem Balken für eine Photoausstellung im Helmhaus, Zurich. (SWI)
318, 319 Vollständiges Plakat und Illustration für eine Ausstellung im Rahmen einer Messe für Comic-Strips (Salon International de la Bande Dessinée). (FRA)

314 Pour l'exposition «Kunstszene Zürich» (La Scène artistique zurichoise) présentée dans 3 musées à la fois et accueillant les œuvres des artistes de l'agglomération. (SWI)
315 Affiche pour une exposition de design au Musée des arts et métiers de Zurich. D noir sur rouge froid, texte rouge et blanc. (SWI)
316 Annonce d'exposition au Musée des arts et métiers (Kunstgewerbemuseum) de Zurich. (SWI)
317 Affiche noir et blanc, avec barre jaune, pour une exposition photo à Zurich. (SWI)
318, 319 Affiche complète et illustration pour une exposition organisée dans le cadre du Salon international de la bande dessinée. (FRA)

320

321

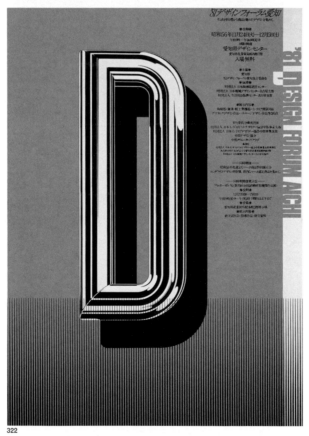

322

323

ARTIST / KÜNSTLER / ARTISTE:

320, 321 Ryosuke Matsuki
322 Shunyo Yamauchi
323 Shin Matsunaga
324, 325 Shigeichi Umemura

DESIGNER / GESTALTER / MAQUETTISTE:

320, 321 Ryosuke Matsuki
322 Shunyo Yamauchi
323 Shin Matsunaga
324, 325 Shigeichi Umemura

ART DIRECTOR / DIRECTEUR ARTISTIQUE:

320, 321 Ryosuke Matsuki
322 Yutaka Takehara
323 Shin Matsunaga
324, 325 Shigeichi Umemura

AGENCY / AGENTUR / AGENCE – STUDIO:

322 Shunyo Yamauchi Design Office
324, 325 Design Studio Flush

320 Announcement of festival weeks organized by the Japanese city of Kumamoto. Japanese letters from yellow-green to sea-green, black ground. (JPN)
321 Poster for a group exhibition of the members of the Kumamoto Arts Association. Green and blue, with white, beige and red. (JPN)
322 Poster for a design exhibition. Black-and-white D on a red ground. (JPN)
323 Full-colour poster for an international design fair in Kanazawa, Japan. (JPN)
324, 325 From a series of *Parco* gallery posters. Fig. 324: orange on blue; Fig. 325: orange, black, white. (JPN)

320 Ankündigung von Festwochen der japanischen Stadt Kumamoto. Japanischer Buchstabe von Gelbgrün in Blaugrün übergehend, auf schwarzem Grund. (JPN)
321 Plakat für eine Gruppenausstellung der Künstlervereinigung von Kumamoto. Grün und Blau, mit Weiss, Beige und Rot. (JPN)
322 Für eine Design-Ausstellung. Schwarzweisses D auf rotem Grund. (JPN)
323 Mehrfarbiges Plakat für eine internationale Design-Messe in Kanazawa, Japan. (JPN)
324, 325 Aus einer Serie von Plakaten für die *Parco*-Galerie. Abb. 324: «Nixen» und Fische orange auf Blau, Abb. 325: orange mit Schwarzweiss. (JPN)

320 Annonce du festival de la ville japonaise de Kumamoto. Caractère japonais variant du vert jaunâtre au vert bleuâtre sur fond noir. (JPN)
321 Affiche pour une exposition collective de l'association des artistes de Kumamoto. Vert et bleu, avec du blanc, du beige et du rouge. (JPN)
322 Pour une exposition de design. D noir et blanc sur fond rouge. (JPN)
323 Affiche polychrome pour un salon international du design à Kanazawa (Japon). (JPN)
324, 325 Exemples d'affiches figurant dans une série réalisée pour la galerie *Parco*. 324: «ondines» et poissons orange sur bleu, 325: orange avec noir-blanc. (JPN)

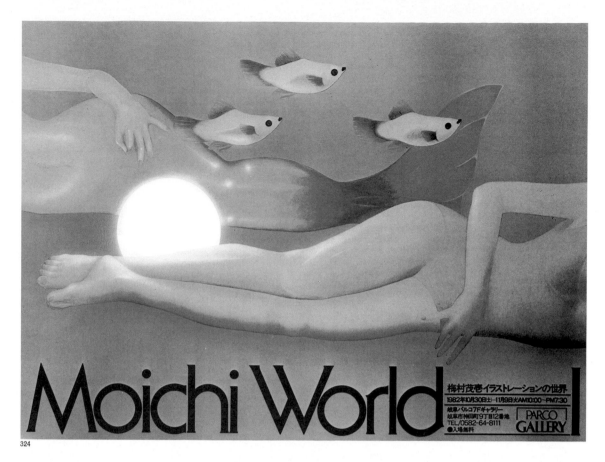

324

325

326 For a Philadelphia College of Art design exhibition showing glass, jewellery and ceramics. Black and white with red. (USA)
327 Announcement of a performance by the Nouveau Théâtre de Poche in Geneva. Black and white on a violet background. (SWI)
328 Invitation to a flower show. Full-colour photograph, black and beige background, white and green lettering. (USA)
329 For an exhibition in Pesaro displaying Belgium's textile culture: "Flanders Linen". In blue and white, black lettering on white. (ITA)
330 Legendary female characters are the subjects of these films shown in an American museum. Black and white. (USA)
331 Small-format poster for a textile fair in Sao Paulo. (BRA)
332 For an arts-and-crafts exhibition in the Kornhaus, Berne. (SWI)
333 Poster announcing the temporary closure of a section of the State Museum of Applied Art in Munich. (GER)

326 Für eine Design-Ausstellung des Philadelphia College of Art, mit Glas, Schmuck und Keramik. Schwarzweiss mit Rot. (USA)
327 Ankündigung einer Aufführung des Nouveau Théâtre de Poche in Genf. Schwarzweiss auf violettem Hintergrund (SWI)
328 Einladung zu einer Blumenausstellung. Farbaufnahme, Hintergrund schwarz und beige, Schrift weiss und grün. (USA)
329 Für eine Ausstellung in Pesaro über die Textil-Kultur Belgiens: «Leinen aus Flandern.» In Blau-Weiss, Schrift schwarz auf Weiss. (ITA)
330 Legendäre Frauengestalten sind Gegenstand der hier angekündigten Film-reihe im Kunstmuseum Worcester. Schwarzweiss. (USA)
331 Kleinformatiges Plakat für eine Textilmesse in Sao Paulo. (BRA)
332 Plakat für eine Kunstgewerbe-Ausstellung im Berner Kornhaus. (SWI)
333 Für die Bekanntgabe einer vorübergehenden Schliessung der Neuen Sammlung des Staatlichen Museums für angewandte Kunst in München. (GER)

ARTIST / KÜNSTLER / ARTISTE:

326 Laurence Bach
327 Roger Pfund/J.-P. Blanchoud
328 Paul Poplis
329 Massimo Dolcini
330 Isolde Monson-Baumgart
331 Ernest Schauder
332 Kurt Wirth/L. Bezzola (Photo)
333 Klaus Oberer

DESIGNER / GESTALTER / MAQUETTISTE:

326 William Longhauser
327 Roger Pfund/
    Jean-Pierre Blanchoud
328 Guy Salvato
329 Massimo Dolcini
332 Kurt Wirth
333 Pierre Mendell

ART DIRECTOR / DIRECTEUR ARTISTIQUE:

326 William Longhauser
327 Roger Pfund/
    Jean-Pierre Blanchoud
328 Guy Salvato
329 Massimo Dolcini
330 Isolde Monson-Baumgart
331 Bjarne Norking
333 Pierre Mendell

AGENCY / AGENTUR / AGENCE – STUDIO:

326 William Longhauser Design
327 Roger Pfund/
    Jean-Pierre Blanchoud
328 Salvato & Coe
329 Fuorischema
330 Isolde Monson-Baumgart
331 Alcantara Machado,
    Periscinoto Comunicaçoes Ltda.
333 Mendell & Oberer

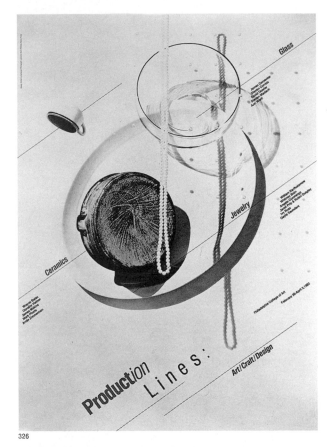

326

327

329

330

326 Pour une exposition d'esthétique industrielle du Philadelphia College of Art – verrerie, bijouterie, céramique. Noir-blanc, rouge. (USA)
327 Annonce d'une représentation au Nouveau Théâtre de Poche de Genève. Noir et blanc sur fond violet. (SWI)
328 Invitation à une exposition florale. Photo couleur, fond noir beige, texte blanc et vert. (USA)
329 Pour une exposition à Pesaro sur l'histoire culturelle du textile belge: «Le lin des Flandres.» Blanc et bleu, texte noir sur blanc. (ITA)
330 Les femmes légendaires constituent le sujet d'une série de films projetés au Musée d'art de Worcester. Noir et blanc. (USA)
331 Affichette pour une foire du textile à São Paulo. (BRA)
332 Pour une exposition d'arts appliqués au Kornhaus de Berne. (SWI)
333 Annonce de la fermeture temporaire des nouvelles collections du Musée d'Etat d'arts appliqués de Munich. (GER)

332

328

31

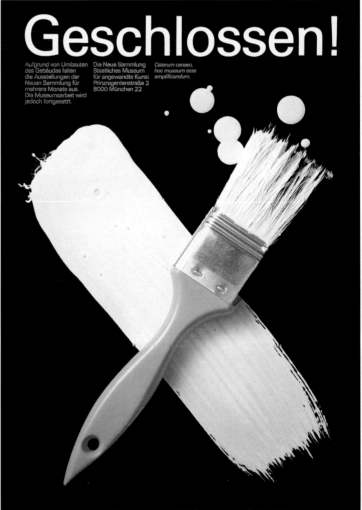

333

334

335

334 Poster for a one-man exhibition of the work of Tom Kamifuji. (USA)
335 Announcement of an exposition on the subject of "Dwellings and Surroundings", planned for 1985 in Japan. Various colours on a turquoise background. (JPN)
336 For a ceramics-design centre. White, carrot-red, green on a dark blue sky. (JPN)
337 For an art exhibition in the Japanese city of Gifu. Full-colour photographs. (JPN)
338 The art of baking is the theme of this poster. (JPN)

334 Pour une exposition de l'œuvre de Tom Kamifuji, artiste habitant la Californie. (USA)
335 Annonce d'une exposition internationale de l'habitat et de l'aménagement urbain prévue pour 1985. Diverses couleurs sur fond turquoise. (JPN)
336 Pour un centre de création en céramique. Blanc, carotte, vert sur ciel bleu nuit. (JPN)
337 Pour une exposition d'art dans la ville japonaise de Gifu. Photos polychromes. (JPN)
338 L'art du boulanger constitue le sujet de cette affiche. (JPN)

334 Für eine Ausstellung des in Kalifornien lebenden Künstlers Tom Kamifuji. (USA)
335 Ankündigung einer für 1985 geplanten internationalen Ausstellung über Wohn- und Umgebungsgestaltung. Verschiedene Farben auf türkisblauem Hintergrund. (JPN)
336 Für ein Keramik-Design-Zentrum. Weiss, karottenrot, grün auf nachtblauem Himmel. (JPN)
337 Für eine Kunstausstellung in der japanischen Stadt Gifu. Mehrfarbige Aufnahmen. (JPN)
338 Die Kunst des Backens ist Gegenstand dieses Plakates. (JPN)

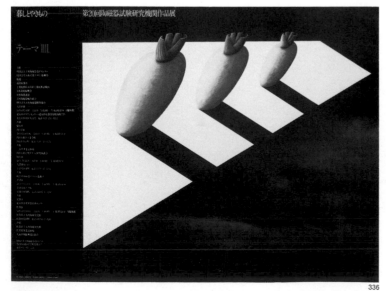

336

337

338

田辺雅一〈原画〉展
1983年4月14日木–4月26日火 午前10時・午後6時30分〈水曜定休〉
ギャラリー絵美時
〒501-02 岐阜県本巣郡穂積町馬場311-1 ユーストア内2F Phone 05832-7-4818〈直通〉

THE EXHIBITION OF ILLUSTRATION 〈WOMEN〉 BY MASAKAZU TANABE

Thursday, April 14th through Tuesday, April 26th, 1983   10:00am to 6:30pm   Gallery ABC (Closed: Wednesday)   U-Store 2F 311-1 Baba Hozumicho Motosugun Gifu 501-02

ART DIRECTOR-DESIGNER: MASAKAZU TANABE   PHOTOGRAPHER: HIROSHI KANAMORI   PRINTED BY TANAKA PRINTING CO. LTD.

339

339 For an exhibition with illustrations by Masakazu Tanabe, entitled "Women", at the ABC Gallery, Gifu. (JPN)
340 "Dialogue on Aesthetics." Announcement of an art exhibition in a museum of modern art in Toyama. (JPN)
341 Collage using multicoloured paper, partly painted, for a poster drawing attention to an Ikebana School (Sogetsu). (JPN)
342 Poster for the Toho-gakuen College, Japan. Full-colour photograph of ears of corn in strong green, background in airbrush technique: mainly blue, with green, white and black. (JPN)
343 Announcement of a design forum for industrial goods and graphic design held in the Aichi prefecture in Japan. (JPN)

339 Für eine Ausstellung mit Illustrationen von Masakazu Tanabe unter dem Titel «Frauen», in der ABC-Galerie, Gifu. (JPN)
340 «Dialog über Ästhetik.» Ankündigung einer Kunstausstellung in einem Museum für moderne Kunst in Toyama. (JPN)
341 Collage mit verschiedenfarbigem, zum Teil bemaltem Papier für das Paket einer Ikebana-Schule (Sogetsu School). (JPN)
342 Plakat für eine Schule (Toho-gakuen College). Farbaufnahme kräftig grüner Ähren; Hintergrund in Spray-Technik: vorwiegend Blau, mit Grün, Weiss und Schwarz. (JPN)
343 Ankündigung eines Design-Forums (Industrie-, Gebrauchsartikel- und graphisches Design) in der japanischen Präfektur Aichi. (JPN)

339 Pour une exposition des illustrations de Masakazu Tanabe organisée sous le titre de «Femmes» à la Galerie ABC de Gifu. (JPN)
340 «Dialogue sur l'esthétique.» Annonce d'une exposition artistique dans un musée d'art moderne de Toyama. (JPN)
341 Collage de papiers de différentes couleurs en partie peints, pour l'affiche d'une école d'ikebana (Ecole Sogetsu). (JPN)
342 Affiche pour une école (le Collège Toho-gakuen). Photo couleur d'épis vert vif; fond au pistolet: bleu prédominant, avec du vert, du blanc et du noir. (JPN)
343 Annonce d'un forum sur le design (esthétique industrielle, art publicitaire) organisé dans la préfecture d'Aichi, au Japon. (JPN)

Cultural Events
Veranstaltungen
Evénements culturels

340

341

342

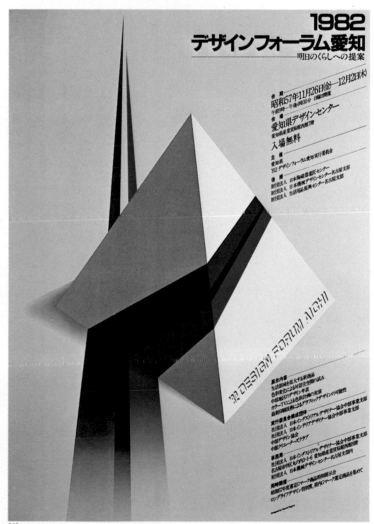

343

ARTIST / KÜNSTLER / ARTISTE:

344 Don Kueker
345 Lonnie Busch
346 Paul Yalowitz
347 James McMullan
348 Stephan Geissbuhler
349 Milton Glaser

DESIGNER / GESTALTER / MAQUETTISTE:

344, 345 David Bartels
346 Bill Kobasz/Susan Spivack
347 James McMullan
348 Stephan Geissbuhler
349 Milton Glaser

ART DIRECTOR / DIRECTEUR ARTISTIQUE:

344, 345 David Bartels
346 Richard Wilde
347 Anthony Hitchcock
348 Stephan Geissbuhler
349 Milton Glaser

AGENCY / AGENTUR / AGENCE – STUDIO:

344, 345 Bartels & Company
346 School of Visual Arts Press, Ltd.
347 Visible Studio, Inc.
348 Stephan Geissbuhler Design
349 Milton Glaser, Inc.

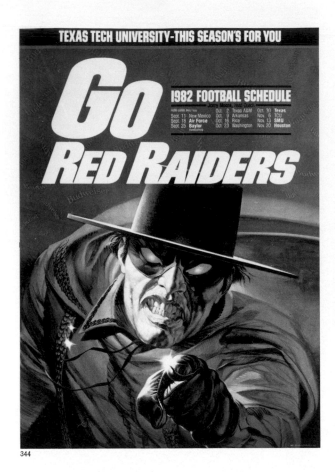

344

345

344, 345 From a series of posters announcing the playing programme of various university American-Football teams, showing the teams' mascots here. Both posters mainly in blue and red, trademark of the sponsor's beer in red. (USA)
346 For an exhibition staged by a New York art school, in which students were given the task of treating life and death, each student being allowed two pictures. Soft colours. (USA)
347 Poster for a horse show. (USA)
348 Small-format poster of the Philadelphia College of Art. (USA)
349 Poster announcing an event devoted to the Snow Leopard, organized by the New York Zoological Society. (USA)

344, 345 Plakate für die Bekanntgabe des Spiel-Terminplans von Football-Universitätsmannschaften, hier jeweils mit den Maskottchen der Teams. Beide Plakate vorwiegend in Blau und Rot, mit Biermarke des Sponsors in Rot, übrige Schrift weiss. (USA)
346 Für die Ausstellung einer Kunstschule unter dem Titel «Eine Sache von Tod und Leben». Aufgabe der Studenten war, dieses Thema in zwei Bildern zu behandeln. Sanfte Farbtöne. (USA)
347 Plakat für eine Pferde-Schau. (USA)
348 Kleinplakat des Philadelphia College of Art für einen Sommer-Kunstkurs. (USA)
349 Für eine dem Schneeleoparden gewidmete Veranstaltung der New Yorker Zoologischen Gesellschaft. (USA)

344, 345 Exemples d'une série d'affiches-calendriers de football pour des équipes universitaires, illustrées des mascottes respectives. Les deux affiches surtout en bleu et en rouge, avec la marque de bière du sponsor en rouge, le texte en blanc. (USA)
346 Pour une exposition d'école d'art intitulée «Une affaire de vie ou de mort». Les étudiants devaient interpréter ce sujet dans deux tableaux. Divers verts, gris, bruns et violets adoucis. (USA)
347 Pour un concours hippique. (USA)
348 Affichette du Philadelphia College of Art pour un cours artistique d'été. (USA)
349 Pour une manifestation de la Société de zoologie de New York axée sur la panthère des neiges. (USA)

347

A matter of
LIFE & DEATH

Life and death touch everything. Places, ideas, emotions, events, favorite sneakers and even Coke® cans may all be said to have a life and death. Students in the Media Arts Department at the School of Visual Arts were asked to express this concept in any example of life and death in two separate images. You are cordially invited to see "A Matter of Life and Death," an exhibition of works of personal perspective on this subject. March 26 through May 20, 1983, Master Eagle Gallery, 40 W. 25 Street, 6th floor, 9:00 a.m.-4:30 p.m., Monday to Friday.

346

Philadelphia College of Art

Art Education
Craft
Ceramics Woodworking Jewelry
Environmental Design
Fabric Design
Graphic Design
Illustration
Industrial Design
Painting
Photography and Film
Printmaking
Sculpture

348

The New York Zoological Society

The Night of the Snow Leopard   June 8, 1983

I know this mountain because I am this mountain, I can feel it breathing at this moment, as its grass tops stray against the snows. If the snow leopard should leap from the rock above and manifest itself before me —S-A-A-O!—then in that moment of pure fright, out of my wits, I might truly perceive it, and be free.
Peter Matthiessen

349

1982 RACING CIRCUIT
NATIONAL OFFSHORE POWERBOAT
NEW ORLEANS   MIAMI   CAPE CORAL   DETROIT   POINT PLEASANT   SAUGATUCK   SAINT AUGUSTINE   FREEPORT, BAHAMAS   IMPERIAL WORLD CUP CHAMPIONSHIP

350

Cultural Events
Veranstaltungen
Evénements culturels

350 Poster announcing various offshore power-boat races in the United States. (USA)
351 For the performance of a play entitled "Petersburg". (USR)
352 Example from a series of posters for the Frankfurt theatre. (GER)
353 "Work in Progress." Poster for an exhibition of modern art held in Bologna. (ITA)
354 Programme announcement for concerts at Zurich's Theatre 11. (SWI)
355 Poster for a Monteverdi cycle at Zurich's opera-house. (SWI)
356 "Thursdays of the Marionette." For puppet shows on each Thursday of the month, organized by the city of Brest's culture department. (FRA)

350 Plakat für die Bekanntgabe von verschiedenen Motorbootrennen in den USA. (USA)
351 Für die Aufführung eines Theaterstücks mit dem Titel «Petersburg». (USR)
352 Beispiel aus einer Serie von Plakaten für das Schauspiel Frankfurt. (GER)
353 «Laufende Arbeiten.» Plakat für eine Ausstellung moderner Kunst in Bologna. (ITA)
354 Programmankündigung für Konzerte im Zürcher Theater 11. (SWI)
355 Plakat für den Monteverdi-Zyklus am Zürcher Opernhaus. (SWI)
356 Für Marionetten-Spiele, die vom Kulturamt der Stadt Brest organisiert wurden, und einen Monat lang jeweils donnerstags stattfanden. (FRA)

350 Affiche annonçant diverses courses de canots automobiles aux Etats-Unis. (USA)
351 Pour la représentation d'une pièce de théâtre intitulée «Petersbourg». (USR)
352 Exemple d'une série d'affiches pour la Comédie de Francfort. (GER)
353 «Travaux en cours.» Affiche pour une exposition d'art moderne à Bologne. (ITA)
354 Affiche-programme de concerts organisés au Théâtre 11 de Zurich. (SWI)
355 Affiche pour un cycle Monteverdi à l'Opéra de Zurich. (SWI)
356 Pour des spectacles de marionnettes organisés par la maison de la Culture de la ville de Brest un mois durant, tous les jeudis. (FRA)

352

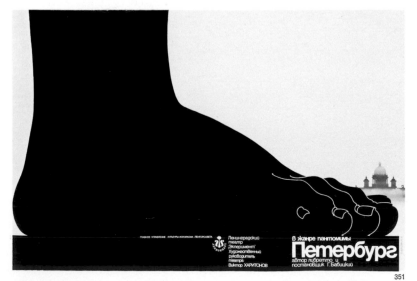

351

353

354

355

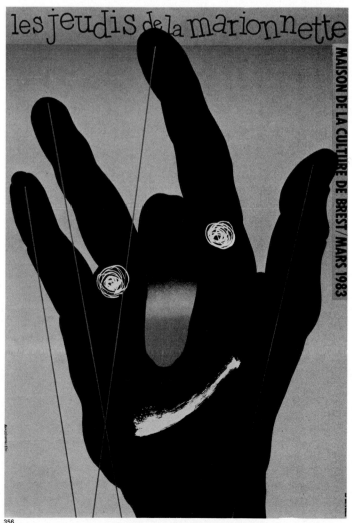

356

357

358

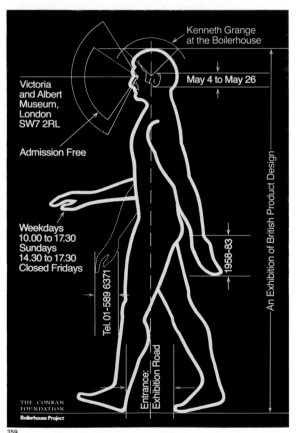

359

360

Cultural Events
Veranstaltungen
Evénements culturels

357 Poster for a puppet-show for children: "The Castle of Pétugnac." (FRA)
358 Announcement of a festival of the Café-Theatre in Paris. Yellow, red, black, white. (FRA)
359 Poster for an exhibition of work by the industrial designer Kenneth Grange. White and red on a dark blue ground. (GBR)
360 Invitation to a special dinner on the occasion of the 21st prize-giving ceremony of the Design & Art Direction-Jury, London. Blue figure on a yellow ground. (GBR)
361, 362 Complete poster and illustration for an exhibition devoted to the theme of Kiss. Fifty-five contemporary artists took part. (FRA)

357 Plakat für ein Marionettenspiel für Kinder. «Das Schloss von Pétugnac.» (FRA)
358 Ankündigung eines Festivals des Café-Theaters. Gelb, rot, schwarz, weiss. (FRA)
359 Für eine Ausstellung des Industrie-Designers Kenneth Grange. Weiss und rot auf dunkelblauem Grund. (GBR)
360 Einladung zu einem Festessen anlässlich der 21. Preisverleihung der Design & Art Direction-Jury in London. Blaue Figur auf Gelb. (GBR)
361, 362 Vollständiges Plakat und Illustration für eine Ausstellung zum Thema Kuss. Teilnehmer sind 55 zeitgenössische Künstler. (FRA)

357 Affiche pour un spectacle de marionnettes pour les petits. (FRA)
358 Annonce d'un festival du café-théâtre. Jaune, rouge, noir, blanc. (FRA)
359 Pour une exposition de l'œuvre de l'esthéticien industriel Kenneth Grange. Blanc, rouge sur fond bleu foncé. (GBR)
360 Invitation à un dîner de gala à l'occasion de la 21e cérémonie de remise des prix par le jury de Design & Art Direction à Londres. Personnage bleu sur fond jaune. (GBR)
361, 362 Affiche complète et illustration pour une exposition sur le thème du Baiser, avec la participation de 55 artistes contemporains. (FRA)

361

ARTIST / KÜNSTLER / ARTISTE:

357, 358 Alain Le Quernec
359 David Hillman
361, 362 Roman Cieslewicz

DESIGNER / GESTALTER / MAQUETTISTE:

357, 358 Alain Le Quernec
359 David Hillman
360 Alan Fletcher/Lisa de Francis
361, 362 Roman Cieslewicz

ART DIRECTOR / DIRECTEUR ARTISTIQUE:

357, 358 Alain Le Quernec
359 David Hillman
360 Alan Fletcher
361, 362 Claudine Martin

AGENCY / AGENTUR / AGENCE – STUDIO:

359, 360 Pentagram

140

363 Poster announcing a lecture by a Polish artist at the University of Maryland. (USA)
364 Poster for a university's fancy-dress ball. (USA)
365 Poster used as an invitation to a Halloween party. (USA)
366 Poster for the 1981 Lille Festival, dedicated to "Portraits of Italy". Towel in Italy's national colours. (FRA)
367 For a series of events entitled "German Culture in Exile" held in Gütersloh on the occasion of the 50th anniversary of the burning of the books by the Nazis. (GER)
368 For aeronautic events held in Mannheim, referring to the first ascent in a balloon from the Mannheim castle in 1784. (GER)
369 For a second-hand market at Verres in the Aosta Valley. (ITA)
370 Poster for the traditional horse-race meeting in Mannheim. (GER)

363 Plakat zur Ankündigung des Vortrags eines polnischen Künstlers an der Universität von Maryland. (USA)
364 Für einen Maskenball an der Pennsylvania State University. (USA)
365 Plakat als Einladung an eine Party am Abend vor Allerheiligen. (USA)
366 Für das Festival von Lille 1981, das «Porträts von Italien» gewidmet war. Tuch in den italienischen Farben. (FRA)
367 Für eine Veranstaltungsreihe «Deutsche Kultur im Exil» in Gütersloh, aus Anlass des 50. Jahrestages der Bücherverbrennung. (GER)
368 Für die Luftschiffertage in Mannheim, mit Bezug auf den ersten Ballonaufstieg im Ehrenhof des Mannheimer Schlosses am 12.2.1784. (GER)
369 Für einen Occasionsmarkt in der Gemeinde Verres im Aosta-Tal. (ITA)
370 Plakat für die Mannheimer Galopprenntage, mit dem historischen Stadtbild als Anspielung auf die lange Tradition dieses Sports in Mannheim. (GER)

ARTIST / KÜNSTLER / ARTISTE:

363 James Thorpe
364 Lanny Sommese
365 Frank Baseman
366 Jacques Leclercq
367 Thomas Steinkämper
368, 370 Anita Büscher
369 Franco Balan

DESIGNER / GESTALTER / MAQUETTISTE:

363 James Thorpe
364 Lanny Sommese
365 Frank Baseman
367 Thomas Steinkämper
369 Franco Balan

ART DIRECTOR / DIRECTEUR ARTISTIQUE:

363 James Thorpe
364 Lanny Sommese
365 Frank Baseman
366 Jacques Leclercq
369 Franco Balan

AGENCY / AGENTUR / AGENCE – STUDIO:

363 The Design Service Project
364 Lanny Sommese Design
365 Frank Baseman Graphic Design
369 Franco Balan

363

364

365

366

Cultural Events
Veranstaltungen
Evénements culturels

363 Affiche annonçant une conférence de l'artiste polonais Jan Sawka à l'Université du Maryland. (USA)

364 Pour un bal masqué à la Pennsylvania State University. (USA)

365 Affiche invitant à une fête la veille de la Toussaint. (USA)

366 Pour le Festival de Lille 1981, qui était consacré à des «Portraits de l'Italie». Linge aux couleurs italiennes. (FRA)

367 Pour une série de manifestations à l'occasion du 50e anniversaire de l'autodafé de livres par les nazis, organisées à Gütersloh. (GER)

368 Pour les Journées de l'aérostat à Mannheim; référence au 1er envol de ballon dans la cour d'honneur du château de Mannheim en 1784. (GER)

369 Pour un marché de la brocante à Verres, au val d'Aoste. (ITA)

370 Affiche pour les Journées de course de plat de Mannheim; la silhouette de la vieille ville évoque la longue tradition locale de ce sport. (GER)

368

367

369

370

371

372

375

376

371 Poster for the 8th stage-décor exhibition in Riga. Girls in lilac skirts, yellow, red and blue stockings, red shoes. (USR)
372 Announcement of an international jazz festival in Pori. (FIN)
373 For the announcement of J. Cvik's poster exhibition in Cheb. (USR)
374 "Time of the Land Surveyors." Full-colour poster for a play commissioned by the State Academic Drama Theatre in Riga. (USR)
375 "Steaming Cabaret." Poster in dark brown on light brown, lilac-light-blue landscape in the middle of the lowest part. (POL)
376 For a performance of *Thomas More* at the municipal theatre in Hildesheim. Full-colour shot, title in magenta, lettering in white. (GER)
377 Poster in lilac, magenta and blue announcing the showing of a Polish film dealing with the critical analysis of the system for university admission in which the more intellectually oriented students find themselves at a disadvantage. (POL)
378 Poster announcing a Sergei Belyatsky concert. (USR)

373

374

ARTIST / KÜNSTLER / ARTISTE:

371 Juris Dimiters
372 Kyösti Varis
373 Jefim Cvik
374 Gunar Zemgal
375 Antoni Chodorowski
376 Fritz Dommel
377 Leszek Drzewiński/Grazyna Drzewińska
378 Alexander Kondurow

DESIGNER / GESTALTER / MAQUETTISTE:

371 Juris Dimiters
372 Kyösti Varis
373 Jefim Cvik
374 Gunar Zemgal
375 Antoni Chodorowski
376 Fritz Dommel
377 Leszek Drzewiński/Grazyna Drzewińska
378 Alexander Kondurow

377

378

371 Plakat für die 8. Bühnenbildausstellung in Riga. Mädchen in lila Röckchen, Strümpfe gelb, rot, blau, Schuhe rot. (USR)
372 Zur Ankündigung des Internationalen Jazz-Festivals in Pori. (FIN)
373 Plakatausstellung von J. Cvik im tschechischen Museum Cheb. (USR)
374 «Zeit der Landbauräte.» Mehrfarbiges Plakat für eine Aufführung des Staatlichen Akademischen Drama-Theaters in Riga. (USR)
375 «Dampfendes Kabarett.» Plakat in Dunkelbraun auf Hellbraun, mit Ausnahme der in Lila-Hellblau gehaltenen Landschaft unten in der Mitte. (POL)
376 Für eine Aufführung von Thomas More im Stadttheater Hildesheim. Farbaufnahme, Titel des Stücks magenta, übrige Schrift weiss. (GER)
377 In Lila, Magenta und Blau gehaltenes Plakat für die Ankündigung des polnischen Films «Punkte für Herkunft», in dem es um die kritische Auseinandersetzung mit dem Hochschulaufnahme-Verfahren geht. Die eher intellektuell orientierten Studenten werden bei diesem System benachteiligt. (POL)
378 Plakat für die Ankündigung eines Konzertes von Sergei Belyatsky. (USR)

371 Pour la 8e Exposition du Décor de théâtre à Riga. Filles aux jupettes lilas, bas jaune, rouge, bleu, chaussures rouges. (USR)
372 Annonce du Festival international de jazz de Pori. (FIN)
373 Exposition des affiches de J. Cvik au Musée tchèque de Cheb. (USR)
374 «Le Temps des inspecteurs agricoles.» Affiche polychrome pour une représentation du Théâtre universitaire de Riga. (USR)
375 «Cabaret fumant.» Affiche en brun foncé sur brun clair, à l'exception du paysage en bas au centre, qui apparaît en lilas et bleu clair. (POL)
376 Pour une représentation de Thomas More au Théâtre municipal de Hildesheim. Photo couleur, titre magenta, reste du texte blanc. (GER)
377 Affiche aux tons lilas, magenta et bleu pour la projection du film polonais «Des Points d'admission en fonction de l'origine», où l'on critique la procédure d'admission à l'université, qui désavantage les intellectuels parmi les étudiants. (POL)
378 Affiche annonçant un concert de Sergei Belyatsky. (USR)

145

379

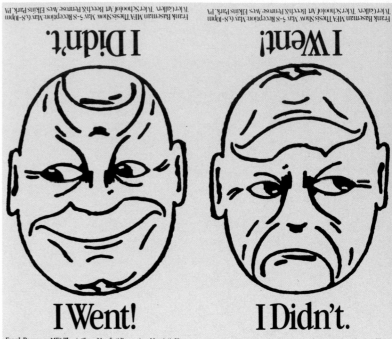

380

ARTIST / KÜNSTLER / ARTISTE:

379 James McMullan
380 Frank Baseman
381, 382, 384 Michael Mathias Prechtl
383 Bob Coonts

DESIGNER / GESTALTER / MAQUETTISTE:

379 James McMullan
380 Frank Baseman
381, 382, 384 Michael Mathias Prechtl
383 Bob Coonts

ART DIRECTOR / DIRECTEUR ARTISTIQUE:

379 James McMullan
380 Frank Baseman
383 Bob Coonts

381

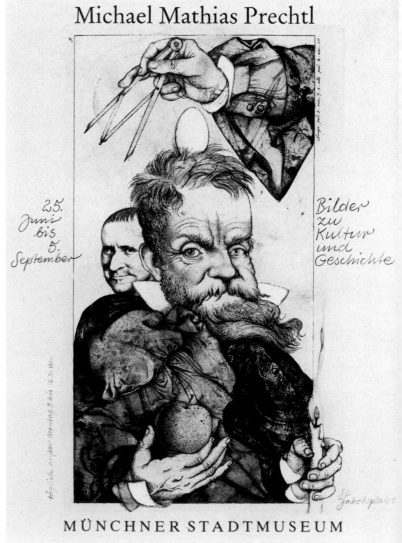

382

383

379 Full-colour poster for an exhibition of "Revealing Illustrations" by James McMullan. (USA)
380 Poster that can be viewed from both ends, announcing an exhibition. (USA)
381 The adaption of a phrase from Dürer, "Martin Luther, inwardly full of figures", is the title of this work by M. M. Prechtl announcing a Luther symposium in Nuremberg. Mixed technique on very old paper. (GER)
382, 384 For exhibitions of works by M. M. Prechtl in Munich's municipal museum. Fig. 382: The title of this graphic plate is "Bertolt Brecht and I", showing Galileo Galilei in the foreground; Fig. 384: "The River Isar, a History", with Lola Montez and Ludwig I. In Munich this portrayal incurred the wrath of the "loyalists to the throne". Mixed technique on early 18th century paper. (GER)
383 Full-colour poster announcing a tennis tournament. (USA)

379 Mehrfarbiges Plakat für eine Ausstellung mit Werken von James McMullan. (USA)
380 Von zwei Seiten zu betrachtendes Plakat für die Ankündigung einer Ausstellung. (USA)
381 «Martin Luther, inwendig voller Figur» (Abwandlung eines Dürerwortes) ist der Titel dieser Arbeit von M. M. Prechtl, die für die Ankündigung eines Luther-Symposiums in Nürnberg verwendet wurde. Mischtechnik, auf sehr altem Papier. (GER)
382, 384 Für Ausstellungen mit Arbeiten von Michael Mathias Prechtl im Münchner Stadtmuseum. Abb. 382: Der Titel des graphischen Blattes ist «Bertolt Brecht and I» (im Vordergrund Galileo Galilei); Abb. 384: «Die Isar, ein Lebenslauf», mit Lola Montez und Ludwig I. (Diese Darstellung erregte in München den Unwillen der «Königstreuen».) Mischtechnik auf Papier aus dem Anfang des 18. Jahrhunderts (s. auch Abb. 381). (GER)
383 Mehrfarbiges Plakat für die Ankündigung eines Tennisturniers. (USA)

379 Affiche polychrome pour une exposition de l'œuvre de James McMullan. (USA)
380 Affiche tête-bêche annonçant une exposition. (USA)
381 «Martin Luther, intérieurement plein de personnages» – c'est le titre, imité de Dürer, que M. M. Prechtl a choisi pour cette affiche annonçant un symposium sur Luther à Nuremberg. Technique mixte, sur du très vieux papier. (GER)
382, 384 Pour des expositions de l'œuvre de Michael Mathias Prechtl au Musée municipal de Munich. Fig. 382: cette composition s'intitule «Bertolt Brecht and I» (au premier plan: Galilée); fig. 384: «L'Isar, un curriculum vitae», avec Lola Montez et Louis Ier de Bavière, ce qui n'a pas manqué d'indigner les royalistes bavarois. Papier du XVIIIe siècle. (GER)
383 Affiche polychrome annonçant un tournois de tennis. (USA)

AGENCY / AGENTUR / AGENCE – STUDIO:

379 Visible Studio, Inc.
380 Frank Baseman Graphic Design
383 Bob Coonts Graphic Design

384

385

386

387

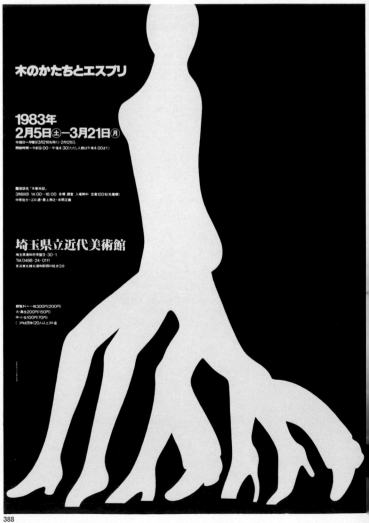

388

musée de l'affiche et de la publicité 18 rue de paradis 75010 paris
11 mai — 12 sept 82

394

De Beyerd
centrum voor beeldende kunst
Boschstraat 22, Breda, Holland
30.4 t.m. 5.6 1983
dinsdag t.m. zaterdag 10-17 uur
zondag 13-17 uur, maandag gesloten

ontwerp:
Total Design

395

California College of Arts + Crafts

396

NEW PHONIC ART

397

ARTIST / KÜNSTLER / ARTISTE:

392 Dana Andreyev
393 Stacey Lewis/Robert Martin/
Michael Furman/
Christopher Ransom
394 Bernard Vidal
396 Charly Franklin
397 Kaviiik

DESIGNER / GESTALTER / MAQUETTISTE:

390 Shaun Dew
391 Ernst Roch
393 Joel Katz
395 Frans Lieshout
396 Michael Manwaring
397 Kaviiik

ART DIRECTOR:

390 Lynn Trickett/Brian Webb
391 Ernst Roch
393 Joel Katz
396 Michael Manwaring
397 Kaviiik

AGENCY / AGENTUR / AGENCE:

390 Trickett & Webb Ltd.
391 Roch Design
393 Katz Wheeler Design
395 Total Design
396 The Office of Michael Manwaring

390 Plakat für eine Ausstellung von *Riba*-Stühlen in London. (GBR)
391 Ankündigung des Nationalen Buch-Festivals in Kanada. (CAN)
392 Plakat für einen polnischen Film («Wünsch mir schlechtes Wetter»). (POL)
393 An Künstler gerichtete Einladung zu einem Wettbewerb der *AIGA*. Himmel (rötlich), Karte und Tuschschreiber photographiert, Notizblatt und Rahmen in Spraytechnik: lila, türkis und rosa auf weissem Grund. (USA)
394 Ankündigung einer Ausstellung von Plakaten («Bilder aus den Jahren der Revolte 1965–1975») in einem Pariser Museum. (FRA)
395 Plakat für eine Ausstellung mit Entwürfen der Gruppe *Total Design*. «Ontwerp» in Gelb, übriger Text schwarz, weiss und grau. (NLD)
396 Kleinformatiges Plakat einer Kunstakademie (California College of Arts + Crafts). Bild in Schwarzweiss, Umrandung in Lila. (USA)
397 Siebdruckplakat zur Ankündigung eines zeitgenössischen Musikkonzerts. Schwarz, weiss, silber, orange, lila auf gelbem Grund. (FRA)

390 Affiche pour une exposition des sièges *Riba* à Londres. (GBR)
391 Annonce du Festival national du Livre au Canada. (CAN)
392 Pour un film polonais («Souhaite-moi du mauvais temps»). (POL)
393 Appel d'envois de l'*AIGA* de Philadelphie. Ciel (rougeâtre), carte et porte-plume à encre de Chine en photo, feuille de calepin et cadre exécutés à l'aérographe: lilas, turquoise, rose sur fond blanc. (USA)
394 Pour une exposition d'affiches organisée par un musé spécialisé. (FRA)
395 Affiche pour une exposition des projets du groupe *Total Design*. «Ontwerp» en jaune, les autres textes noir, blanc, gris. (NLD)
396 Affichette d'une académie des beaux-arts (California College of Arts + Crafts). Composition noir et blanc dans encadrement lilas. (USA)
397 Affiche sérigraphique annonçant un concert de musique contemporaine. Les couleurs employées sont le noir, le blanc, l'argent, l'orange et le lilas sur fond jaune. (FRA)

398

399

400

401

402

403

404

ARTIST / KÜNSTLER / ARTISTE:

398 Rolf Felix Müller
399 Magdalena Abakanowicz
400 Stasys Eidrigevičius
401 Rambow, Lienemeyer, van de Sand
402 Alain Le Quernec
403 Martti Mykkänen
404 René Gruau

DESIGNER / GESTALTER / MAQUETTISTE:

398 Rolf Felix Müller
401 Rambow, Lienemeyer, van de Sand
402 Alain Le Quernec
403 Martti Mykkänen
404 Bartsch & Chariau

ART DIRECTOR / DIRECTEUR ARTISTIQUE:

401 Rambow, Lienemeyer, van de Sand
402 Alain Le Quernec

AGENCY / AGENTUR / AGENCE – STUDIO:

401 Rambow, Lienemeyer, van de Sand

398 Small-format poster for an exhibition of posters and book illustrations by Rolf Felix Müller, held in Bad Köstritz. Green iris, brown background. (GDR)
399 For an exhibition of works by Abakanowicz, held in Lausanne. (SWI)
400 Poster for an exhibition of a Polish artist, in Toruń. (POL)
401 For an exhibition about exiled writers during the Nazi era. (GER)
402 For an exhibition about Anne de Bretagne, held in a Nantes castle. (FRA)
403 For the 5th poster biennale in Lahti. Winner of a competition. (FIN)
404 For an exhibition in Munich about René Gruau, fashion illustrator. (GER)

398 Kleinplakat für eine Ausstellung der Plakate und Buchillustrationen von Rolf Felix Müller in Bad Köstritz. Grüne Iris, brauner Hintergrund. (GDR)
399 Für eine Ausstellung mit Werken von Abakanowicz in Lausanne. (SWI)
400 Plakat für die Ausstellung eines polnischen Künstlers in Toruń. (POL)
401 Für eine Ausstellung über Schriftsteller im Exil in der Nazizeit. (GER)
402 Für eine Ausstellung über Anne de Bretagne in einem Schloss in Nantes. (FRA)
403 Für die 5. Plakatbiennale in Lahti. Gewinner eines Wettbewerbs. (FIN)
404 Für eine Ausstellung über den Mode-Illustrator René Gruau in München. (GER)

398 Affichette pour une exposition des affiches et illustrations de livres de Rolf Felix Müller à Bad Köstritz. Iris vert, fond brun. (GDR)
399 Pour une exposition de l'œuvre d'Abakanowicz à Lausanne. (SWI)
400 Affiche pour l'exposition de l'œuvre d'un artiste polonais à Toruń. (POL)
401 Pour une exposition des écrivains allemands en exil sous le nazisme. (GER)
402 Pour une exposition consacrée à Anne de Bretagne dans un château de Nantes. (FRA)
403 Pour la 5e Biennale de l'Affiche de Lahti. Affiche primée. (FIN)
404 Pour une exposition à Munich consacrée à l'illustrateur de mode René Gruau. (GER)

ARTIST / KÜNSTLER / ARTISTE:

405 Niklaus Troxler
406 Lanny Sommese
407 Gary Viskupic
408 Mary Lynn Blasutta
409 Saul Bass
410 Felix & Doris Gyssler
411 Per Arnoldi

DESIGNER / GESTALTER:

405 Niklaus Troxler
406 Lanny Sommese
407 Gary Viskupic
408 Eric Rickabaugh
409 Saul Bass
410 Felix & Doris Gyssler
411 Per Arnoldi

ART DIRECTOR:

405 Niklaus Troxler
406 Lanny Sommese
407 Gary Viskupic
408 Eric Rickabaugh
410 Felix & Doris Gyssler

AGENCY / AGENTUR / AGENCE:

405 Grafik-Studio
    Niklaus Troxler
406 Lanny Sommese Design
407 Viskupic Design
408 Salvato & Coe
409 Saul Bass/Herb Yager
    & Associates

405

406

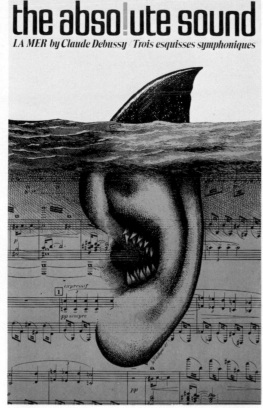

407

408

409

410

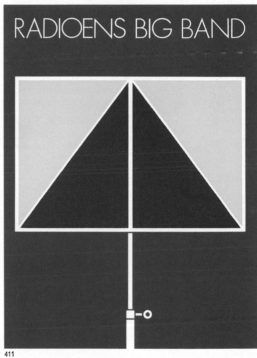

411

405 Small-format poster displaying the programme for the Jazz Festival in Willisau, Switzerland. (SWI)
406 Announcement of performances by the Penn State University Choir. Blue and pink with yellow. (USA)
407 Claude Debussy's "The Sea" is the subject of this poster issued by the magazine *The Absolute Sound*. (USA)
408 Poster announcing outdoor concerts. Yellow flower on a light blue background. (USA)
409 Poster for a music centre in Los Angeles uniting four performing arts organizations. (USA)
410 Large-format poster with a portrait of the famous composer, for the 1983 Haydn Festival in Basle. Violet-grey, grey-brown, red, black and white. (SWI)
411 Poster for Danish Radio's big band. (DEN)

405 Kleinformatiges Plakat mit Programmvorschau für das Jazz-Festival im schweizerischen Willisau. (SWI)
406 Für die Ankündigung eines Konzert- und Kammerchors der Penn State Universität. Blau und Rosa mit Gelb. (USA)
407 Claude Debussys Orchestersuite «Das Meer» ist Gegenstand dieses Plakates, das von der Zeitschrift *The Absolute Sound* herausgegeben wurde. (USA)
408 Für die Bekanntgabe von Konzertveranstaltungen im Freien. Gelbe Blume auf hellblauem Hintergrund. (USA)
409 Plakat für ein Musik-Zentrum in Los Angeles, das vier künstlerische Organisationen vereint. (USA)
410 Grossformatiges Plakat für das Haydn-Fest in Basel. Violettgrau, Graubraun, Rot, Schwarz und Weiss. (SWI)
411 Für die Big Band des dänischen Radios. (DEN)

405 Affichette-programme du festival de jazz organisé à Willisau en Suisse. (SWI)
406 Pour la présentation d'un chœur d'orchestre et ensemble vocal de la Penn State University. Bleu, rose, jaune. (USA)
407 «La Mer», trois esquisses symphoniques du compositeur français Claude Debussy, fournit le thème de cette affiche publiée par le magazine *The Absolute Sound*. (USA)
408 Pour l'annonce de concerts en plein air. Fleur jaune sur fond bleu clair. (USA)
409 Affiche pour un centre de musique de Los Angeles auquel participent quatre sociétés artistiques. (USA)
410 Affiche au grand format pour le festival Haydn organisé à Bâle. Gris violet, brun gris, rouge, noir et blanc. (SWI)
411 Pour le Grand Orchestre de la Radiodiffusion danoise. (DEN)

412

BOUQUET

413

412, 413 Illustration and complete poster for a small party on the occasion of the introduction of "Bouquet", a book of fables by Myrna Davis with pictures by Paul Davis. (USA)
414 Poster for an exhibition of Grapus, a collective organization of poster designers. (FRA)
415 Poster for an exhibition of works by the Swiss artist Celestino Piatti. (SWI)
416 For a retrospective of Tom Eckersley's graphic work. (GBR)
417 Announcement of a festival of European puppet-theatres, here for the tour of the Sicilian puppet-show. Orange and green landscape, yellowish ground. (ITA)
418 Poster advertising a patents exhibition in Jerusalem. Bright yellow and green on a red ground. (ISR)

412, 413 Illustration und vollständiges Plakat für ein kleines Fest anlässlich der Vorstellung des Fabelbuches «Bouquet» von Myrna Davis, mit Bildern von Paul Davis. (USA)
414 Plakat für eine Ausstellung von Grapus, einem Kollektiv von Plakatgestaltern. (FRA)
415 Plakat für eine Ausstellung mit Werken des Schweizer Künstlers Celestino Piatti. (SWI)
416 Für eine Retrospektive des britischen Künstlers Tom Eckersley. (GBR)
417 Ankündigung eines Festivals europäischer Marionetten, hier für die Tournee sizilianischer Puppenspieler. Orange und grüne Landschaft, gelblicher Grund. (ITA)
418 Plakat für eine Patentausstellung in Jerusalem. Leuchtendes Gelb und Grün auf rotem Grund. (ISR)

412, 413 Illustration et affiche complète pour une fête organisée lors de la parution du recueil de fables «Bouquet» de Myrna Davis illustré par Paul Davis. (USA)
414 Affiche pour une exposition de Grapus, un collectif d'affichistes. (FRA)
415 Affiche pour une exposition de l'œuvre de l'artiste suisse Celestino Piatti. (SWI)
416 Pour une rétrospective de l'œuvre de l'artiste britannique Tom Eckersley. (GBR)
417 Annonce d'un festival de la marionnette européenne, ici pour une tournée de marionnettistes siciliens. Paysage vert et orange, fond jaune. (ITA)
418 Affiche pour une exposition de brevets à Jérusalem. Jaune et vert lumineux sur fond rouge. (ISR)

414

ARTIST / KÜNSTLER / ARTISTE:

412, 413 Paul Davis
414 Grapus/Pierre Bernard
415 Celestino Piatti
416 Tom Eckersley
417 Andrea Rauch
418 Dan Reisinger

DESIGNER / GESTALTER / MAQUETTISTE:

412, 413 Paul Davis
414 Grapus
415 Celestino Piatti
416 Tom Eckersley
417 Andrea Rauch
418 Dan Reisinger

ART DIRECTOR / DIRECTEUR ARTISTIQUE:

417 Andrea Rauch
418 Dan Reisinger

AGENCY / AGENTUR / AGENCE – STUDIO:

414 Grapus
417 Graphiti
418 Dan Reisinger

415

416

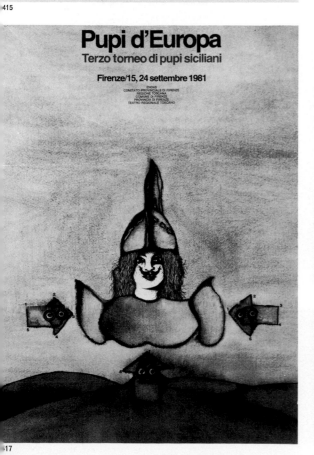

417

418

Louis Armstrong 1900-1971

419

Charles Mingus

420

421

422

SURBOUM Sixties

21H SAM. 30 OCTOBRE 82. OUVERTURE MPT KERFEUNTEUN. QUIMPER

423

JAZZ E BREIZ

TEL 96 95.62.35. PLOEZAL 22 260

LA ROCHE JAGU. 18.19.20.21 AOUT 1983

425

ARTIST / KÜNSTLER / ARTISTE:

419, 420 Waldemar Swierzy
421 Gancho St. Ganev
422 Volker Hartmann
423, 425 Alain Le Quernec

DESIGNER / GESTALTER:

419, 420 Waldemar Swierzy
421 Gancho St. Ganev
422 Günther Kieser
423, 425 Alain Le Quernec
424 Douglas Scott

ART DIRECTOR:

419, 420 Waldemar Swierzy
422 Günther Kieser
423, 425 Alain Le Quernec
424 Douglas Scott

AGENCY / AGENTUR / AGENCE:

422 Günther Kieser
424 WGBH Design

424

Cultural Events
Veranstaltungen
Evénements culturels

419, 420 From a series of posters issued in Poland and dedicated to famous jazz musicians. Fig. 419: mainly in red shades, Fig. 420: in blue shades. (POL)
421 Poster for a Bulgarian production of Molière's *George Dandin*. (BUL)
422 From a series of posters for a folk- and blues-festival. (GER)
423 The 60's are the theme of the dancing announced here. (FRA)
424 For the announcement of radio programmes dedicated to jazz. Dark blue on beige. (USA)
425 "Jazz in Bretagne." Poster for a jazz festival. (FRA)

419, 420 Beispiele aus einer in Polen herausgegebenen Reihe von Plakaten, die berühmten Jazz-Musikern gewidmet sind. Abb. 419 vorwiegend in Rot, Abb. 420 in Blau. (POL)
421 Für eine bulgarische Inszenierung von Molières *George Dandin*. (BUL)
422 Aus einer Serie von Plakaten für ein Folk- und Blues-Festival. (GER)
423 Die sechziger Jahre sind Thema des hier angekündigten Balls. (FRA)
424 Für die Ankündigung von Radio-Programmen, die dem Jazz gewidmet sind. Dunkelblau auf Beige. (USA)
425 «Jazz in der Bretagne.» Plakat für ein Jazz-Festival. (FRA)

419, 420 Exemples d'affiches publiées dans une série polonaise consacrée aux grands musiciens de jazz. Fig. 419: rouge prédominant. Fig. 420: exécutée en bleu. (POL)
421 Pour une interprétation bulgare du *George Dandin* de Molière. (BUL)
422 Affiche dans une série présentant un festival de folk et blues. (GER)
423 Affiche pour un bal des jeunes axée sur les années soixante. (FRA)
424 Annonce d'une série de programmes radio consacrés au jazz. Bleu foncé sur beige. (USA)
425 «Jazz en Bretagne» (en breton). Affiche pour un festival de jazz. (FRA)

426

ARTIST / KUNSTLER / ARTISTE:

426 Günther Kieser
427 Holger Matthies
428 Tomasz Ruminski
429 Volker Hartmann
430 Roswitha & Eberhard Marhold

DESIGNER / GESTALTER / MAQUETTISTE:

426, 429 Günther Kieser
427 Holger Matthies
428 Rolf Müller
430 Roswitha & Eberhard Marhold

ART DIRECTOR / DIRECTEUR ARTISTIQUE:

426, 429 Günther Kieser
427 Holger Matthies
428 Rolf Müller

AGENCY / AGENTUR / AGENCE – STUDIO:

428 Büro Rolf Müller

426 Poster announcing various programmes to be broadcast by the Hessian radio company. (GER)
427 Full-colour collage on a light blue ground for a poster announcing various musical events. (GER)
428 Poster announcing topical discussions on the radio. Lilac-white clouds on a blue ground. (GER)
429 Announcement of concerts during the "Days of Improvised Music" in Frankfurt. Black guitar on an olive-green background. (GER)
430 Colourful poster announcing various children's programmes on the radio, here for "Dino's Children's Radio" broadcast by the Hessian radio company. (GER)

426 Plakat zur Ankündigung von diversen Rundfunksendungen. (GER)
427 Farbenfrohe Collage auf hellblauem Grund für verschiedene Musikveranstaltungen. (GER)
428 Ankündigung von aktuellen Diskussionen am Radio. Lila-weisse Wolken auf Blau. (GER)
429 Konzertankündigungen für die «Tage improvisierter Musik» in Frankfurt am Main. Schwarze Gitarre auf olivgrünem Hintergrund. (GER)
430 Buntes Plakat zur Bekanntgabe von verschiedenen Kinderveranstaltungen im Rundfunk. (GER)

426 Affiche annonçant diverses émissions de radio en période de Noël. (GER)
427 Collage multicolore sur fond bleu ciel pour une série de manifestations musicales. (GER)
428 Annonce de débats d'actualité à la radio. Nuages blanc lilas sur fond bleu. (GER)
429 Annonce de concerts pour les «Journées de musique improvisée» à Francfort-sur-le-Main. Guitare noire sur fond olive. (GER)
430 Affiche haute en couleur annonçant diverses émissions enfantines à la radio. (GER)

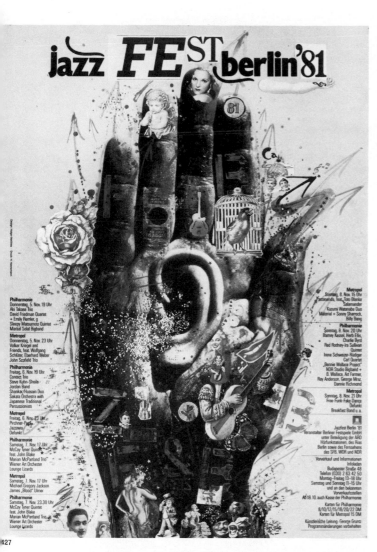

427

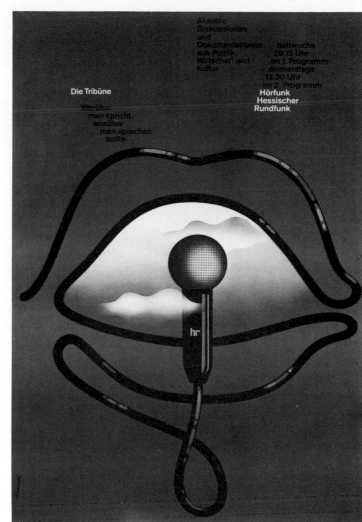

428

429

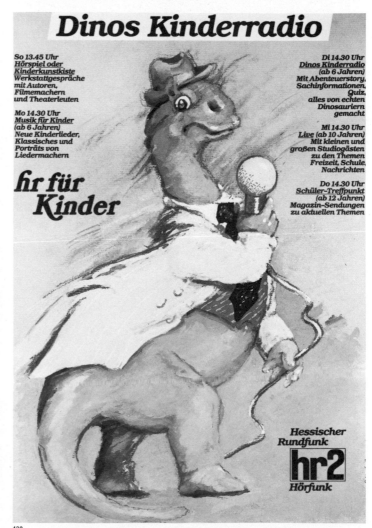

430

THE AMERICAN BOOK AWARDS

1982

PRODUCED FOR THE AMERICAN BOOK AWARDS BY HARLIN QUIST · ART COPYRIGHT © BY BRAD HOLLAND · LITHOGRAPHED ON MOHAWK POSEIDON COVER

431

431 Announcement of the 1982 book awards in America. Illustration mainly in subdued, dark shades on a violet-gre[y] ground. (USA)
432 Poster for a special international art festival for handi[-] capped artists sponsored by Moss Hospital. (USA)
433 Announcement of the opening times of a museum o[f] natural history in New York. (USA)
434 Small-format poster for the announcement of an exhi[-] bition of graphic works by Seymour Chwast at the Guten[-] berg Museum in Mainz. In full colour. (GER)
435 For an exhibition devoted to New York's Grand Centra[l] Station. Brown-yellow, orange, grey shades and lig[ht] green. (USA)

431 Ankündigung der Verleihung der amerikanische[n] Buchpreise. Illustration in verhaltenen, vorwiegend dunk[-] len Farbtönen auf violettgrauem Grund. (USA)
432 Plakat für ein internationales Kunst-Festival für behin[-] derte Künstler. (USA)
433 Bekanntgabe der Öffnungszeiten des amerikanische[n] naturhistorischen Museums, mit freiem Eintritt. (USA)
434 Kleinformatiges Plakat für die Ankündigung einer Aus[-] stellung mit graphischen Arbeiten von Seymour Chwast i[m] Mainzer Gutenberg-Museum. In Farbe. (GER)
435 Für eine Ausstellung, die dem New Yorker Grand[-] Central-Bahnhof, «einer Stadt in der Stadt», gewidmet is[t]. Braungelb-, Orange-, Grautöne und Hellgrün. (USA)

431 Annonce de la cérémonie de remise des Prix du Liv[re] américain. Illustration exécutée en tons adoucis, surtou[t] sombres, sur fond gris violacé. (USA)
432 Affiche pour un festival international réunissant le[s] œuvres d'artistes handicapés. (USA)
433 Annonce des heures d'ouverture du Muséum améri[-] cain d'histoire naturelle, dont l'entrée est gratuite. (USA)
434 Affichette annonçant une exposition de l'œuvre grav[ée] de Seymour Chwast au Musée Gutenberg de Mayence. E[n] couleurs. (GER)
435 Pour une exposition consacrée à la gare Grand Centra[l] de New York, «une ville dans la ville». Divers tons jaun[e] brun, orange et gris, ainsi que du vert clair. (USA)

432

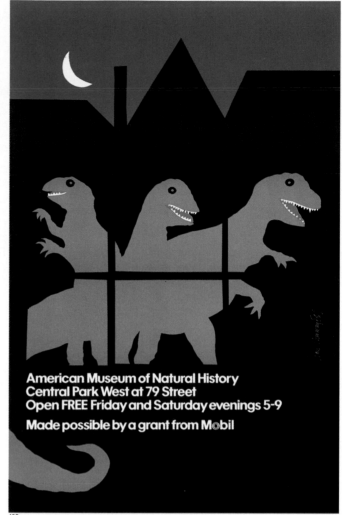

American Museum of Natural History
Central Park West at 79 Street
Open FREE Friday and Saturday evenings 5-9

Made possible by a grant from Mobil

433

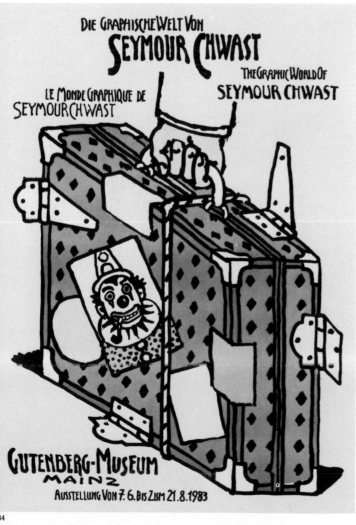

434

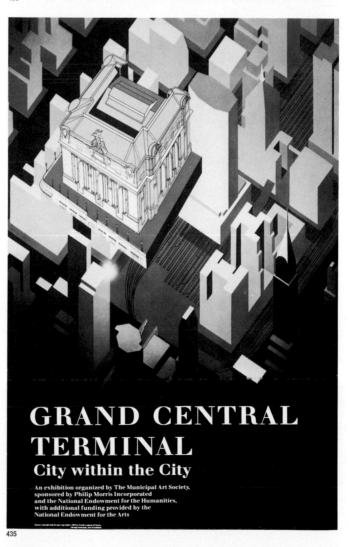

GRAND CENTRAL
TERMINAL
City within the City

An exhibition organized by The Municipal Art Society,
sponsored by Philip Morris Incorporated
and the National Endowment for the Humanities,
with additional funding provided by the
National Endowment for the Arts

435

436

437

440

44

436 Plakat für eine Kunstausstellung in London. (GBR)

437 Für eine Kunstausstellung in der Galerie Bartsch & Chariau. (GER)

438 Ankündigung von Konzerten im Park, organisiert von der *Denver Post.* Zarte Farben auf weissem Grund. (USA)

439 Einladung zu einem Ball, dessen Ziel eine bessere Verständigung zwischen Einheimischen und Ausländern ist. (GER)

440 Ankündigung eines Nô-Theaters an der Universität von Kalifornien, Los Angeles. Grau-schwarz auf gedämpftem Lila. (USA)

441 Programmankündigung für eine Sendereihe über die Nazis und Hinweis auf das Buch «Europa unterm Hakenkreuz». (GER)

442 Plakat für eine mehrtägige Konferenz mit dem Thema «Wirtschaftlichkeit versus Ästhetik». (USA)

443 Plakat für eine Ausstellung neuer Grafiken und visueller Kunst aus Europa, vom MIT und dem Goethe-Institut Boston organisiert. (USA)

436 Affiche pour une exposition d'art à Londres. (GBR)

437 Pour une exposition d'art à la Galerie Bartsch & Chariau. (GER)

438 Annonce de concerts dans un parc organisés par le journal *Denver Post.* Coloris délicats sur fonc blanc. (USA)

439 Invitation à un bal destiné à promouvoir une meilleure compréhension entre les autochtones et les immigrés. (GER)

440 Annonce d'une représentation Nô à l'Université de Californie à Los Angeles. Noir gris sur lilas mat. (USA)

441 Annonce de programme pour une série d'émissions sur le thème du nazisme, avec référence à l'ouvrage intitulé «L'Europe sous la croix gammée». (GER)

442 Affiche pour des journées de conférences sur le thème «Rendement publicitaire ou esthétique». (USA)

443 Affiche pour une exposition de travaux graphiques et de productions de l'art visuel européen récent. (USA)

438

439

442

443

ARTIST / KÜNSTLER / ARTISTE:

436 Allen Jones
437 Karl Arnold
438 Bonnie Timmons
439 Eduard Prüssen
440 Takenobu Igarashi
441 Frieder Grindler

DESIGNER / GESTALTER:

437 Galerie Bartsch & Chariau
438 Howard Klein
439 Eduard Prüssen
440 Takenobu Igarashi
441 Frieder Grindler
442 Michael Vanderbyl
443 Jacqueline S. Casey

ART DIRECTOR:

438 Howard Klein
441 Frieder Grindler
442 Michael Vanderbyl

AGENCY / AGENTUR / AGENCE:

438 The Denver Post
440 Takenobu Igarashi Design
442 Vanderbyl Design
443 MIT Design Services

3

Social Posters

Soziale Plakate

Affiches sociales

ARTIST / KÜNSTLER / ARTISTE:

444, 445 Massimo Dolcini
446 Franco Balan
447, 449 Bruno Magno
448 Massimo Dolcini/Iole Bortoli
450 Dario Neglia
451 Tullio Pericoli

DESIGNER / GESTALTER / MAQUETTISTE:

444, 445 Massimo Dolcini
446 Franco Balan
447, 449 Bruno Magno
448 Massimo Dolcini/Iole Bortoli
450 Guiseppe De Liso

ART DIRECTOR / DIRECTEUR ARTISTIQUE:

444, 445, 448 Massimo Dolcini
446 Franco Balan
447, 449 Bruno Magno
450 Giuseppe De Liso

AGENCY / AGENTUR / AGENCE – STUDIO:

444, 445, 448 Furioschema
446 Franco Balan
450 Studio De Liso

444

445

447

448

444, 445, 448 Posters of the city of Pesaro, dealing with the following subjects. Fig. 444: A discussion about the problems and prospects of reconstructing villages on hills. Hill in green, white hen, blue sky, light brown houses; Fig. 445: A call upon people to make their old paper available in exchange for plants; Fig. 448: The national society for the protection of animals offers its services, here for cats and dogs. (ITA)
446 Announcement of a regional conference of Italy's Communist Party. Yellow hammer and sickle on a red ground. (ITA)
447 Invitation to a party organized by Pisa's Communists. Both lower lines of lettering in red, other text and picture in blue on white ground. (ITA)
449 National gathering of the Communist Party of Italy, dealing with the subject of university structures. Black and white and orange. (ITA)
450 A political manifesto of Italy's Socialist Party, dealing with changes in the municipal concept. (ITA)
451 Exhibition of architectural plans for Milan's cathedral square. (ITA)

444, 445, 448 Plakate der Stadt Pesaro zu folgenden Themen: Abb. 444: Diskussion der Probleme und Aussichten des Wiederaufbaus von Hügeldörfern. Hügel in Grün, weisse Henne, blauer Himmel, hellbraune Häuser. Abb. 445: Aufforderung an die Bevölkerung, im Austausch gegen Grünpflanzen ihr Altpapier zur Verfügung zu stellen. Abb. 448: Der Nationale Tierschutzverein bietet seine Dienste an, hier speziell für Hunde und Katzen. (ITA)
446 Ankündigung eines regionalen Parteitages der Kommunistischen Partei Italiens. Gelbe Sichel und Hammer auf rotem Grund. (ITA)
447 Einladung zu einem Fest der Kommunisten in Pisa. Schrift der beiden unteren Zeilen in Rot, übriger Text und Bild in Blau auf weissem Grund. (ITA)
449 Zusammenkunft der Kommunistischen Partei Italiens zum Thema «Abteilungen und Lehrmethoden an der Universität». Schwarzweiss und orange. (ITA)
450 Ein politisches Manifest der Sozialistischen Partei Italiens über Veränderungen im Stadtbild. (ITA)
451 Ausstellung von Bauplänen für den Mailänder Domplatz. (ITA)

446

450

449

444, 445, 448 Affiches de la ville de Pesaro traitant des sujets suivants: fig. 444: discussion des problèmes et perspectives de la reconstruction des villages de collines. Colline verte, poule blanche, ciel bleu, maisons brun clair. Fig. 445: appel à l'échange de vieux papiers contre des plantes vertes. Fig. 448: la société nationale de protection des animaux offre ici ses services, notamment pour «chiens et chats». (ITA)

446 Annonce d'un congrès régional du parti communiste italien. Marteau et faucille en jaune sur fond rouge. (ITA)

447 Invitation à une fête communiste à Pise. Les deux lignes inférieures en rouge, le reste du texte et l'image en bleu sur fond blanc. (ITA)

449 Réunion du parti communiste au plan national sur le thème «Départements et méthodes d'enseignement universitaires». Noir-blanc, orange. (ITA)

450 Manifeste politique du parti socialiste italien au sujet des progrès de l'urbanisme. (ITA)

451 Exposition de plans d'urbanisme pour la place du Dôme de Milan. (ITA)

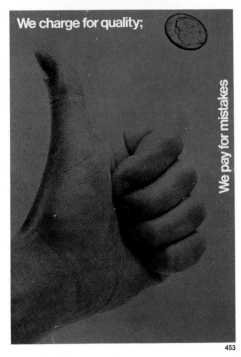

Educative Posters
Erzieherische Plakate
Affiches éducatives

DESIGNER / GESTALTER / MAQUETTISTE:

452–454 Kerry Grady
455 John Massey
456, 458 Alan Fletcher
457, 459, 460 Tom Bluhm
461 Bob Ryf

ART DIRECTOR / DIRECTEUR ARTISTIQUE:

452–454 Kerry Grady
455 John Massey
456, 458 Alan Fletcher
457, 459, 460 Tom Bluhm
461 Bob Ryf

ARTIST / KÜNSTLER / ARTISTE:

452, 453 Jerry Kalyniuk
454 Kerry Grady
455 Rufino Tamayo
456, 458 Alan Fletcher

AGENCY / AGENTUR / AGENCE – STUDIO:

452–455 Container Corporation of America
456, 458 Pentagram
457, 459, 460 IBM Boulder Graphic Design
461 IBM Design, Kingston

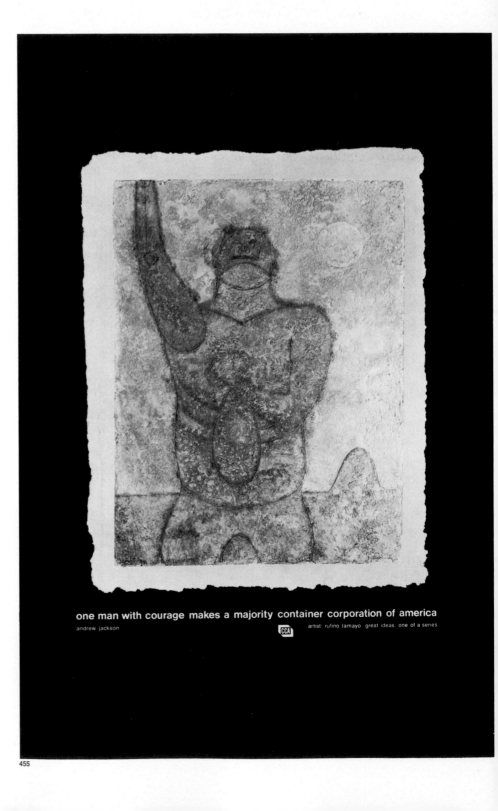

one man with courage makes a majority container corporation of america
andrew jackson
artist: rufino tamayo great ideas one of a series

452–454 From a series of silkscreen posters appealing to employees to be conscious of quality. The aphorisms were coined by the employees themselves. Fig. 452: red Q, light brown "cardboard head" on white; Fig. 453: black and white and light blue; Fig. 454: blue and green blocks, yellow circle. (USA)
455 Poster from a series devoted to great thoughts. Illustration in yellow, beige and grey shades on black. (USA)
456, 458 From a series of posters of the IBM company, for the opening of its art programme at the firm's Paris offices. (USA)
457, 459, 460 More examples of IBM posters, here small-format posters for internal display. Fig. 457: light grey on a dark red ground, with the EO signifying equal opportunity; Fig. 459: black and white with blue lettering; Fig. 460: brownish ground, white lettering, colour photographs. (USA)
461 Appeal to personnel to change defective industrial gloves before dangerous chemicals can seep through them. (USA)

452–454 Aus einer Serie von Siebdruckplakaten, die an das Qualitätsbewusstsein der Angestellten appellieren. Die Aphorismen stammen von den Angestellten selber. Abb. 452: Rotes Q, hellbrauner «Karton-Kopf» auf Weiss; Abb. 453: Schwarzweiss und hellblau; Abb. 454: Blöcke blau und grün, Kreis gelb. (USA)
455 Plakat aus einer Serie mit dem Motto «Grosse Gedanken». Illustration in Gelb-, Beige- und Grautönen auf Schwarz. (USA)
456, 458 Aus einer Serie von Plakaten der Firma IBM zur Eröffnung des Kunstprogramms des europäischen Firmensitzes in Paris. (USA)
457, 459, 460 Weitere Beispiele von IBM-Plakaten, hier innerbetriebliche Kleinplakate. Abb. 457: Helles Grau auf dunkelrotem Grund, EO = Equal Opportunity (gleiche Chancen für alle); Abb. 459: Schwarzweiss mit blauer Schrift; Abb. 460: Bräunlicher Grund, Schrift weiss, Farbphotos. (USA)
461 Aufforderung, defekte Schutzhandschuhe auszuwechseln, bevor mit gefährlichen Chemikalien hantiert wird. (USA)

452–454 Exemples d'une série d'affiches sérigraphiques incitant le personnel à se concentrer sur la qualité. Les slogans ont été contribués par le personnel. Fig. 452: Q rouge , «tête-carton» brun clair sur blanc; fig. 453: noir-blanc et bleu clair; fig. 454: blocs bleus et verts, cercle jaune. (USA)
455 Elément d'une série d'affiches intitulée «Grandes Pensées». Illustration en divers tons jaunes, beiges, gris sur noir. (USA)
456, 458 Série d'affiches IBM pour le lancement d'un programme artistique au siège européen de cette société, à Paris. (USA)
457, 459, 460 Autres exemples d'affiches IBM destinées à la publication dans l'entreprise sous forme d'affichettes. 457: gris clair sur rouge foncé, EO = Equal Opportunity, les mêmes chances pour tous; 459: noir et blanc, texte bleu; 460: fond brunâtre, texte blanc, photos couleur. (USA)
461 Invitation à changer de gants de protection avant de risquer un contact direct avec des produits chimiques dangereux. (USA)

456

457

458

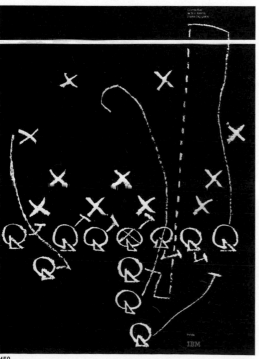

459

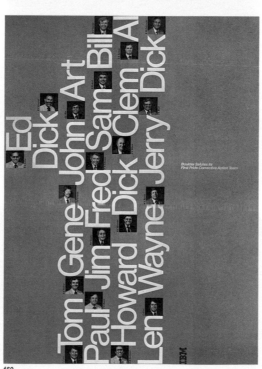

460

461

462

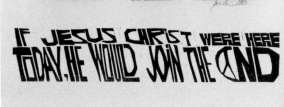

463

462–469 From a series of full-colour linocut posters by Paul Peter Piech who works with his own hand-operated press. Fig. 462: Two-colour poster for a citation from the Bible. Dark red lettering, lower half in dark yellow. Fig. 463: Poster for the CND peace movement in England. Dark red lettering, figure in dark blue. Fig. 464: A peace poster for the anti-war documentation centre in Germany. Fig. 465: Poster for the rights of Third World people to alternative sources of energy and to the development of their environment and culture. Bright red lettering in a blue figure. Fig. 466: Small-format poster for the CND peace movement. Blue and red on white. Fig. 467: The poem by Len Dennis in the upper part of this poster refers to the Hiroshima catastrophe, which should never happen again. Fig. 468: Poster for the CND peace movement. Fig. 469: Poster announcing a play on the theme of war. (GBR)

462–469 Aus einer Serie farbiger Linolschnitt-Plakate von Paul Peter Piech, der mit eigener Handpresse arbeitet. Abb. 462: Zweifarbiges Plakat zu einem Bibelzitat. Schrift in Dunkelrot, untere Hälfte in Dunkelgelb. Abb. 463: Plakat für die englische Friedensbewegung CND. Schrift in Dunkelrot, Figur in Dunkelblau. Abb. 464: Friedensplakat für ein Anti-Kriegs-Dokumentationszentrum in Deutschland. Abb. 465: «Das Recht der Völker dor Dritten Welt auf alternative Energiequellen zur Entwicklung ihrer Umgebung und Kultur.» Schrift leuchtend rot in blauer Figur. Abb. 466: Kleinplakat für die CND-Friedensbewegung. Blau und Rot auf Weiss. Abb. 467: Das Gedicht von Len Dennis im oberen Teil mahnt an die Katastrophe von Hiroshima, die sich nicht wiederholen darf. Abb. 468: Plakat für die CND-Friedensbewegung. Abb. 469: Plakat für ein Theaterstück zum Thema Krieg. (GBR)

ARTIST / KÜNSTLER / ARTISTE:
462–469 Paul Peter Piech

DESIGNER / GESTALTER / MAQUETTISTE:
462–469 Paul Peter Piech

ART DIRECTOR / DIRECTEUR ARTISTIQUE:
462–469 Paul Peter Piech

465

466

464

462–469 Série d'affiches réalisées en linogravure couleur par Paul Peter Piech et tirées sur sa presse à bras. Fig. 462: affiche bichrome sur une citation de la Bible. Texte rouge sombre, moitié inférieure jaune sombre. Fig. 463: pour le mouvement pacifiste anglais CND. Texte rouge sombre, personnage bleu foncé. Fig. 464: pour un centre documentaire antimilitariste en Allemagne. Fig. 465: «Le droit des peuples du Tiers Monde à des énergies nouvelles pour le développement de leur environnement et de leur culture.» Texte rouge vif dans personnage bleu. Fig. 466: affichette pour le CND; bleu, rouge sur blanc. Fig. 467: poème rappelant Hiroshima. Fig. 468: pour le mouvement pacifiste CND. Fig. 469: affiche pour une pièce de théâtre traitant de la guerre. (GBR)

468

467

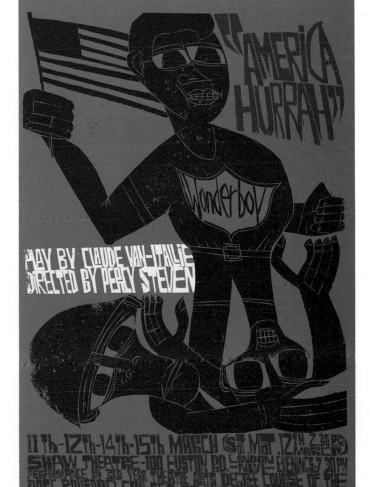

469

470

471

472

473

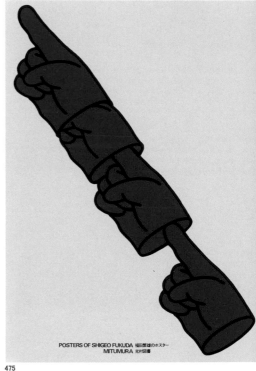

474

475

Political Posters
Politische Plakate
Affiches politiques

ARTIST / KÜNSTLER / ARTISTE:

470–475 Shigeo Fukuda
476 Volker Hartmann

DESIGNER / GESTALTER / MAQUETTISTE:

470–475 Shigeo Fukuda
476 Günther Kieser

ART DIRECTOR / DIRECTEUR ARTISTIQUE:

470–475 Shigeo Fukuda
476 Günther Kieser

AGENCY / AGENTUR / AGENCE – STUDIO:

476 Günther Kieser

470–475 Six posters by Shigeo Fukuda, who expresses himself here in terms of topical subjects such as ecology, an international understanding between peoples, brotherhood and peace. Figs. 470, 473: Ecological posters from a series entitled "Happy Earthday" in which Fig. 473 uses the UNICEF symbol for impact. Fig. 472: Poster as an anti-war communication. Figs. 471, 474, 475: These posters were also employed to announce exhibitions by the artist. (JPN)
476 Poster for an event devoted to peace. Full-colour photograph on a black ground, text in white. (BRD)

470–475 Sechs Plakate von Shigeo Fukuda, der sich hier zu aktuellen Themen wie Ökologie, internationale Verständigung zwischen den Menschen, Brüderlichkeit und Frieden äussert. Abb. 470, 473: Ökologische Plakate einer Serie mit dem Titel «Happy Earthday»; bei Abb. 473 wurde das UNICEF-Symbol verwendet. Abb. 472: Plakat gegen den Krieg. Abb. 471, 474, 475: Diese Plakate dienten auch für die Ankündigung von Ausstellungen des Künstlers. (JPN)
476 Plakat für eine Friedensveranstaltung. Farbaufnahme auf schwarzem Grund, Text in Weiss. (BRD)

470–475 Six affiches de l'artiste japonais Shigeo Fukuda sur des thèmes d'actualité: l'écologie, la fraternité entre les hommes, la paix. Fig. 470, 473: affiches écologiques d'une série intitulée «Bonjour la Terre», avec le symbole de l'UNICEF pour la fig. 473. Fig. 472: affiche contre la guerre. Fig. 471, 474, 475: ces affiches ont aussi servi à annoncer des expositions de l'œuvre de l'artiste. (JPN)
476 Affiche pour une manifestation pacifiste – «mais pourquoi donc pas la paix?» Photo couleur sur fond noir, sur lequel le texte apparaît en blanc. (BRD)

Warum denn nicht Frieden?

GEORGE F. KENNAN 1982

477

Political Posters
Politische Plakate
Affiches politiques

ARTIST / KÜNSTLER / ARTISTE:

477 Akira Yokoyama
478, 480–482 Kenny-Lui Kam Yuen
479 Hiroshi Koiwai

DESIGNER / GESTALTER / MAQUETTISTE:

477 Yusaku Kamekura
478–482 Masuteru Aoba/Kenny-Lui Kam Yuen

ART DIRECTOR / DIRECTEUR ARTISTIQUE:

477 Yusaku Kamekura
478–482 Masuteru Aoba

AGENCY / AGENTUR / AGENCE – STUDIO:

478–482 Sasaki Studio

477 The JAGDA (Japan Graphic Designers Association) was contracted by the citizens of Hiroshima and the Hiroshima International Cultural Foundation Inc. to create a campaign using posters to draw attention on an annual basis—for the first time in 1983—to the Hiroshima catastrophe "because words alone cannot suffice". An aim of this campaign is to distribute these posters worldwide, the proceeds of the sales to be put into a special fund. (Posters can be ordered from: JAGDA, Daiichi Naoki Bldg. 5F, 2-11-14 Minami-Aoyama Minato-ku, Tokyo 107, Japan. Price approx. 5 US dollars per poster). The 1983 poster shows burning butterflies on light grey-blue. (JPN)

478–482 From a series of full-colour posters on the subject of peace. Figs. 478, 481, 482 cite in ten languages the Preamble to the Constitution of UNESCO: "Since wars begin in the minds of men, it is in the minds of men that the defences of peace must be constructed." Figs. 479, 480: Posters proclaiming that the world armaments expenditure runs at a million dollars a minute. (JPN)

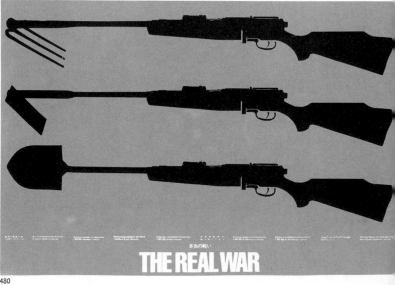

480

477 Die JAGDA (Japan Graphic Designers Association) kreierte im Auftrag der Bürger von Hiroshima und der Hiroshima International Cultural Foundation Inc. eine Kampagne mit Plakaten, die jedes Jahr – erstmals 1983 – an die Katastrophe von Hiroshima mahnen sollen. Ein Ziel der Kampagne ist, diese Plakate möglichst weltweit zu verbreiten. Der Erlös aus dem Verkauf soll einem Fonds zugute kommen. (Plakate können bestellt werden bei: JAGDA, Daiichi Naoki Bldg. 5F, 2-11-14 Minami-Aoyama Minato-ku, Tokio 107, Japan; Einzelpreis ca. US$ 5.00). Das 1983er Plakat zeigt brennende Schmetterlinge auf hellem Grau-Blau. (JPN)
478–482 Aus einer Serie von mehrfarbigen Plakaten zum Thema «Frieden». Abb. 478, 481, 482 erwähnen in zehn Sprachen die Präambel der UNESCO-Satzungen: «Weil Kriege in den Köpfen der Menschen entstehen, muss auch die Verteidigung des Friedens in ihren Köpfen grossgezogen werden.» Abb. 479, 480: «Rüstungsausgaben der Welt: 1 Million Dollar pro Minute». (JPN)

477 La JAGDA (Japan Graphic Designers Association) a réalisé pour les citoyens de Hiroshima et la Hiroshima International Cultural Foundation Inc. une campagne d'affiches destinées depuis 1983 à rappeler la catastrophe de Hiroshima; «puisque les mots seuls ne suffisent pas.» A cet effet, on envisage une diffusion mondiale, le produit des ventes revenant à un fonds spécial. (Ces affiches peuvent être commandées au prix d'environ 5 dollars américains à JAGDA, Daiichi Naoki Bldg. 5F, 2-11-14 Minami-Aoyama Minato-ku, Tōkyō 107, Japon.) La première affiche, celle qui a été diffusée en 1983, montre des papillons en flammes, sur fond gris bleu clair. (JPN)
478-482 Exemples d'une série d'affiches polychromes sur le thème de la «Paix». Les fig. 478, 481, 482 citent en dix langues le préambule de l'acte constitutif de l'UNESCO «Les guerres prenant naissance dans l'esprit des hommes, c'est dans l'esprit des hommes que doivent être élevées les défenses de la paix.» Fig. 479, 480: «Dépenses mondiales d'armement: 1 million dollars/minute.» (JPN)

478

479

481

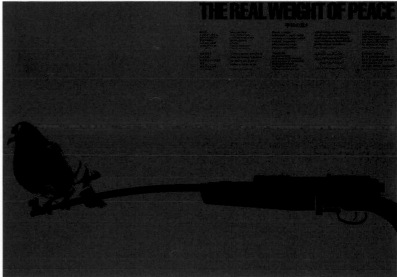

482

483 "Stop Nazi terror and warmongering." Poster issued by an anti-fascist group. (GER)
484–487 From a series of anti-nuclear-arms posters. Fig. 484: Full colour on a black ground. Fig. 487: White dove on a black rocket device, red ground, black lettering. (JPN)
488, 489 Satirical posters dealing with the American president's current policies. Fig. 488: Green lettering, dark-grey illustration on beige paper; Fig. 489: rusty-red lettering, dark-grey illustration on beige paper. (USA)

483 Ein vom Bund der Antifaschisten herausgegebenes Plakat. (GER)
484–487 Aus einer Serie von Anti-Atomwaffen-Plakaten. Abb. 484: Mehrfarbig auf Schwarz. Abb. 487: Weisse Taube auf schwarzem Raketengeschoss. Grund rot, Text schwarz. (JPN)
488, 489 Satirische Plakate, auf die Politik des gegenwärtigen amerikanischen Präsidenten anspielend. Abb. 488: Grüne Schrift, Illustration dunkelgrau auf beigem Papier. Abb. 489: Rostrote Schrift, Illustration dunkelgrau auf beigem Papier. (USA)

483 Affiche publiée par la Ligue antifasciste. (GER)
484–487 Série d'affiches antinucléaires. Fig. 484: polychrome sur fond noir. Fig. 487: colombe blanche sur missile noir. Fond rouge, texte noir. (JPN)
488, 489 Affiches satiriques stigmatisant la politique du président américain actuel. Fig. 488: texte vert, illustration gris foncé sur papier beige. Fig. 489: texte rouille, illustration gris foncé sur papier beige. (USA)

ARTIST / KÜNSTLER / ARTISTE:

483 Wolfgang Freitag
484 Naoki Ohno
485 Noboru Matsuura
486, 487 Hirokatsu Hijikata
488, 489 Lanny Sommese

ART DIRECTOR / DIRECTEUR ARTISTIQUE:

483 Wolfgang Freitag
484 Naoki Ohno
485 Noboru Matsuura
486, 487 Hirokatsu Hijikata
488, 489 Lanny Sommese

AGENCY / AGENTUR / AGENCE – STUDIO:

488, 489 Lanny Sommese Design

484

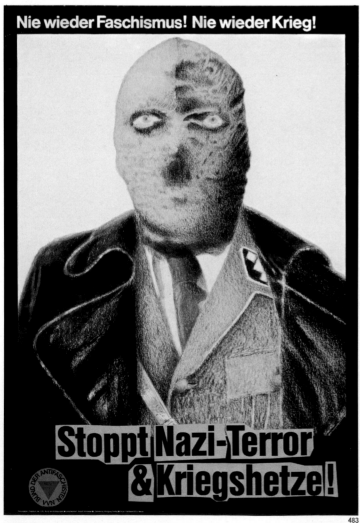

483

486

485

487

488

489

179

490

490 From a series of posters for environmental protection. (JPN)
491, 492 Posters designed under the auspices of an organization for cooperation in developing countries and humanitarian help: "Each minute 23 hectares of forest are felled in the world...", "...the DDA reacts against this." Silkscreen by Albin Uldry, Berne. (SWI)
493 Small-format poster used as an appeal to save our forests. (SWI)

490 Aus einer Reihe von Plakaten, die der Erhaltung der Umwelt gewidmet sind. (JPN)
491, 492 Im Auftrag der Direktion für Entwicklungszusammenarbeit und humanitäre Hilfe entstandene Plakate: «Jede Minute verschwinden 23 ha Wald in der Welt...», «...die DDA tut etwas dagegen.» (Siebdruck Albin Uldry, Bern.) (SWI)
493 Kleinformatiges Plakat als Appell zur Rettung des Waldes. (SWI)

490 Affiche dans une série consacrée à la protection de l'environnement. (JPN)
491, 492 Affiches réalisées à la demande de la Direction de la coopération au dévelopement et de l'aide humanitaire. Le texte allemand de l'affiche de la fig. 491 parle de la disparition de 23 ha de forêts par minute. (Sérigraphie d'Albin Uldry, Berne.) (SWI)
493 Affichette appelant à la sauvegarde des espaces forestiers. (SWI)

491

492

ARTIST / KÜNSTLER / ARTISTE:

490 Kazumasa Nagai
491, 492 Laurent Cocchi
493 Hans Erni

DESIGNER / GESTALTER / MAQUETTISTE:

490 Kazumasa Nagai
491, 492 Laurent Cocchi
493 Hans Erni

ART DIRECTOR / DIRECTEUR ARTISTIQUE:

490 Kazumasa Nagai
491, 492 Laurent Cocchi
493 Hans Erni

AGENCY / AGENTUR / AGENCE – STUDIO:

490 Nippon Design Center
491, 492 Laurent Cocchi

493

494, 495 Complete poster and illustration for the UCLA College of Fine Arts, announcing cultural studies and various events. (USA)
496 Invitation to participate in a competition for design students. (IRL)
497 Announcement of *Reuter* scholarships. In black and white. (GBR)
498 Poster for a New York art school. Mainly blue shades. (USA)
499 Full-colour poster for display in schools. (USA)

494, 495 Vollständiges Plakat und Illustration, mit dem kulturellen Studien- und Veranstaltungsprogramm der Universität von Kalifornien. (USA)
496 Einladung zu einem Wettbewerb für Design-Studenten. (IRL)
497 Bekanntgabe von *Reuter*-Stipendien für Journalisten. (GBR)
498 Für eine New Yorker Kunstschule; vorwiegend Blautöne. (USA)
499 Für den Aushang in Schulen bestimmtes, mehrfarbiges Plakat. (USA)

494, 495 Affiche complète et illustration qui y figure: programme d'études culturelles et de manifestations de l'Université de Californie. (USA)
496 Invitation à participer à un concours du meilleur design estudiantin en Irlande. (IRL)
497 Annonce de bourses *Reuter* pour journalistes. En noir et blanc. (GBR)
498 Pour une école d'art newyorkaise; tons bleus prédominants. (USA)
499 Affiche polychrome destinée à l'enseignement. (USA)

ARTIST / KÜNSTLER / ARTISTE:
494, 495 Don Weller
496 Anthony O'Hawlon
498 Robert Weaver
499 James McMullan

DESIGNER / GESTALTER:
494, 495 Don Weller
496 Anthony O'Hawlon
497 Mervyn Kurlansky/
Robert Maude/
Karen Blincoe
498 Bill Kobasz
499 Carol Carson

ART DIRECTOR:
494, 495 M. Reingold
496 Anthony O'Hawlon
497 Mervyn Kurlansky
498 Silas Rhodes
499 Carol Carson

AGENCY / AGENTUR:
494, 495 The Weller
Institute for the Cure
of Design, Inc.
496 Kilkenny Design
497 Pentagram
498 School of Visual Arts
Press, Ltd.
499 Visible Studio, Inc.

494

495

496

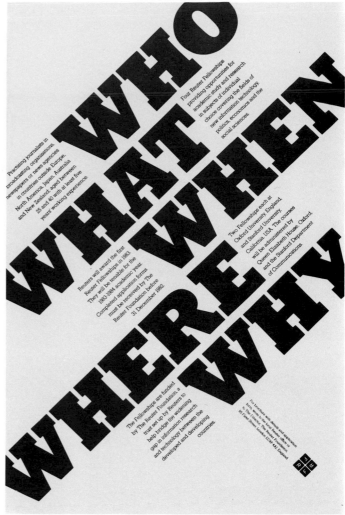

497

498

499

500

501

502

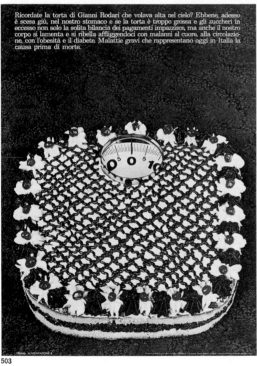

503

504

505

ARTIST / KÜNSTLER / ARTISTE:

500, 501 Luciano Padovani
502, 505 Alain Le Quernec
503, 504 James Saldani
506 Jacques Monory
507 Arroyo
508 Cueco

500, 501 Examples from a series of posters issued by the newspaper *L'Unità*, official organ of Italy's Communist Party. Fig. 500 deals with reasonable, progressive methods of production and manufacturing: Fig. 501: The quality of life in cities—sufficient green areas as opposed to real-estate speculators. (ITA)
502 "Who killed *FACT*?" The theme of this poster is the broken promise from official quarters regarding the support of an architectural project. (FRA)
503, 504 Two further posters by the newspaper *L'Unità*, official organ of Italy's Communist Party. This series deals with nutrition. In Fig. 503 a warning about the overindulgence in sweets is made; Fig. 504 deals with hunger in the Third World and the practical help that can be effected. (ITA)
505 An appeal to the candidates of France's political parties to pay attention to children's needs. (FRA)
506–508 Examples from a series of posters for a peace rally in Paris organized by the peace organization "Appel des 100". (FRA)

500, 501 Beispiele aus einer Serie von Plakaten, die von der Zeitung *L'Unità*, dem Parteiorgan der KPI, herausgegeben wurden. In Abb. 500 geht es um angemessene, fortschrittliche Produktionsmethoden, in Abb. 501 um die Lebensqualität in den Städten, d.h. genügend Grünflächen statt Bodenspekulation. (ITA)
502 Die Nichteinhaltung der Versprechen von offizieller Seite zur Unterstützung eines der Architektur gewidmeten Projektes ist Gegenstand dieses Plakates: «Wer hat *FACT* getötet?» (FRA)
503, 504 Zwei weitere Plakate, hier mit Farbaufnahmen, aus einer Serie der *L'Unità*, Organ der KPI (s. auch Abb. 500, 501), zum Thema Ernährung. In Abb. 503 wird vor übertriebenem Genuss von Süssigkeiten gewarnt, in Abb. 504 geht es um den Hunger in der Dritten Welt und sinnvolle Hilfe zur Eigenhilfe. (ITA)
505 Aufruf an die Kandidaten der politischen Parteien Frankreichs, sich auch um die Belange der Kinder zu kümmern. (FRA)
506–508 Plakate, die für das von der Friedensorganisation «Appell der 100» organisierte Friedensfest in Paris entworfen wurden. (FRA)

500, 501 Affiches dans une série publiée par le journal *L'Unità*, l'organe du parti communiste italien. La fig. 500 se réfère aux méthodes de production modernes humanisant le travail, la fig. 501 à la qualité de vie dans les villes où les espaces verts doivent être préservés de la spéculation. (ITA)
502 Affiche de protestation contre le manque de soutien officiel à un projet d'architecture, contrairement aux promesses faites. (FRA)
503, 504 Deux autres affiches (ici avec photos couleurs) dans une série réalisée pour *L'Unità*, organe du PC italien (cf. les fig. 500, 501), sur le thème de l'alimentation. Fig. 503: mise en garde contre l'abus de friandises. Fig. 504: la faim dans le monde et l'aide raisonnée au développement. (ITA)
505 Appel aux candidats des partis politiques français pour qu'ils se fassent les avocats des enfants et des jeunes. (FRA)
506–508 Exemples d'affiches créées à l'occasion de la Fête pour la paix, une initiative parisienne des pacifistes réunis dans «L'Appel des 100». (FRA)

Fête pour la Paix/Appel des 100/19 juin 1983/Paris

506

DESIGNER / GESTALTER / MAQUETTISTE:

502, 505 Alain Le Quernec
503, 504 Celestino Pantaleoni

ART DIRECTOR / DIRECTEUR ARTISTIQUE:

502, 505 Alain Le Quernec
503, 504 Celestino Pantaleoni

AGENCY / AGENTUR / AGENCE – STUDIO:

506–508 PPI Bagnolet

Political Posters
Politische Plakate
Affiches politiques

507

508

509

510

511

512

The ocean surface has a changing topography of hills and valleys. These are coupled to currents which alter temperature patterns and influence global climate. Satellite altimeters can measure this relief along the track beneath the orbiting spacecraft. For one month in 1978 SEASAT had a repeating orbit. Every three days the satellite passed over the same track on the sea surface and recorded changes in topography. The large image shows the extent of these changes. This time-varying topography is directly related to the variability of ocean currents. Maximum variability (red-orange) is associated with the energetic Gulf Stream, Kuroshio and Antarctic Circumpolar Currents, while broad areas are relatively steady (light blue).

This image shows the long-term average of ocean surface topography — the marine geoid — acquired by SEASAT over a three month period in 1978. Irregularities in the sea floor are reflected on the sea surface. Sharp depressions (dark blues) appear above trenches while gradual rises (lighter shades) are above mid-ocean ridges.

513

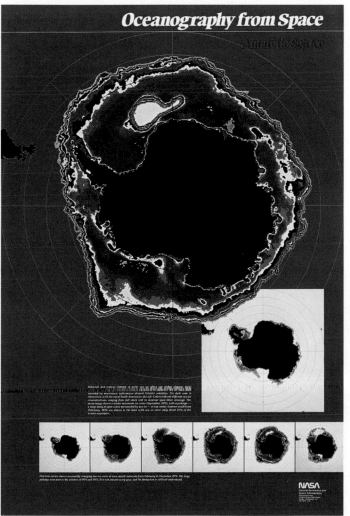

Oceanography from Space
Antarctic Sea Ice

514

ARTIST / KÜNSTLER / ARTISTE:

509 Tomek Kawiak
510 Kenji Nakahara
511, 512 René Burri/Magnum

DESIGNER / GESTALTER / MAQUETTISTE:

509 Tomek Kawiak
510 Kenji Nakahara
511, 512 Richard Danne
513, 514 Leonard Sirota

ART DIRECTOR / DIRECTEUR ARTISTIQUE:

509 Tomek Kawiak
511, 512 Richard Danne
513, 514 Payson R. Stevens

AGENCY / AGENTUR / AGENCE – STUDIO:

509 Tomek Kawiak
510 Design Office Nakahara
511, 512 Danne & Blackburn, Inc.
513, 514 InterNetwork, Inc.

509 "Black holes, the energy of tomorrow." Poster against energy wastage. (FRA)
510 Poster entitled "Infinite Cosmos". Blue with yellow. (JPN)
511, 512 Posters for two of Columbia's flights into space. (USA)
513, 514 From a series of NASA posters devoted to oceanography from space, the first that have ever been published on this subject. Fig. 513: The surface topography of the ocean, at the upper left a representation of the long-term average picture, below the time-varying topography (maximum variations in red and orange) directly related to the ocean currents; Fig. 514: The winter maximum ice cover of the Antarctic (centre) and the dramatic variations in Antarctic sea ice revealed by microwave radiometers. (USA)

509 «Schwarze Löcher, die Energie von morgen.» Aufruf gegen die Energieverschwendung. (FRA)
510 Plakat mit dem Titel «Unendlicher Kosmos». Blau mit Gelb. (JPN)
511, 512 Zur Erinnerung an den Jungfernflug der Raumfähre Columbia herausgegebene Plakate. (USA)
513, 514 Aus einer von der NASA herausgegebenen Reihe von Plakaten über Ozeanographie, die ersten, die je zu diesem Thema veröffentlicht wurden. Abb. 513: Darstellung der Oberflächentopographie des Meeres oben links Durchschnittswerte, in einer Dreimonatsphase von dem Satelliten aufgezeichnet, unten durch Strömungen verursachte Abweichungen (Maximalwerte rot und orange); Abb. 514: Darstellung der maximalen Eisfläche der Antarktis im Winter (Mitte) und die dramatischen Veränderungen des Meereeises, durch Mikrowellen-Radiometer der Satelliten festgestellt. (USA)

509 «Les trous noirs, l'énergie de demain.» Appel aux économies d'énergie. (FRA)
510 Affiche intitulée «Cosmos infini». Bleue, avec du jaune. (JPN)
511, 512 Affiches publiées en souvenir du premier vol de la navette spatiale Columbia. (USA)
513, 514 «L'Océanographie vue de l'espace»: affiches dans une série publiée par la NASA. Fig. 513: représentation topographique de la surface des mers, avec en haut à gauche les valeurs moyennes enregistrées par satellite sur trois mois, en bas les écarts dus aux courants marins (maxima rouge et orange); fig. 514: représentation du maximum de glaciation de l'Antarctique en hiver (au centre) et des variations dramatiques des glaces marines déterminées par radiomètre satellisé à micro-ondes. (USA)

jog your mind   run to your library

515

Your Lifemeter

516

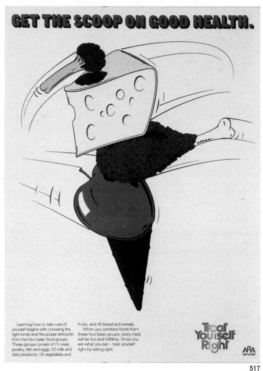

GET THE SCOOP ON GOOD HEALTH.

Treat
Yourself
Right

517

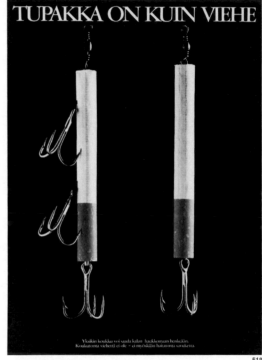

TUPAKKA ON KUIN VIEHE

518

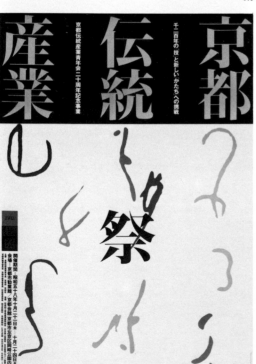

519

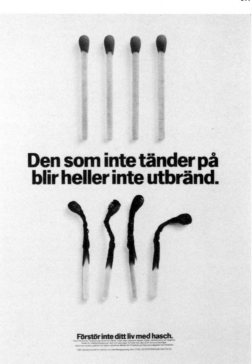

**Den som inte tänder på
blir heller inte utbränd.**

Förstör inte ditt liv med hasch.

520

Il verde non è solo un colore

Regione Toscana Giunta Regionale

521

522

515 Poster challenging people to train their minds by jogging to the library. (USA)
516 A burning cigarette and an ominous scale serve as a warning. Dark ground. (FIN)
517 Poster appealing for sensible nutrition. (USA)
518 Poster warning cigarette smokers: "Even if there are a number of hooks, one is enough to kill a fish." It does not matter whether a cigarette contains more or less tar. (FIN)
519 For the 20th anniversary of the artisans' and tradesmen's association in Kyoto. (JPN)
520 "Hashish makes you burn like a flame; don't burn yourself out." (SWE)
521 "Green is not only a colour." Full-colour poster from a campaign to encourage more public green zones in the Toscana region. (ITA)
522, 523 From a series of posters issued by Israel's Ministry of Education and Culture, drawing attention to various institutions and establishments in that country. (ISR)
524 Poster for a writers' congress in Cologne concentrating on the subject of "Peace." (GER)

515 Das Plakat fordert auf, seinen Geist durch «Joggen zur Bibliothek» zu trainieren. (USA)
516 «Ihr Lebensmeter» in Form einer brennenden Zigarette mit Skala. Dunkler Grund. (FIN)
517 «Schöpf Dir Gesundheit» als Aufforderung, auf ausgewogene Nahrung zu achten. (USA)
518 Gegen den Zigarettenkonsum: «Auch wenn's mehrere Angeln gibt, eine genügt, um den Fisch zu töten.» Ob eine Zigarette mehr oder weniger Teer enthält, zählt nicht. (FIN)
519 Zum 20jährigen Jubiläum der Handwerks- und Handelsvereinigung in Kyoto. (JPN)
520 «Haschisch lässt Dich brennen wie eine Flamme; lass Dich nicht ausbrennen.» (SWE)
521 «Grün ist nicht nur eine Farbe.» Mehrfarbiges Plakat aus einer Kampagne zur Förderung von öffentlichen Grünflächen in der Toskana. (ITA)
522, 523 Vom Kultur- und Erziehungsdepartement herausgegebene Plakate, die auf verschiedene Institutionen und Einrichtungen in Israel aufmerksam machen. (ISR)
524 Plakat für den Schriftstellerkongress in Köln zum Thema «Frieden». (GER)

515 Affiche invitant à faire du jogging en direction des bibliothèques. (USA)
516 «Votre compte-vie»: cigarette allumée, avec échelle de vie. Fond sombre. (FIN)
517 Appel à la raison du consommateur en faveur d'une alimentation équilibrée. (USA)
518 Contre l'abus de tabac: «Même s'il existe plusieurs types de hameçons, un seul suffit à ferrer et à tuer le poisson.» La teneur des cigarettes en goudron compte peu. (FIN)
519 Pour le 20e anniversaire de la Chambre de commerce et d'artisanat de Kyōto. (JPN)
520 «Le haschisch te consume comme une flamme; ne te laisse pas brûler en entier.» (SWE)
521 «Le vert n'est pas seulement une couleur.» Affiche polychrome pour une campagne en faveur du développement des espaces verts publics en Toscane. (ITA)
522, 523 Affiches publiées par le Département de l'Instruction publique et des Affaires culturelles, mettant en vedette des institutions et établissements israéliens. (ISR)
524 Affiche pour le congrès des écrivains de Cologne, sur le thème de la «paix». (GER)

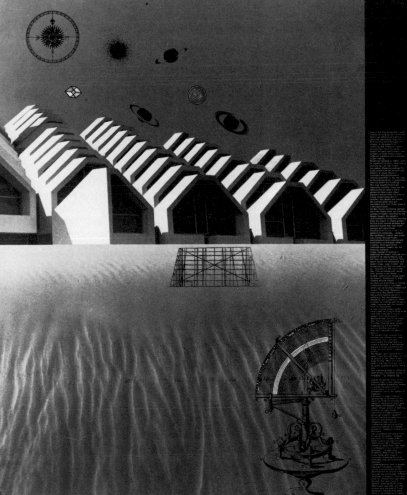

523

524

525

526

527

525–527 From a series of small-format posters with portraits of jazz musicians. The back of each poster supplies details on the musician in question as well as on the poster's designer. Fig. 525: In black and white; Fig. 526: Full-colour poster dedicated to Thelonious Monk; Fig. 527: Full-colour poster portraying the jazz musician Charlie Christian. (ITA)
528, 529 Silkscreen posters mainly in pastel shades, on the subject of graphic design. Grey frames. (JPN)
530 "Give us strength." Pope John Paul II portrayed on a poster displayed in Poland. (POL)

525–527 Aus einer Serie von Kleinplakaten mit Jazzmusiker-Porträts. Auf der Rückseite sind nähere Angaben zur Person und deren Werke sowie über den Künstler des Plakats aufgeführt. Abb. 525: Schwarzweiss; Abb. 526: Mehrfarbiges Plakat über den Musiker Thelonious Monk; Abb. 527: Mehrfarbiges Plakat über den Jazzmusiker Charlie Christian. (ITA)
528, 529 Vorwiegend pastellfarbige Siebdruckplakate zum Thema der graphischen Darstellung. Graue Rahmen. (JPN)
530 «Gib uns Kraft.» Papst Johannes Paul II. auf einem in Polen herausgegebenen Plakat. (POL)

525–527 Exemples d'une série d'affichettes présentant des musiciens de jazz. Au verso, on trouve une notice sur le musicien et son œuvre, ainsi que sur l'auteur de l'affiche. Fig. 525: noir et blanc. Fig. 526: affiche polychrome consacrée au musicien Thelonious Monk. Fig. 527: affiche polychrome présentant le musicien de jazz Charlie Christian. (ITA)
528, 529 Affiches sérigraphiques sur le thème de la conception graphique. Cadre gris, tons pastel prédominants. (JPN)
530 «Donne-nous de la force.» Le pape Jean-Paul II sur une affiche publiée en Pologne. (POL)

Social Posters
Soziale Plakate
Affiches sociales

ARTIST / KÜNSTLER / ARTISTE:

525 Guido Rosa
526 Milvio Cereseto
527 Nicola Bucci
528, 529 Masakazu Tanabe
530 Waldemar Swierzy

DESIGNER / GESTALTER / MAQUETTISTE:

525–527 Fernanda Maset
528, 529 Masakazu Tanabe
530 Waldemar Swierzy

ART DIRECTOR / DIRECTEUR ARTISTIQUE:

525–527 Marino Benedetti
528, 529 Masakazu Tanabe
530 Waldemar Swierzy

AGENCY / AGENTUR / AGENCE – STUDIO:

525–527 Metra Ads
528, 529 Media Co., Ltd.

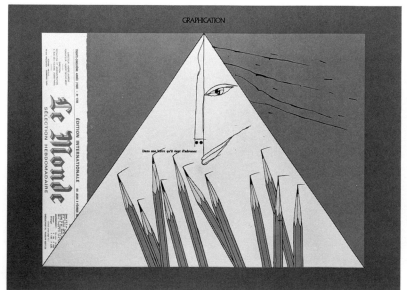

528

529

532

531

536

ARTIST / KÜNSTLER / ARTISTE:

531 Roman Cieslewicz
532–535 Bernard Chadebec
536 François Fabrizi
537–539 Celestino Piatti

DESIGNER / GESTALTER / MAQUETTISTE:

531 Roman Cieslewicz
536 François Fabrizi
537–539 Celestino Piatti

ART DIRECTOR / DIRECTEUR ARTISTIQUE:

531 Roman Cieslewicz
536 François Fabrizi
537–539 Celestino Piatti

AGENCY / AGENTUR / AGENCE – STUDIO:

536 Fabrizi/Loyau

CONTRE LES BRULURES

533

CONTRE LES COUPURES

534

CONTRE LES PIQURES

535

GEBORGEN BEI UNS

FLÜCHTLINGE
AUS KAMBODSCHA
LAOS VIETNAM

537

EL SALVADOR
REVOLUCION
O MUERTE

538

SUCHTKRANK
DIE GRUPPE HILFT
SOFORT VERTRAULICH UNBÜROKRATISCH
CARITAS ✛ KREUZBUND

539

531 The local government committee of the city of Montreuil offers its services. (FRA)
532–535 From a series of accident-prevention posters. (FRA)
536 Poster issued by a French union for the social, economic and cultural development of the island of Corsica. Yellow lettering, CGT in white on blue and red, blue ground. (FRA)
537, 539 Examples from a series of small-format posters by Celestino Piatti in which he turns to various social and political problems. Fig. 537 draws attention to the integration of refugees; Fig. 539 "Addiction. The Group helps." Shades of violet, white and blue, border in black. (GER)
538 "Revolution or Death." Commentary on the political situation in El Salvador. Blue on white, red letters and tears. (SWI)

531 Mit diesem Plakat bietet die Gemeindeverwaltung der Stadt Montreuil ihre Dienste an. (FRA)
532–535 Aus einer Serie von Plakaten zur Unfallverhütung. (FRA)
536 Plakat einer französischen Arbeitergewerkschaft für die soziale, wirtschaftliche und kulturelle Entwicklung der Insel Korsika. Schrift gelb, CGT in Weiss auf Blau und Rot, blauer Grund. (FRA)
537, 539 Beispiele aus einer Reihe von Kleinplakaten von Celestino Piatti zu verschiedenen sozialen und politischen Problemen. Abb. 537 fordert die Flüchtlingsintegration; Abb. 539 plädiert für Hilfe durch die Gruppe bei Suchtkrankheit. Violett-, Weiss-, Blautöne, Rahmen schwarz. (GER)
538 «Revolution oder Tod»: Kommentar zur politischen Situation in El Salvador. Blau auf Weiss, Schrift und Tränen rot. (SWI)

531 La municipalité de Montreuil offre ses services à la population par voie d'affiche. (FRA)
532–535 Série d'affiches pour la prévention des accidents. (FRA)
536 Affiche du syndicat français C.G.T. (Confédération Générale du Travail) pour le développement de la Corse aux plans social, économique et culturel. Texte en jaune, CGT en blanc sur bleu et rouge, fond bleu. (FRA)
537, 539 Exemples d'affichettes réalisées par Celestino Piatti sur divers thèmes sociaux et politiques. Fig. 537: l'intégration des réfugiés; fig. 539: l'aide apportée aux toxicomanes par des groupes bénévoles. Violets, blancs, bleus, cadre noir. (GER)
538 «La révolution ou la mort»: commentaire de la situation politique au Salvador. Bleu sur blanc, texte et larmes rouges. (SWI)

ENDANGERED

540 Example from a series of posters on endangered species, designed by The Graphic Workshop. (USA)
541 Poster issued by the committee protesting the planned Trans-Jura motorway in Switzerland. (SWI)
542 "Fine, thanks! And the others?" Full-colour poster for the December collections of the Swiss section of Caritas. (SWI)
543 Poster to encourage the protection of trees and forests, issued by the Minnesota Department of Agriculture and the Shade Tree Program. (USA)

540 Beispiel aus einer Reihe von Plakaten, welche den vom Aussterben bedrohten Tierarten gewidmet sind, von einem Graphik-Studio in Boston herausgegeben. (USA)
541 Gegen die in der Schweiz geplante Trans-Jura-Autobahn veröffentlichtes Plakat. (SWI)
542 Mehrfarbiges Plakat für die Dezember-Sammlung der Schweizerischen Caritas. (SWI)
543 Dem Schutz von Bäumen und Wäldern gewidmetes Plakat, herausgegeben vom Landwirtschafts-ministerium Minnesota und vom Shade Tree Program, im «Monat des Baumes». (USA)

540 Exemple des affiches publiées par un studio d'art graphique de Boston en faveur des espèces animales menacées de disparition. (USA)
541 Affiche publiée par le Comité contre la Transjurane, une autoroute dont la construction est envisagée dans le canton suisse du Jura. (SWI)
542 «Merci, je vais bien. Et les autres?» Affiche polychrome pour la collecte de décembre de la Caritas suisse. (SWI)
543 Affiche appelant à la protection des arbres et des forêts publiée par le Département de l'agriculture de l'Etat du Minnesota et le Shade Tree Program au «mois de l'arbre». (USA)

ARTIST / KÜNSTLER / ARTISTE:

540 Agusta Agustsson
541 Franco Balan

DESIGNER / GESTALTER:

540 Agusta Agustsson
541 Franco Balan
542 Regina Wyss
543 Hideki Yamamoto/
    Miranda Moss

ART DIRECTOR:

541 Franco Balan
542 Mark Zeugin
543 Hideki Yamamoto/
    Miranda Moss

AGENCY / AGENTUR / AGENCE:

540 The Graphic Workshop
541 Franco Balan
542 Mark Zeugin
543 Seitz Yamamoto Moss

Social Posters
Soziale Plakate
Affiches sociales

544 Poster issued on the occasion of a plebiscite in Yugoslavia: "Where there's a will, there's a way." (YUG)
545 "Every grain counts." Ears of corn form the word "bread". (POL)
546 Poster published and displayed in order to demonstrate solidarity for the outlawed Polish union "Solidarność". (ITA)
547 Another poster supporting the "Solidarność" movement. (USA)
548 Poster entitled "Nature + human being = life". (USR)
549 For an art school, announcing an exhibition of graduate work. (POL)

544 Anlässlich einer Volksabstimmung herausgegebenes Plakat: «Wo ein Wille ist, ist auch ein Weg.» (YUG)
545 «Jede Ähre zählt.» Das mit Ähren gebildete Wort heisst «Brot». (POL)
546 Aus Solidarität mit der verbotenen polnischen Gewerkschaft «Solidarność» veröffentlichtes Plakat. (ITA)
547 Ein weiteres Plakat zur Unterstützung der «Solidarność». (USA)
548 Plakat mit dem Titel «Natur + Mensch = Leben». (USR)
549 Für eine Kunstschule, mit Hinweis auf eine Diplom-Ausstellung. (POL)

544 Affiche publiée à l'occasion d'une consultation populaire: «Vouloir, c'est pouvoir.» (YUG)
545 «Chaque épi compte.» Les épis composent le mot «pain». (POL)
546 Affiche publiée par solidarité avec le syndicat «Solidarność» interdit en Pologne. En couleurs. (ITA)
547 Une autre affiche de soutien à «Solidarność». (USA)
548 Affiche intitulée «La nature + l'homme = la vie». (USR)
549 Pour une école d'art; référence à une exposition de travaux diplômés. (POL)

544

Social Posters
Soziale Plakate
Affiches sociales

547

545

546

ARTIST / KÜNSTLER / ARTISTE:

544 Radovan Jenko
545, 549 Wladyslaw Pluta
546 Ferenc Pintér
547 Jan Sawka
548 Yuri Nikolaev

ART DIRECTOR / DIRECTEUR ARTISTIQUE:

544 Radovan Jenko
546 Ferenc Pintér
547 Jan Sawka

AGENCY / AGENTUR / AGENCE – STUDIO:

544 Aero-Design

548

549

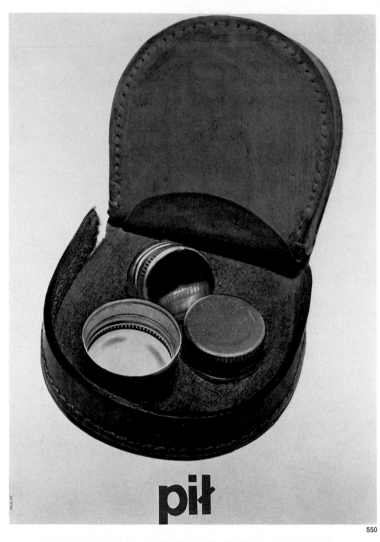

pił

550

551

552

553

550 Alcoholism and its consequences (here especially as regards the purse) are the subject of this poster. (POL)
551–553 Examples from a series of full-colour posters issued by the Evangelical Forum in Berlin on the subject of adult education, and entitled "Future? Yes, please". Fig. 551 deals with the problem of older women trying to find employment within the current market conditions; Fig. 552 deals with the senseless increase in growth, and Fig. 553 points to the hostile environment in cities for children. (GER)
554 "World Savings Day. 28 October 1983." From a series of artistic posters issued regulary for the savings day by the publishing organ of the German Savings Banks. This series was designed for the savings banks' public work. (GER)

550 Trunksucht und ihre Folgen (hier speziell für den Geldbeutel) sind Gegenstand dieses Plakates. (POL)
551–553 Aus einer Serie von Plakaten, die vom Evangelischen Forum Berlin zum Thema Erwachsenenbildung unter dem Titel «Zukunft? ja bitte» veröffentlicht wurden. In Abb. 551 geht es um die Probleme älterer Bewerberinnen auf dem Arbeitsmarkt, in Abb. 552 um die sinnlose Steigerung des Wachstums, in Abb. 553 um die kinderfeindliche Umwelt in den Städten. (GER)
554 Aus einer Serie von Künstlerplakaten, die vom Deutschen Sparkassenverlag regelmässig zum Weltspartag herausgegeben werden. Die Reihe wurde für die Öffentlichkeitsarbeit der Sparkassen konzipiert, als Ergänzung zu den Werbeplakaten. (GER)

550 L'alcoolisme et son incidence sur le porte-monnaie constituent le thème de cette affiche. (POL)
551–553 Exemples d'une série d'affiches polychromes publiées par le Forum évangélique de Berlin sur la formation continue sous le titre générique de «L'avenir? Oh oui, s'il vous plaît». Fig. 551: les problèmes des femmes âgées à la recherche d'un emploi; fig. 552: la croissance sans frein; fig. 553: l'environnement urbain hostile aux enfants. (GER)
554 Exemple d'affiches d'artistes publiées à intervalles réguliers par le Deutsche Sparkassenverlag à l'occasion de la Journée mondiale de l'épargne. Série réalisée pour les relations publiques des caisses d'épargne. (GER)

ARTIST / KÜNSTLER / ARTISTE:

550 Wladyslaw Pluta
551–553 Inge Pape
554 Herbert Leupin

DESIGNER / GESTALTER / MAQUETTISTE:

551–553 Inge Pape
554 Herbert Leupin

WELTSPARTAG
28. OKTOBER 1983
SPARKASSE

554

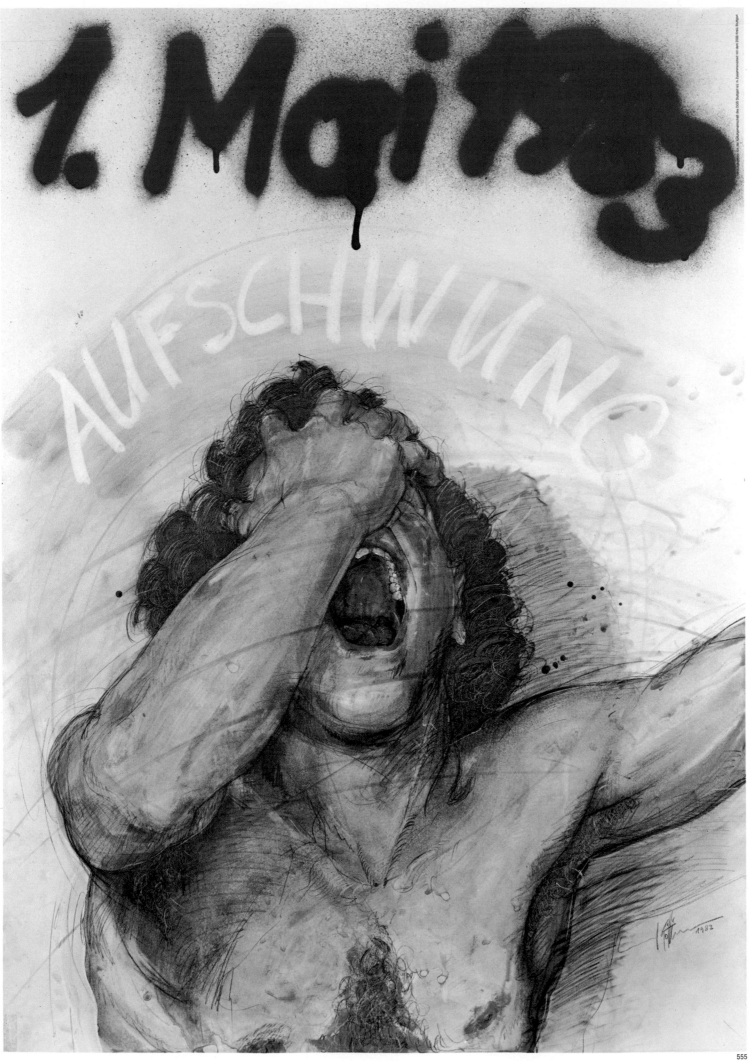

556

ARTIST / KÜNSTLER / ARTISTE:

555 Erhard Göttlicher
556 Tadanori Yokoo
557 James Thorpe
558 Paul Davis

DESIGNER / GESTALTER / MAQUETTISTE:

555 Erhard Göttlicher
556 Tadanori Yokoo
557 James Thorpe
558 Paul Davis

ART DIRECTOR / DIRECTEUR ARTISTIQUE:

556 Tadanori Yokoo
557 James Thorpe

AGENCY / AGENTUR / AGENCE – STUDIO:

557 The Design Service Project

555 Example from a series of 1st May posters issued by the Stuttgart section of the German Trades-Union Congress. 100×70 cm, five-colour offset. (GER)
556 Poster designed as part of a save-nature series. (JPN)
557 Announcement of lectures dealing with the poster as a medium. (USA)
558 Poster issued to encourage people to participate in a demonstration supporting Jews in the Soviet Union. (USA)

555 Beispiel aus der Reihe der 1.-Mai-Plakate des DGB-Kreises Stuttgart. (Format 100×70 cm, Fünffarben-Offsetdruck, bei der Büchergilde Gutenberg erhältlich.) (GER)
556 Im Rahmen einer dem Naturschutz gewidmeten Reihe entstandenes Plakat. (JPN)
557 Ankündigung von Vorlesungen über «Plakate als Ausdruck ihrer Zeit». (USA)
558 «Sprich für die, die es nicht können.» Aufruf zur Teilnahme an einer Demonstration für die jüdische Bevölkerung der Sowjetunion. (USA)

555 L'une des affiches de l'arrondissement de Stuttgart du syndicat allemand DGB pour le 1er mai. (Format: 100×70 cm, réalisation offset 5 couleurs.) (GER)
556 Affiche réalisée dans le cadre d'une série destinée à l'écologie. (JPN)
557 Annonce de conférences sur «l'affiche porte-parole de son époque». (USA)
558 «Exprimez-vous au nom de ceux qui sont réduits au silence.» Appel à une manifestation en faveur de la population juive de l'Union soviétique. (USA)

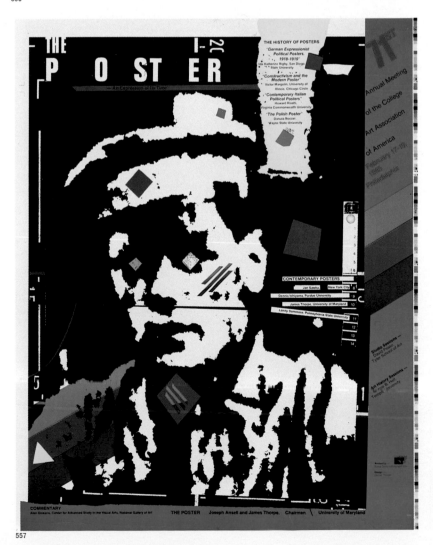

557

558

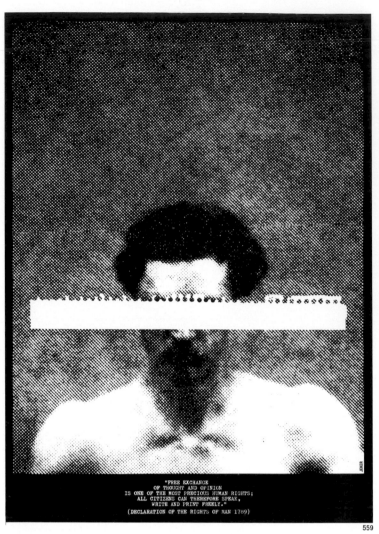

"FREE EXCHANGE
OF THOUGHT AND OPINION
IS ONE OF THE MOST PRECIOUS HUMAN RIGHTS;
ALL CITIZENS CAN THEREFORE SPEAK,
WRITE AND PRINT FREELY."
(DECLARATION OF THE RIGHTS OF MAN 1789)

559

560

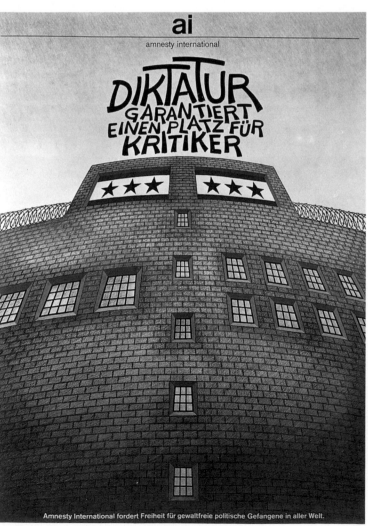

Amnesty International fordert Freiheit für gewaltfreie politische Gefangene in aller Welt.

561

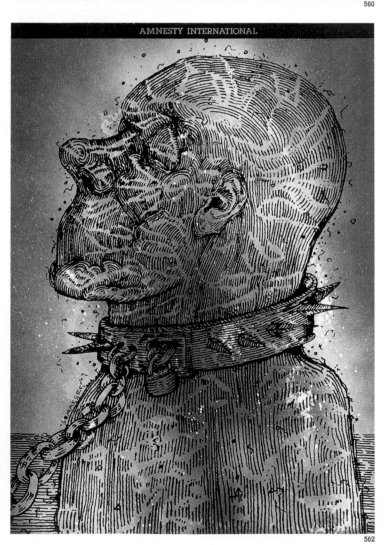

562

202

**Political Posters
Politische Plakate
Affiches politiques**

ARTIST / KÜNSTLER / ARTISTE:

559 Werner Jeker
561 Wolfgang Storbakken
562, 563 Lanny Sommese

DESIGNER / GESTALTER / MAQUETTISTE:

559 Werner Jeker
560 Ute Berner
561 Wolfgang Storbakken
562, 563 Lanny Sommese

ART DIRECTOR / DIRECTEUR ARTISTIQUE:

559 Werner Jeker
562, 563 Lanny Sommese

AGENCY / AGENTUR / AGENCE – STUDIO:

559 Werner Jeker
562, 563 Lanny Sommese Design

559 Silkscreen poster in black and white with an excerpt from the Declaration of the Rights of Man 1789. (SWI)
560, 561 "No More Torture" and "Dictatorship guarantees a place for critics": examples from a series of posters designed for the Amnesty International organization in Germany. (GER)
562, 563 For Amnesty International (see also Figs. 560, 561), dealing with the torture of prisoners. Fig. 562: Black, white, silver and orange on violet paper; Fig. 563: Pink and dark blue on grey paper. (USA)

559 Siebdruckplakat in Schwarzweiss mit einem Auszug aus den 1789 in den Vereinigten Staaten niedergelegten Menschenrechten, hier über das Recht auf freie Meinungsäusserung. (SWI)
560, 561 Beispiele aus einer Reihe von Plakaten für die Gefangenen-Hilfsorganisation Amnesty International in Deutschland. (GER)
562, 563 Die Folter von Gefangenen ist Gegenstand dieser in den USA erschienenen Plakate für Amnesty International (s. auch Abb. 560, 561). Abb. 562: Schwarz, weiss, silber und orange auf violettem Papier; Abb. 563: Rosa und dunkelblau auf grauem Papier. (USA)

559 Affiche sérigraphique, noir et blanc, avec un extrait des Droits de l'homme formulés en 1789 aux Etats-Unis, ici sur la garantie de la liberté d'expression. (SWI)
560, 561 Exemples d'affiches dans une série réalisée pour le siège allemand d'Amnesty International, l'organisation internationale d'aide aux prisonniers. (GER)
562, 563 La torture appliquée aux prisonniers, voilà le thème de ces affiches parues aux Etats-Unis en faveur d'Amnesty International (cf. les fig. 560, 561). Fig. 562 noir, blanc, argent, orange sur violet; fig. 563: rose et bleu foncé sur gris. (USA)

563

203

Paper / Papier: Papierfabrik Biberist–Biber art paper, super white, glaced, 130 gm² and Biber Offset SK3, pure white, machine-finished, 140 gm² / Biber-Kunstdruck ultra weiss, glaciert, 130 gm² und Biber-Offset SK3, hochweiss, maschinenglatt, 140 gm²

Printed by / gedruckt von: Offset + Buchdruck AG, Staffelstrasse 12, CH-8021 Zürich

Typesetting / Lichtsatz: Sauerländer AG, Aarau (Univers, MONOTYPE-Lasercomp)

Binding / Einband: Buchbinderei Schumacher AG, Bern / Schmitten

Glossy lamination / Glanzfoliierung: Durolit AG, Pfäffikon SZ